CAMBRIDGE
UNIVERSITY PRESS

CAMBRIDGE

nary Computing

Learner's Book 5

Ceredig Cattanach-Chell,
Yianni Dimitriadis & Bernie Fishpool

CAMBRIDGE
UNIVERSITY PRESS

University Printing House, Cambridge CB2 8BS, United Kingdom

One Liberty Plaza, 20th Floor, New York, NY 10006, USA

477 Williamstown Road, Port Melbourne, VIC 3207, Australia

314–321, 3rd Floor, Plot 3, Splendor Forum, Jasola District Centre, New Delhi – 110025, India

103 Penang Road, #05–06/07, Visioncrest Commercial, Singapore 238467

Cambridge University Press is part of the University of Cambridge.

It furthers the University's mission by disseminating knowledge in the pursuit of education, learning and resea ch at the highest international levels of excellence.

www.cambridge.org
Information on this title: www.cambridge.org/9780009309288

© Cambridge University Press & Assessment 2023

20 19 18 17 16 15 14 13 12 11 10 9 8 7

Printed in Malaysia by Vivar Printing

A catalogue record for this publication is available from the British Library

ISBN 978-1-009-30928-8 Paperback with Digital Access (1 Year)
ISBN 978-1-009-32051-1 Digital Learner's Book (1 Year)
ISBN 978-1-009-32052-8 eBook

Additional resources for this publication at www.cambridge.org/go

....

....

Endorsement statement

Endorsement indicates that a resource has passed Cambridge International's rigorous quality-assurance process and is suitable to support the delivery of a Cambridge International curriculum framework. However, endorsed resources are not the only suitable materials available to support teaching and learning, and are not essential to be used to achieve the qualification. Resource lists found on the Cambridge International website will include this resource and other endorsed resources.

Any example answers to questions taken from past question papers, practice questions, accompanying marks and mark schemes included in this resource have been written by the authors and are for guidance only. They do not replicate examination papers. In examinations the way marks are awarded may be different. Any references to assessment and/or assessment preparation are the publisher's interpretation of the curriculum framework requirements. Examiners will not use endorsed resources as a source of material for any assessment set by Cambridge International.

While the publishers have made every attempt to ensure that advice on the qualification and its assessment is accurate, the official curriculum framework, specimen assessment materials and any associated assessment guidance materials produced by the awarding body are the only authoritative source of information and should always be referred to for definitive guidance. Cambridge International recommends that teachers consider using a range of teaching and learning resources based on their own professional judgement of their students' needs.

Cambridge International has not paid for the production of this resource, nor does Cambridge International receive any royalties from its sale. For more information about the endorsement process, please visit www.cambridgeinternational.org/endorsed-resources

Cambridge International copyright material in this publication is reproduced under licence and remains the intellectual property of Cambridge Assessment International Education.

Third party websites and resources referred to in this publication have not been endorsed by Cambridge Assessment International Education.

Introduction

Welcome to Stage 5 of Cambridge Primary Computing!

The world of computing is incredibly exciting. Many of the things you see around you every day are linked to computing.

In this book you will:

- plan and develop computer programs in Scratch using selection and operators
- learn how to collect, store and use data
- investigate networks and how data travels over the internet
- learn how data is saved in a computer system
- find out about artificial intelligence (AI) and how it is used.

These computing ideas affect our daily lives. Learning about them will help you to see how computers are a part of the world we live in now and how they might impact it in the future. Many of these ideas can be used both in the classroom and outside of school.

This book has lots of activities and questions where you can work with a partner or a group. Sharing your ideas with others is fun and helps you to explore the ideas in the book. Maybe you can share your knowledge with other friends and family who have not learnt about computing.

There is also a project for you to complete at the end of each unit. The projects will help you to use and share what you have learnt in each unit.

We hope that these topics will inspire you to learn more about computing and to keep learning about computers as you grow older.

You may even think about getting a job in computing and help to shape the future of computing in the world!

Ceredig Cattanach-Chell, Yianni Dimitriadis and Bernie Fishpool

Contents

Note for teachers: Throughout the resource there is a symbol to indicate where additional digital only content is required. This content can be accessed through the Digital Learner's Book on Cambridge GO. It can be launched either from the Media tab or directly from the page. The symbol that denotes additional digital content is: [⬀]. The source files can also be downloaded from the Source files tab on Cambridge GO. In addition, this tab contains a teacher guidance document which supports the delivery of digital activities and programing tasks in this Learner's Book.

How to use this book

In this book you will find lots of different features to help your learning.

What you will learn in the topic.

> **We are going to:**
> - investigate the computing tools we use in a statistical investigation
> - understand how to use questions to collect different types of data
> - find out how to make rules in spreadsheet cells to help avoid mistakes in data.

Important words to learn.

> assign   temporary   variable
> meaningful   value   variable assignment

A reminder about what you already know and an activity to start you off.

> **Getting started**
>
> **What do you already know?**
> - Algorithms are sets of instructions, written in a specific order.
> - You can use indefinite loops and count-controlled loops to repeat instructions, like the same steps of a dance or a verse in a song.

Fun activities about computing. Sometimes, you will use a computer.

> **Activity 2**
>
> You will need: a desktop computer, laptop or tablet and word-processing software
>
> Use a computer to create a poster that explains what variables are and how we use them.

Some activities don't need a computer. These are called unplugged activities. They help you to understand important ideas about computing.

> **Unplugged activity 4**
>
> You will need: a paper copy of your line graph from Practical task 3, pen and paper
>
> Get into pairs and look at the table below. One person will think about Situation A; the other person will think about Situation B. What changes would make the chart as useful as possible in your situation? Write or draw ideas for changes on your chart or on a separate sheet of paper.
>
> | Situation A | Situation B |
> | --- | --- |
> | The person reading the chart is hard of hearing. | The person reading the chart is colour-blind and cannot tell the difference between red and green. |
> | The person reading the chart is only interested in the temperature in July. | The person reading the chart wants to be able to see all of the data points with lots of detail. |
> | It will be viewed on a small screen. | It will be viewed on a big screen. |

Sometimes, you will see this question. It will help you to think about your work.

> **How are we doing?**
>
> Swap notes with your partner and think about their situation. Look at the ideas they have written.
> - What have they done well?
> - Do you disagree with any of their ideas? If so, why?
> - Can you think of any other ideas to add to theirs? If so, discuss them together and add them if your partner agrees.

Tasks to help you to practise what you have learnt.

Programming tasks are in Unit 1. ———————————→

Programming task 3

You will need: a pen and paper; a desktop computer or laptop, a micro:bit, a mini USB cable and access to the MakeCode website; or a tablet, a micro:bit, a battery pack and access to the MakeCode app

Part A

Work with a partner to plan and then make a 'Guess the Press' game.

The game will be for two players. Player one will press button A on the micro:bit a secret number of times. Player two will then have to guess the number of times button A has been pressed by using button B.

Read the criteria for this game:

1 When button A is pressed, 1 will be added to player one's number.

Practical tasks are in Unit 2. ———————————→

Practical task 1

You will need: a desktop computer, laptop or tablet with spreadsheet software (such as Microsoft Excel) and source file **2.2_Marcus_game_data_class**

We are going to look at the data from Marcus's computer game investigation. Marcus organised the data in his spreadsheet to count how many people said each game type was their favourite. He called these 'votes up' and made a bar chart of this data.

1 Open source file **2.2_Marcus_game_data_class**.

First, let's create a bar chart that shows the votes down next to the votes up, so that we can compare them.

Look out for this icon. You are going to do an activity at the computer using a source file or website link. This content can be found in the Digital Learner's Book on Cambridge GO. Your teacher will help you to get started. ———————————→

Questions that help you to practise what you have just learnt. Are you ready to move on? →

Questions

Which of the following questions could be conditions?

1 What colour is your T-shirt?
2 Is dinner time at 6.00 p.m.?
3 Which button are you pressing?

Things to remember when you are doing a task. ———————————→

Stay safe!

Remember to only use websites that you trust and are safe. Always check with a teacher or adult before going on a website you do not know.

Interesting facts connected to the topic. ———————————→

Did you know?

It takes up to 22 minutes for an input command to be sent to Mars. If we drove to Mars, it would take over 350 years to get there.

Questions to help you think about how you learn.

How did the programming tasks help you to learn today?
How do you remember the difference between variables and values?

What you have learnt in the topic.

Look what I can do!

☐ I can identify the different roles and skills of people involved in creating a program.
☐ I understand the five stages of the project life cycle.
☐ I understand why creating clear criteria at the start of a project is important.
☐ I can evaluate how successful a final program is based on criteria.

At the end of each unit, there is a project for you to carry out, using what you have learnt. You might make something or solve a problem.

Project

In this project you will imagine you are setting up a dessert café business. You will collect data using a form, then organise this data in a spreadsheet and use it to help you make decisions.

Step 1: Create a form

- With a partner, decide what kind of imaginary café you will run. Will you serve cupcakes? Or maybe milkshakes? How about ice cream? You could choose pies – or all of these.

- You are going to create a form to find out what customers would want from your café. You will use this data to make decisions about what to serve and what prices to charge. Decide on three pieces of data you will need to collect. For example, you might collect data on:
  - what people's favourite flavours are
  - whether people need non-dairy options
  - how much people are willing to pay per item.
- With your partner, write questions to collect your data.
- Create your form. Think about how easy your form will be to use. What things have you learnt that you could use to help you?

Questions that cover what you have learnt in the unit. If you can answer these, you are ready to move on to the next unit.

Check your progress

1 What device allows a network to access the internet?
2 What allows devices to connect wirelessly to a network?
3 Why do we need IP addresses?
4 Give two advantages of a cellular network.
5 When data is split into smaller pieces, what do we call these pieces?
6 Say two things that a packet should have in it.
7 What is a disadvantage of using packets?
8 What is an advantage of using packets?
9 Give two examples of the effects of internet connection failure.
10 Explain how an email message is sent across the internet. Use the following key terms:

| IP address | internet connection | routes | packets | destination |

1 Computational thinking and programming

> 1.1 Assigning variables

We are going to:

- define a variable as something that holds a value that can change
- identify that algorithms hold values that can change
- assign (give) variables to values such as text or numbers
- create variables with meaningful names to hold values in algorithms
- modify an existing variable in Scratch and make a new variable to hold a value that can change.

| assign | temporary | variable |
| meaningful | value | variable assignment |

Getting started

What do you already know?

- Algorithms are sets of instructions, written in a specific order.
- You can use indefinite loops and count-controlled loops to repeat instructions, like the same steps of a dance or a verse in a song.

Continued

Now try this!

You will need: a pen and paper

You are going to write an algorithm that gets the ladybug to the bug hotel.

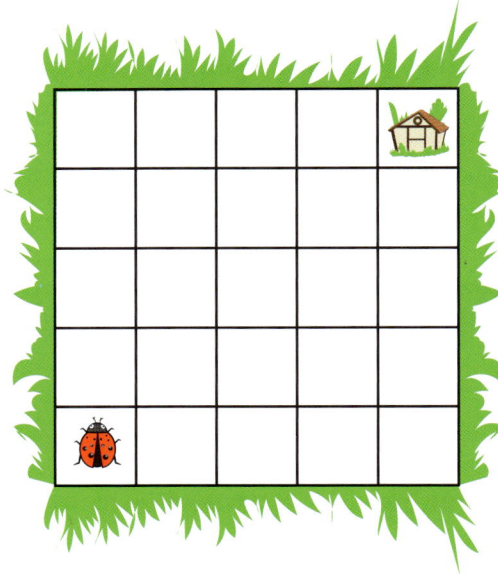

1. Write the instructions for the ladybug as a linear algorithm. The ladybug understands the following instructions: Move forward; Turn right; Turn left.
2. Write the instructions using a count-controlled loop to make the algorithm shorter.

Introducing variables

In an algorithm or a program, a variable stores data that can change. The data that variables store can be set and changed throughout the running of a program. We can use variables to store data and then return to use them later. Variables can only store one item of data at a time.

Look at the algorithm that you wrote to get the ladybug to the bug hotel. Use the grid in the Now try this! activity to help you. The algorithm uses a count-controlled loop.

> Remember, loops repeat instructions, making algorithms more efficient. A count-controlled loop repeats instructions an exact number of times.

1	Set Count to 2
2	REPEAT Count
3	Move forward
4	Turn right
5	Move forward
6	Turn left

In this algorithm, the word 'Count' in line 1 is a variable. Variable names need to be meaningful. A meaningful variable name gives us information about the data that is stored in the variable. For example, we know the variable Count stores how many times the loop will repeat.

Imagine the variable Count is a box and we are using it to store the number of repetitions for the loop.

Questions

The number stored inside the variable Count is 2. This means the loop will repeat twice.

In pairs, discuss the following questions.

1   The ladybug starts in the bottom left square. What number should the variable Count hold to make sure the ladybug can get to the bug hotel?

2   What value would we need to assign to Count if we moved the ladybug one square up and right, as shown in the picture?

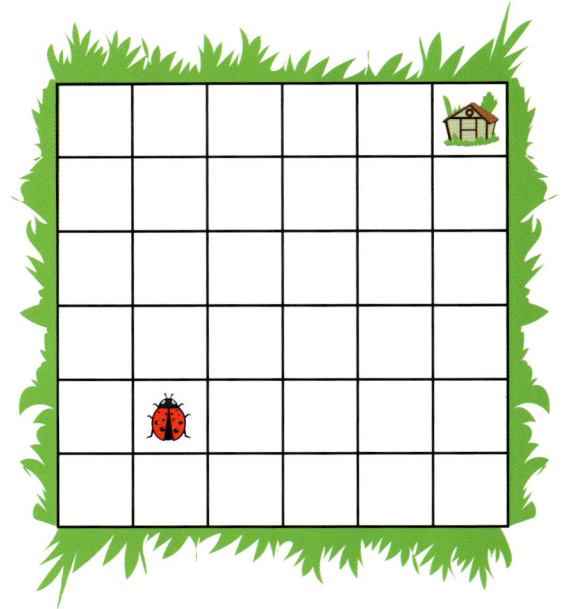

We can write our algorithm like this:

1	set Count to 5
2	REPEAT Count
3	Move forward
4	Turn right
5	Move forward
6	Turn left

In this algorithm, we use the variable Count to store the number of repetitions. We instruct the variable to store the number of repetitions like this:

set Count to 5

This is like putting the number 5 into our box.

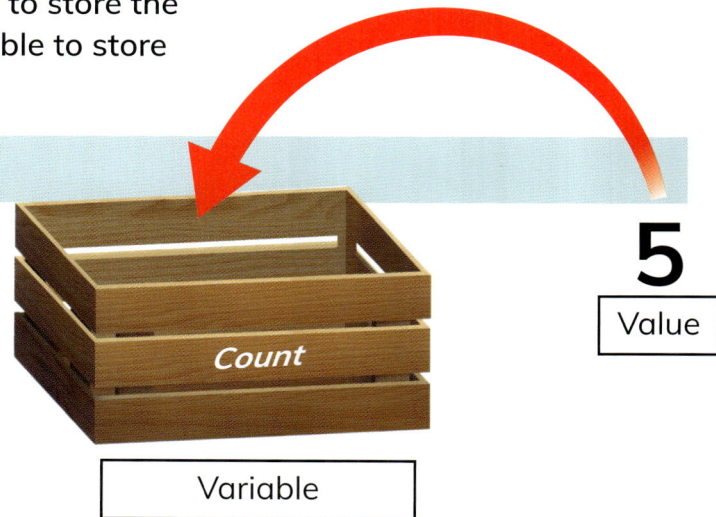

5

Value

Count

Variable

If we move our ladybug closer to the bug hotel, we can change the number of repetitions by changing the number we give to *Count*:

```
1        set Count to 4
2        REPEAT Count
3            Move forward
4            Turn right
5            Move forward
6            Turn left
```

Now the number 4 is stored in the Count variable.

Note that the number 5 is no longer in the box because a variable can only hold one item of data.

5

4

Value

Count

Variable

Values that can change

When writing algorithms, we often want to use and store data, such as numbers and words, that can change. The numbers and words we use in our algorithms are called values. Values can be text (such as letters), numbers or some symbols.

Imagine a program for creating an electronic birthday card. The electronic birthday card says Happy Birthday, your name and how old you are. The name and age in the message will change depending on whose birthday it is.

For the birthday party in this photo we use the values 'Miah' for her name and 8 for her age. For the birthday party on the next page, we use the value 'Mike' for his name and 9 for his age.

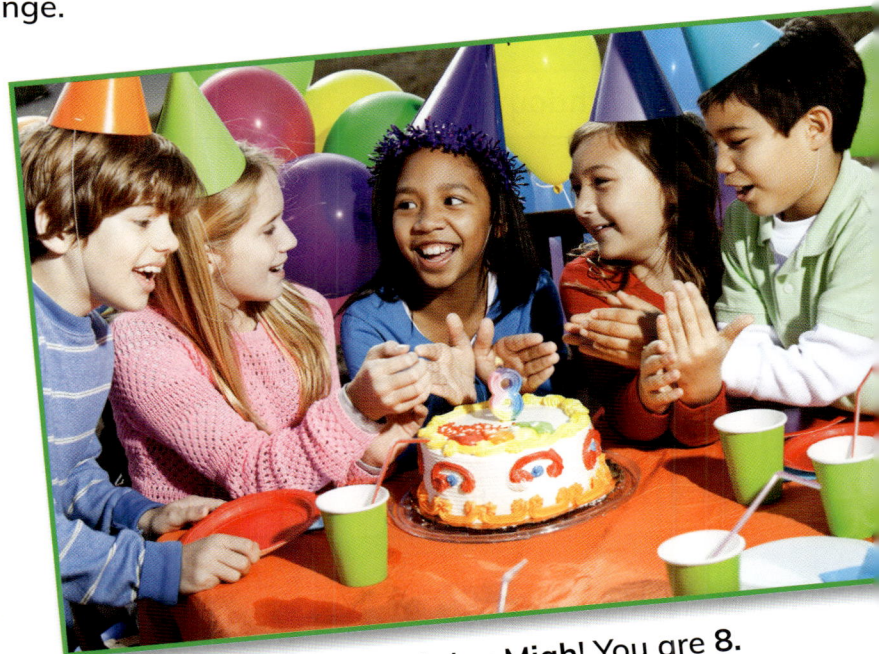

Happy Birthday Miah! You are 8.

The happy birthday algorithm could be written like this:

| 1 | say "Happy Birthday", "Miah" |
| 2 | say "You are", 8 |

The second algorithm could be written like this with different values for name and age:

| 1 | say "Happy Birthday", "Mike" |
| 2 | say "You are", 9 |

We can see that the happy birthday message is the same, but the values change depending on whose birthday it is and how old they are.

Happy Birthday **Mike**! You are **9**.

Question

3   What type of value (number or word) would you give to each of the things listed in the table?

Item	Value
Birthday	
Age	
Name	
Height	
Colour of your T-shirt	
Shoe size	
Favourite colour	

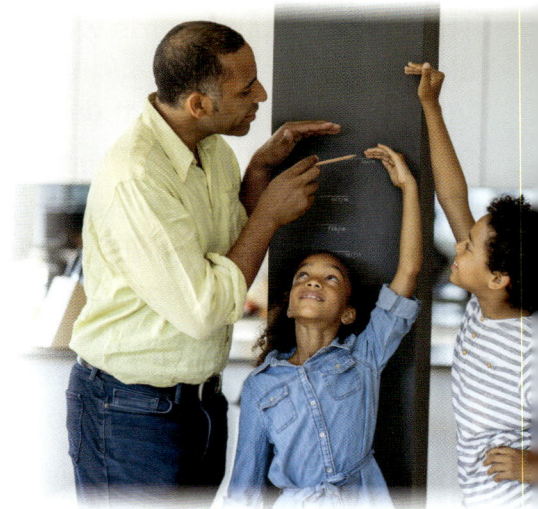

Assigning variables to values

Remember, computer programs use variables to store values that can change. For example, our happy birthday algorithm could use a variable to store the values for Mike and Miah's names and ages. These values can change depending on whose birthday it is and how old they are.

We need meaningful variable names to give us information about the value that is stored in the variable. Name will store the person's name and the variable Age will store their age.

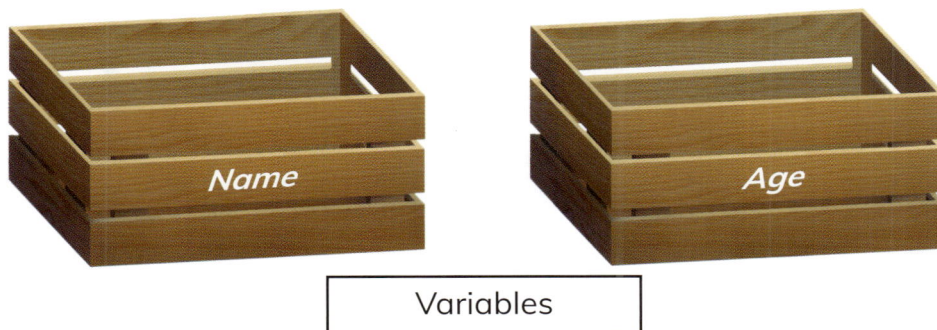

Variables

We can write the happy birthday algorithm like this, using variables to store the values for name and age:

```
1          say "Happy Birthday", Name
2          say "You are", Age
```

We can use this algorithm for anyone's birthday. We just need to store the correct values inside the variables.

Before we use a variable, we need to assign the variable a value. Assign means to give. A variable assignment is when we give a value to a variable to store. We can then use the value assigned to the variable in our program when we need it.

For example, to assign the variable Name to the value Mike, we say:

```
           set Name to Mike
```

To assign the variable Age to the value 9, we say:

set Age to 9

We can now use the variables assigned to the values in our program by referring to the variable name. Our happy birthday algorithm for Mike now looks like this:

1	set Name to Mike
2	set Age to 9
3	say Happy Birthday, Name
4	say You are, Age

Unplugged activity 1

You will need: a pen and paper

Look at these pictures from some children's birthday parties.

A  B  C

Now copy and complete the table. Add the correct values to the table, then write the message that would be output if the happy birthday algorithm was followed.

Child	A	B	C
Value for *Name* variable			
Value for *Age* variable			
Happy birthday message			

Question

If you want to challenge yourself, discuss the following question with a partner:

4 If you wanted to add who the birthday card was from, why would you use a variable?

Let's think about a different example.

Marcus is creating a program for buying his favourite things from the supermarket. He can set what his favourite items are in the program, and this makes it quicker for him to do his shopping. Marcus uses variables to store his favourite items from the supermarket.

Let's look at how Marcus uses the variable for storing his favourite vegetable. He gives the variable the name: *MyFavouriteVegetable*.

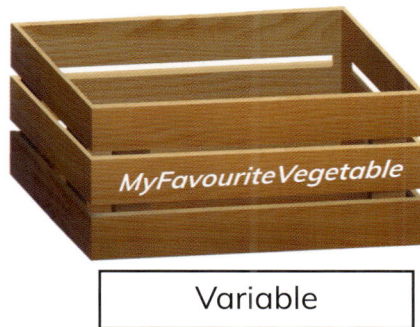

Variable

Marcus wants the program to store his favourite vegetable: broccoli.
He assigns the *MyFavouriteVegetable* variable to the value 'broccoli' like this:

set *MyFavouriteVegetable* to broccoli

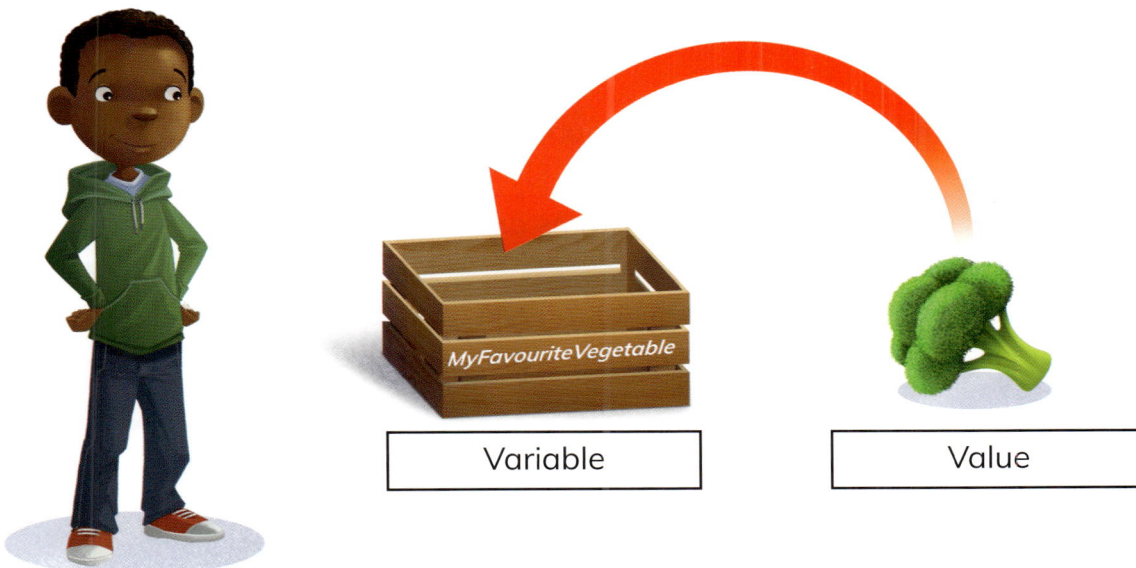

Variable   Value

If we look inside the variable, we can see the value broccoli. *MyFavouriteVegetable* is the variable assigned to the value broccoli in this algorithm.

Imagine Marcus wants to display what is inside the variable. The instruction to output what is inside the variable would be:

> say *MyFavouriteVegetable*

The value, broccoli, is the output.

Marcus's algorithm for assigning the variable *MyFavouriteVegetable* to the value broccoli, and then displaying the value, would look like this.

| 1 | set *MyFavouriteVegetable* to broccoli |
| 2 | say *MyFavouriteVegetable* |

A variable holds a temporary value that can change. Temporary means that the value is not kept forever. For example, we use the variable *MyFavouriteVegetable* because not everyone has the same favourite vegetable. So, depending on who is using the program, we can store a different value inside the variable.

When Sofia uses the variable, her algorithm looks like this:

| 1 | set *MyFavouriteVegetable* to carrot |
| 2 | say *MyFavouriteVegetable* |

Questions

5   Write an algorithm to assign the *MyFavouriteVegetable* variable to your own favourite vegetable.

6   With your partner, compare your algorithms and discuss the differences.

7   Marcus wants to add a variable to his algorithm that stores his favourite fruit. What meaningful name would you give this variable?

Activity 2

You will need: a desktop computer, laptop or tablet and word-processing software

Use a computer to create a poster that explains what variables are and how we use them.

Unplugged activity 3

You will need: a pen and paper or a whiteboard pen and mini whiteboard

Look at the picture of the football game. Notice how the screen displays different values. The values are numbers and letters.

Continued

Part A

In pairs, look at the picture and discuss the following questions.

1 How many different values are there on the screen?
2 What do the different values represent?
3 Which values might change during the football game?
4 Why is it useful to hold each value inside a variable?

Part B

In pairs, write an algorithm for assigning the variables to the values at the start of the match. Use the picture and your answers from Part A. Each variable should have a meaningful name so that everyone can understand what is stored inside it. One variable has been done for you.

set *Team1* to Python

How are we doing?

Work with your partner. Compare your algorithms, then read the success criteria below. Record your answers in a table like this. Draw a tick if your algorithm matches the success criteria. Draw a cross if it does not.

Success criteria	🙂	🙁
My algorithm has five variables.		
My variables have meaningful names.		
Each variable has been assigned a value.		

Programming task 1

You will need: a pen and paper, a desktop computer, laptop or tablet with access to Scratch, source file **1.1_basketball**

Part A

With a partner, look at source file 1.1_basketball. Discuss what you think will happen when you click on the basketball. What will happen if you click on the basketball three times? What happens when you click the 'Reset Score' button? Identify any variables in this program.

Score   0

Reset Score

```
when this sprite clicked
change  Score ▼  by  1
```

Part B

Run the program and click on the basketball to see if your predictions were correct.

Write down what happens to the value of the variable 'Score' when you click the basketball.

Write down what happens when you click the 'Reset Score' button.

The 'Reset Score' button does not work in the way I predicted. I thought it would reset the score to zero.

Continued

Click on the Button sprite to see the Reset Score script.

Change the variable from 'my variable' to 'Score'.

Now the 'Reset Score' button should work as expected, setting the score to 0 when clicked.

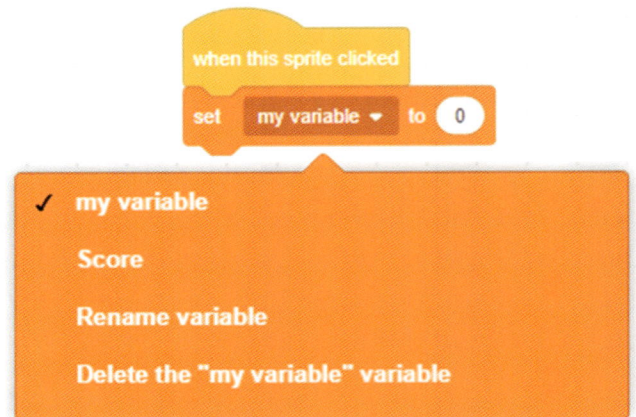

Part C

In basketball, if you throw the ball from inside the three-point line and it goes in the hoop you get two points. If you throw the ball from outside the three-point line and it goes in the hoop, you get three points.

when this sprite clicked
set my variable to 0

✓ my variable

Score

Rename variable

Delete the "my variable" variable

1   Modify the code for the Basketball1 sprite so that the score changes by two points each time the sprite is clicked.

Score   0
Shot Counter   0
Reset Score

This is where your next sprite needs to be.

This is the 3-point line. You get 3 points for shooting the ball outside this line.

Continued

2   Add another Basketball sprite to the project and place it outside the three-point line.

3   Add code to the second basketball sprite so that the score changes by three points each time the sprite is clicked.

Part D

With your partner, follow the steps below to add a shot counter to your code. A shot counter tells you how many times you make a shot (throw the ball at the hoop).

Each time you click either basketball, the shot counter should increase by one.

You will need to:

1   Make a new variable. Click on 'Variables' in the blocks palette and then click 'Make a variable'. Remember, you need to give your variable a meaningful name. Both basketballs will need to use the variable, so click 'for all sprites'.

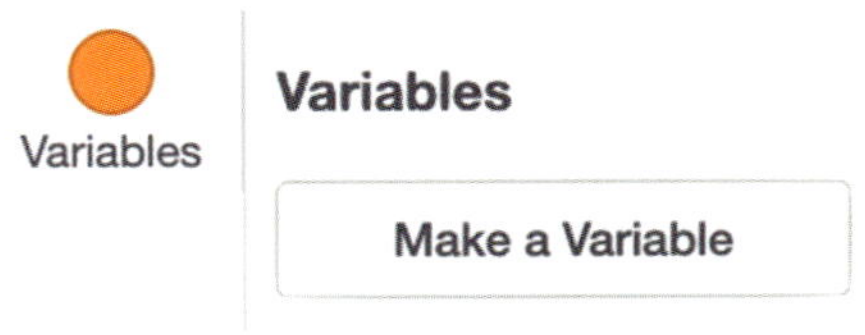

Variables

Variables

Make a Variable

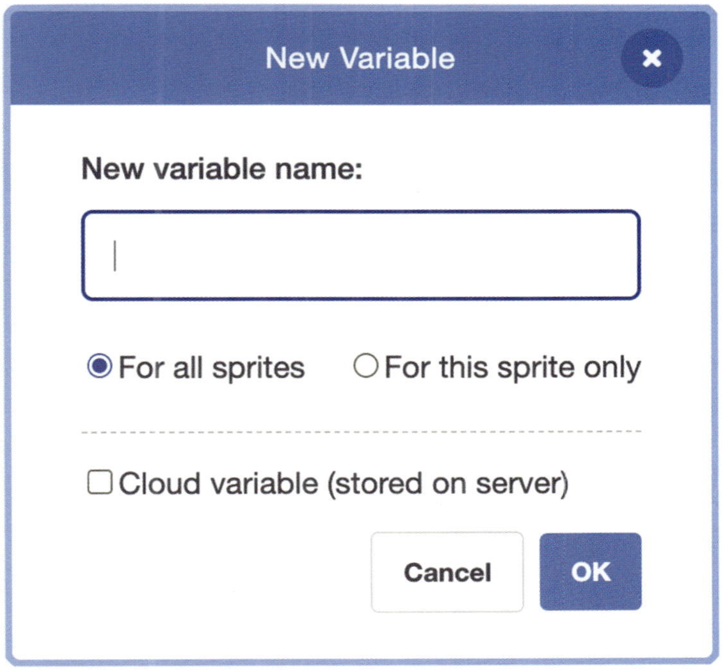

New Variable ✖

New variable name:

|

● For all sprites   ○ For this sprite only

☐ Cloud variable (stored on server)

Cancel   OK

Continued

2   Add code to each of the basketball sprites to change the value of the new shot count variable by one each time the balls are clicked.

3   Add code to the Button sprite so that when it is clicked, the Shot Counter also resets to zero.

> Remember it is important to always use meaningful variable names. This makes it easier for us to know what type of value our variables should hold. It also means that when other people use our programs they can understand what the variables are for.

How are we doing?

Swap your program with another pair. Now check your partner's program. Record your answers in a table like this. Draw a smiley face each time their program meets the success criteria here.

Success criteria	🙂	☹
There is a clearly named variable for the number of shots.		
The score increases by the correct amount when the ball inside the three-point line is clicked (two points) and the ball outside the three-point line is clicked (three points).		
The score and number of shots reset to zero when the 'Reset Score' button is clicked.		

How will you remember the definition of a variable?
Is there anything about variables that confuses you?
What could help you to understand variables better?

Look what I can do!

- [ ] I can define a variable as something that holds a value that can change.
- [ ] I can identify that algorithms hold values that can change.
- [ ] I can assign variables to values such as text or numbers.
- [ ] I can create variables with meaningful names to hold values in algorithms.
- [ ] I can modify an existing variable in Scratch and make a new variable.

> 1.2 Using operators

We are going to:

- follow instructions for adding and subtracting numbers using the plus (+) and minus (–) symbols

- add and subtract values held inside variables and output the answer

- store values that a user inputs, in variables, to perform calculations

- use the 'equal to' comparison operator in algorithms to check if values are the same

- modify and develop a calculator program to perform simple calculations using arithmetic operators.

arithmetic
arithmetic operator
comparison operator

condition
user input

Getting started

What do you already know?

- Variables hold values that can change.

- How to create and assign a value to a variable in Scratch.

- How to take a user input from the keyboard in Scratch.

- A calculator is a computing device that takes inputs, processes those inputs and produces outputs.

Continued

Now try this!

Work with a partner.

Imagine you are helping to prepare a meal. You need to follow the recipe. Read the instructions below and work out the total number of vegetables for each.

1   set *SweetCornAmount* to 1 + 2

2   set *CarrotAmount* to 5 + 2

3   set *BeansAmount* to 20 + 10

With your partner, discuss the following questions.

1   What is the same about the maths problems?

2   What is different about the problems?

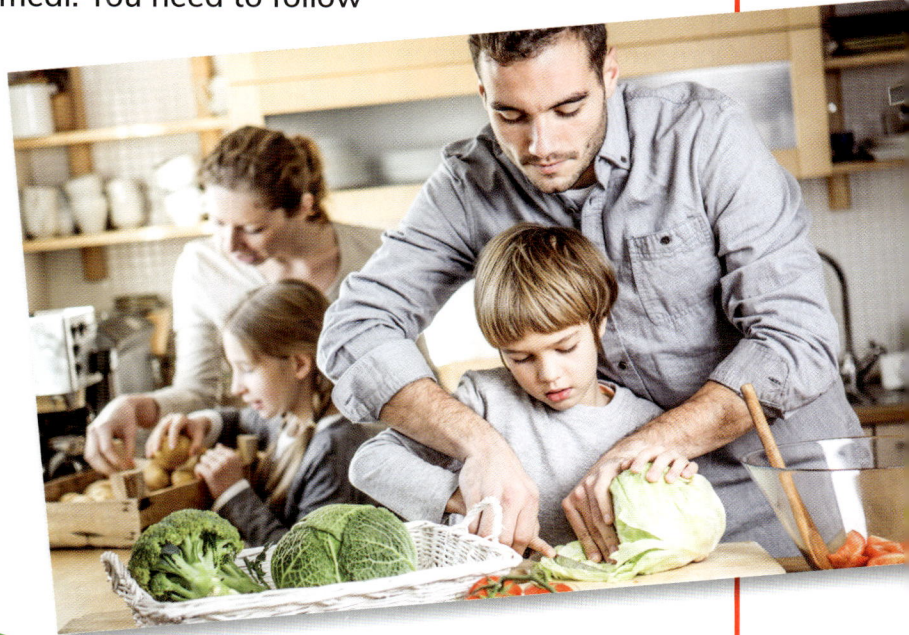

set *CarrotAmount*
to 5 + 2
So *CarrotAmount*
is a variable?

Yes! This variable stores the amount of carrots – this value can change. This is useful because different algorithms for recipes might need different amounts of carrots.

Arithmetic

Arithmetic is the use of numbers in calculations and counting, for example adding numbers together or subtracting numbers from each other.

Computers can do complicated arithmetic more quickly than people can. A calculator is a hand-held computer.

To make a computer carry out arithmetic, we need to give it a clear set of instructions to follow. We can instruct computers to calculate the score in a video game or the total cost of a shopping bill.

Arithmetic operators

Arithmetic operators are the symbols we use to do maths, such as + (add) and / (divide). They tell a computer what type of calculation to carry out on two or more values.

The two most important arithmetic operators we use on a computer are the + symbol for addition and the − symbol for subtraction.

To add two numbers together, we use the arithmetic operator for addition: the + symbol.

For example, 7 + 6, instructs the computer to add the first number, 7, to the second number, 6.

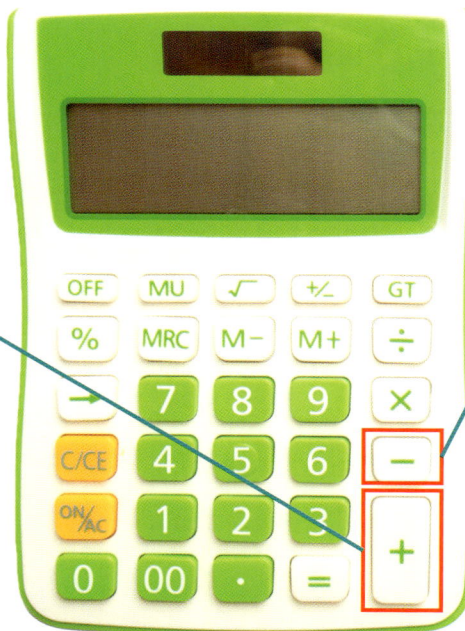

To subtract two numbers, we use the arithmetic operator for subtraction: the − symbol.

For example, 10 − 3, instructs the computer to subtract the second number, 3, from the first number, 10.

Arithmetic operators and variables

We use arithmetic operators in maths problems to add or subtract two or more numbers. For example:

7 + 6 = 13

We can also use arithmetic operators with variables to perform calculations in programs.

For example, the above calculation could be written like this.

1	set *FirstNumber* to 7
2	set *SecondNumber* to 6
3	set *Result* to *FirstNumber* + *SecondNumber*

Sofia, let's follow the algorithm above to find the value of **Result**. First, the values 7 and 6 are assigned to the variables **FirstNumber** and **SecondNumber**.

Then the values assigned to **FirstNumber** and **SecondNumber** are added together. 7 + 6 The answer 13, is assigned to the variable **Result**. So, the value assigned to **Result** is 13.

Unplugged activity 1

You will need: a pen and paper

With a partner, follow each algorithm and write down the value assigned to the last variable in the sequence of instructions. Talk about how you worked out your answer using the key words 'variable', 'assigned' and 'value'.

Remember, variables can only hold one value at a time and algorithms carry out instructions in sequence.

So if we run the following instructions:
set *Basketballs* to 1
set *Basketballs* to 2
set *Basketballs* to 3
the variable *Basketballs* stores the value 3. That is because 3 was the last value assigned to *Basketballs*.

Score   0

Shot Counter   0

Reset Score

Continued

1 What is the value of *Result*?

1	set *NumberOne* to 5
2	set *NumberTwo* to 5
3	set *Result* to *NumberOne* + *NumberTwo*

2 What is the value of *TotalApples*?

1	set *RedApples* to 20
2	set *GreenApples* to 5
3	set *TotalApples* to *RedApples* + *GreenApples*

3 What is the value of *SportsBalls*?

1	set *Basketball* to 3
2	set *Volleyball* to 1
3	set *SportsBalls* to *Basketball* + *Volleyball*

4 What is the value of *Birds*?

1	set *Ducks* to 20
2	set *Chickens* to 4
3	set *Birds* to *Ducks* + *Chickens*
4	set *Ducks* to 2
5	set *Birds* to *Birds* + *Ducks*

5 Create your own two variables.
Assign values to them.
Add the variables together and assign the result to a third variable.

How are we doing?

- Tell your partner what was easy and what was difficult about this task.

- Describe this instruction to a partner using the key words: variable, assign, value and arithmetic operator: set *Birds* to *Ducks* + 5.

Assigning values to a variable from a user input

We can write an algorithm that uses one or more variables with values already assigned to them.

For example, the following algorithm helps Mario, a fruit seller, to count how many fruits he has in the baskets in total. Mario uses variables because the numbers of fruits can change. Mario knows the number of bananas, papayas, pomegranates and oranges so he assigns these values to the variables.

1	set *BananasAmount* to 200
2	set *PapayasAmount* to 100
3	set *PomegranatesAmount* to 300
4	set *OrangesAmount* to 50
5	set *TotalFruits* to *BananasAmount* + *PapayasAmount* + *PomegranatesAmount* + *OrangesAmount*

As a programmer, when we write an algorithm that uses variables, we should know what type of values the variables will hold, such as text or number. For example, we should know that the variable *TotalFruits* is going to store a number.

Sometimes we want to write an algorithm where we only assign a value to a variable when we run the algorithm. For example, we cannot assign a value to *BananasAmount* because the fruit seller has not yet counted all the bananas.

When this happens, we can write the algorithm but allow a user to input the values that they want to assign to the variables. This is called user input. This means that a user provides data to a computer.

For example, we could write the algorithm for Mario like this.

1	set *BananasAmount* to USER INPUT
2	set *PapayasAmount* to USER INPUT
3	set *PomegranatesAmount* to USER INPUT
4	set *OrangesAmount* to USER INPUT
5	set *TotalFruits* to *BananasAmount* + *PapayasAmount* + *PomegranatesAmount* + *OrangesAmount*

Here, the user inputs the value for each variable. This algorithm allows Mario to input how many fruits there are at the start of the day. He could also use the algorithm to input how many fruits there are at the end of the day.

Let's think about using a calculator again. When you use a calculator, the values you input change depending on the calculation you want to perform.

1 Input the number 7

2 Press the arithmetic operator for addition

3 Input the number 6

4 Press the = sign to output the answer

> When I use a calculator, I assign values to variables when I press the buttons – this is my user input.

The algorithm for the calculation in the picture can be written like this.

1	set *FirstNumber* to USER INPUT
2	set *SecondNumber* to USER INPUT
3	set *Answer* to *FirstNumber* + *SecondNumber*

Activity 2

You will need: a desktop computer, laptop or tablet and a calculator

Use a calculator to calculate a difficult sum, like 3941 + 678. Explain what you are doing using words like: input, arithmetic operator, output, assign, variable.

Using a variable to hold numbers is useful because we do not need to change the algorithm every time we want to add together two different numbers.

In Scratch, the Ask block (in Sensing) allows you to enter a user input with the keyboard. The user input is always stored in a variable called *answer*.

Sensing

We can assign the user input stored in the *answer* to a variable with a meaningful name by using the Set To block.

It is a good idea to assign the user input stored in *answer* to a variable with a meaningful name, as shown here:

This is because the value stored in the *answer* variable will change if the user inputs another value.

Question

1   Compare the Scratch code below with the algorithm that Zara used for her calculator. Which one is easier to understand?

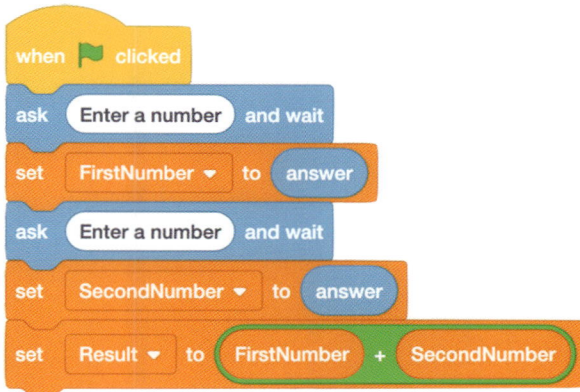

> **Did you know?**
>
> The word 'algorithm' comes from the name of a 9th century Persian mathematician, Muhammad ibn Mūsā al'Khwārizmī. In Latin, his name was Algoritmi, after the title of his famous book of arithmetic, *Algoritmi de numero Indorum*. Algoritmi means 'the decimal number system'.

Comparison operators

Sometimes we want to check the values in our algorithms by comparing them to other values. For example, when a user inputs their password into a computer, the input is compared with the stored password to check that the password the user entered is correct.

Comparison operators allow us to do this. Comparison operators compare two values and then provide the answer True or False. In programming, we say that they return True or False.

The comparison operator for comparing and checking if two values are the same is 'equal to'. The 'equal to' comparison operator checks if one value is the same as another value. If the values are the same, True is returned. If they are not the same, False is returned.

Imagine you are at a theme park. To ride the roller coaster, you have to be exactly 150 cm. You cannot be taller or shorter.

If you were 150 cm, the comparison would look like this:

Height = 150 cm

| 1 | set *Height* to 150 |
| 2 | *Height* equal to 150 |

The comparison will return True because the value of *Height* is 150. So *Height* is the same as 150.

If you were 160 cm, the comparison would look like this:

| 1 | set *Height* to 160 |
| 2 | *Height* equal to 150 |

The comparison will return False because the value of *Height* is 160. Here, *Height* is not the same as 150.

Comparison operators are used to create conditions. Conditions are like questions that need to be checked in an algorithm. Conditions have either a yes or a no answer which we write as True or False.

For example, 'Height equal to 150' can be read as a question: Is height equal to 150? The answer is either True or False.

Questions

2   With a partner, look at the sets of instructions that end with a condition. Write down whether the instructions will return True or False.

a

| 1 | set *Volume* to full |
| 2 | *Volume* equal to full |

b

1	set *CorrectPassword* to 123ABC
2	set *UserPassword* to CBA321
3	*CorrectPassword* equal to *UserPassword*

3 What would the variable *Volume* need to be for False to be returned?

4 What would the variable *UserPassword* need to be for True to be returned?

5 Can you think of situations in your everyday life where you use the 'equal to' comparison operator?

Stay safe!

123ABC is a weak password. A strong password is one that is long (over 16 characters) and easy to remember. Three random words is best practice, such as scissorswindowtree. Never write your password down or share it with other people.

I used to think a strong password needed a mix of special characters, upper-case and lower-case letters.

Many systems haven't updated their rules for passwords yet.

Programming task 1

You will need: a pen and paper, a desktop computer, laptop or tablet, and access to the source file **1.2_Frank_counts_balls**

Part A

Work in pairs. Look at the programs in source file **1.2_Frank_counts_balls**. In each program, Frank the sprite will say something about the number of balls he has collected from children throwing them into his garden.

Predict what Frank will say when the green flag is clicked for each program. Hint: *Balls* is a variable; Frank will say what is stored inside the variable. Think about what you know about arithmetic operators and variables.

Write your predictions on a piece of paper.

1

```
when [flag] clicked
set Football ▾ to 15
set TennisBall ▾ to 20
set SportsBalls ▾ to (Football + TennisBall)
say (join (I have) (join SportsBalls (sports balls))) for 5 seconds
```

2

```
when [flag] clicked
set PingPongBall ▾ to 5
set Football ▾ to 15
set TennisBall ▾ to 20
set SportsBalls ▾ to (Football + TennisBall)
set SportsBalls ▾ to (SportsBalls - TennisBall)
say (join (I have) (join SportsBalls (sports balls))) for 5 seconds
```

3

```
when [flag] clicked
set SportsBalls ▾ to (10 - 7)
say SportsBalls for 5 seconds
```

4

```
when [flag] clicked
set Basketball ▾ to 5
set PingPongBall ▾ to 6
set SportsBalls ▾ to (Basketball + PingPongBall)
say SportsBalls for 5 seconds
```

Continued

Part B

Click the 'See inside' button. Then click the green flag to run the fourth block of code from the predict activity.

```
when [flag] clicked
set PingPongBall ▾ to 5
set Football ▾ to 15
set TennisBall ▾ to 20
set SportsBalls ▾ to (Football + TennisBall)
set SportsBalls ▾ to (SportsBalls - TennisBall)
say (join (I have) (join (SportsBalls) (sports balls))) for 5 seconds
```

Work with your partner. Discuss the answers to the following questions.

1   What did Frank the sprite say when you ran the code?
2   Was your prediction from Part A correct? If not, why?
3   Explain what is happening in each line of the program.
    Try to use the words: values, variables, assign, arithmetic operator, display.

How are we doing?

- Did your partner use the keywords when describing each line of code?

- Did your partner predict the correct output?

- If your partner did not predict the correct output, could they explain what they got wrong?

Programming task 2

You will need: a desktop computer, laptop or tablet with access to Scratch and source file **1.3_calculator**

Arun made a calculator in Scratch but it does not work. All of the instructions for the addition sprite button are there but not in the right order. And there are no instructions for the subtraction sprite button.

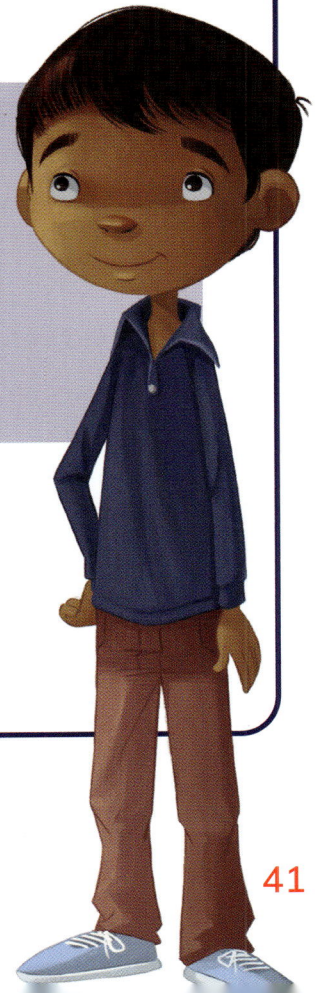

Luckily, Arun wrote his calculator algorithm first.

1	When the addition sign is clicked
2	Ask user to enter the first number
3	set Number1 to answer
4	Ask user to enter the second number
5	Set Number2 to answer
6	set Result to Number1 + Number2
7	Say Result

Open source file **1.3_calculator**. Using the algorithm above, put the Scratch instructions for the addition sprite in the correct order.

After you have ordered the code for the addition button, create the code for the subtraction sprite button.

Continued

How am I doing?

Work in pairs. Check your partner's algorithm against the success criteria below. Record your findings in a table like this.

Success criteria	☺	☹
The answer variable is assigned to Number1 and Number2.		
The instructions are in the correct order.		
When the 'addition' arithmetic operator is clicked and 7 and 5 are input, the answer 12 is displayed.		
When the 'subtraction' arithmetic operator is clicked and 7 and 5 are input, the answer 2 is displayed.		

How did the programming tasks help you to learn today?

How do you remember the difference between variables and values?

Look what I can do!

☐ I can follow instructions for adding and subtracting numbers using the plus (+) and minus (−) symbols.

☐ I can add and subtract values held inside variables and output the answer.

☐ I can store values that a user inputs, in variables, to perform calculations.

☐ I can use the 'equal to' comparison operator in algorithms to check if values are the same.

☐ I can modify and develop a calculator program to perform simple calculations using arithmetic operators.

> 1.3 Selection

We are going to:

- **follow and edit selection statements in everyday algorithms**
- **predict the outcome of algorithms using IF THEN ELSE statements**
- **follow and correct an algorithm using selection with IF statements**
- **develop programs to control a spaceship using IF THEN ELSE statements and the 'equal to' comparison operator.**

comments   selection
condition block   selection statement
IF statements   sequence
iteration

Getting started

What do you already know?

- Algorithms can produce different outputs based on different inputs.
- Pressing different combinations of buttons on a video game controller produces different outcomes.
- Programs can store user inputs in variables to use in calculations, like in a calculator.
- How to use an indefinite (forever) loop in Scratch to repeat instructions forever.
- The comparison operator 'equal to' is used to check if two things are the same.

43 >

Continued

Now try this!

You will need: a pen and paper

Traffic lights work differently depending on where you live in the world. Computer programs control traffic light sequences. The image shows the four different stages of a traffic light sequence. The lights follow this sequence in a forever loop.

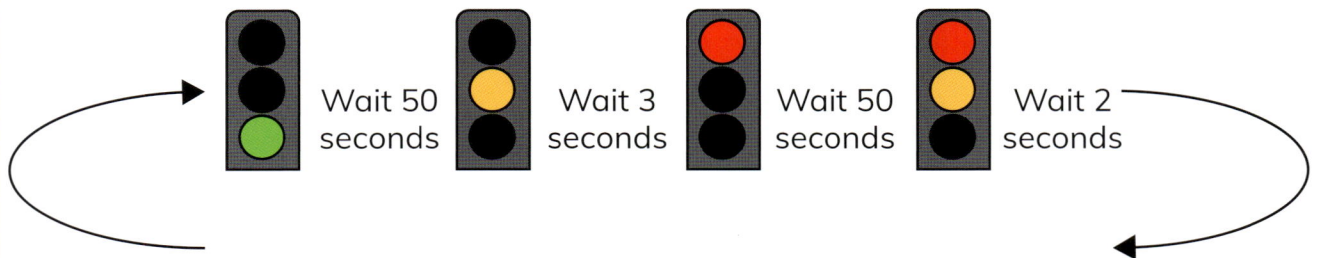

Write instructions for sequencing each stage of the traffic lights in the correct order forever.

The instructions for the first stage have been done for you. Use a variable for each traffic light: red, amber and green. The variables can be set to ON or OFF.

Write and complete the algorithm:

1	REPEAT FOREVER
2	set *RedLight* to OFF
3	set *AmberLight* to OFF
4	set *GreenLight* to ON
5	wait 50

Selection in algorithms

Remember: **sequence** is the order in which code or instructions are carried out.

Remember: **iteration** is where code or instructions are being repeated.

Sequence and iteration control the order in which code or instructions are carried out.

So is selection another way we can control the order in which instructions are carried out?

Selection lets our algorithms and programs decide what to do next. The next instructions or code that are carried out will depend on the answer to a question. You already know that we call these True or False conditions.

Selection statements have a condition and instructions or code that is carried out only if that condition is True. There may be an instruction to carry out if the condition is False, otherwise the program or algorithm just continues in the normal sequence.

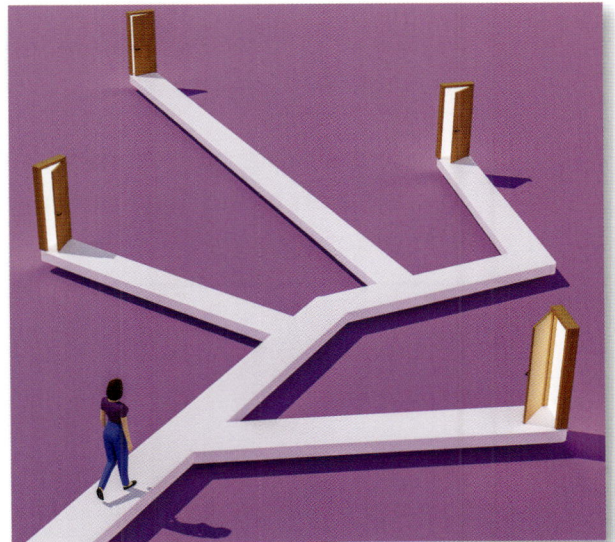

We use selection and conditions in real life to help us make decisions about what to do.

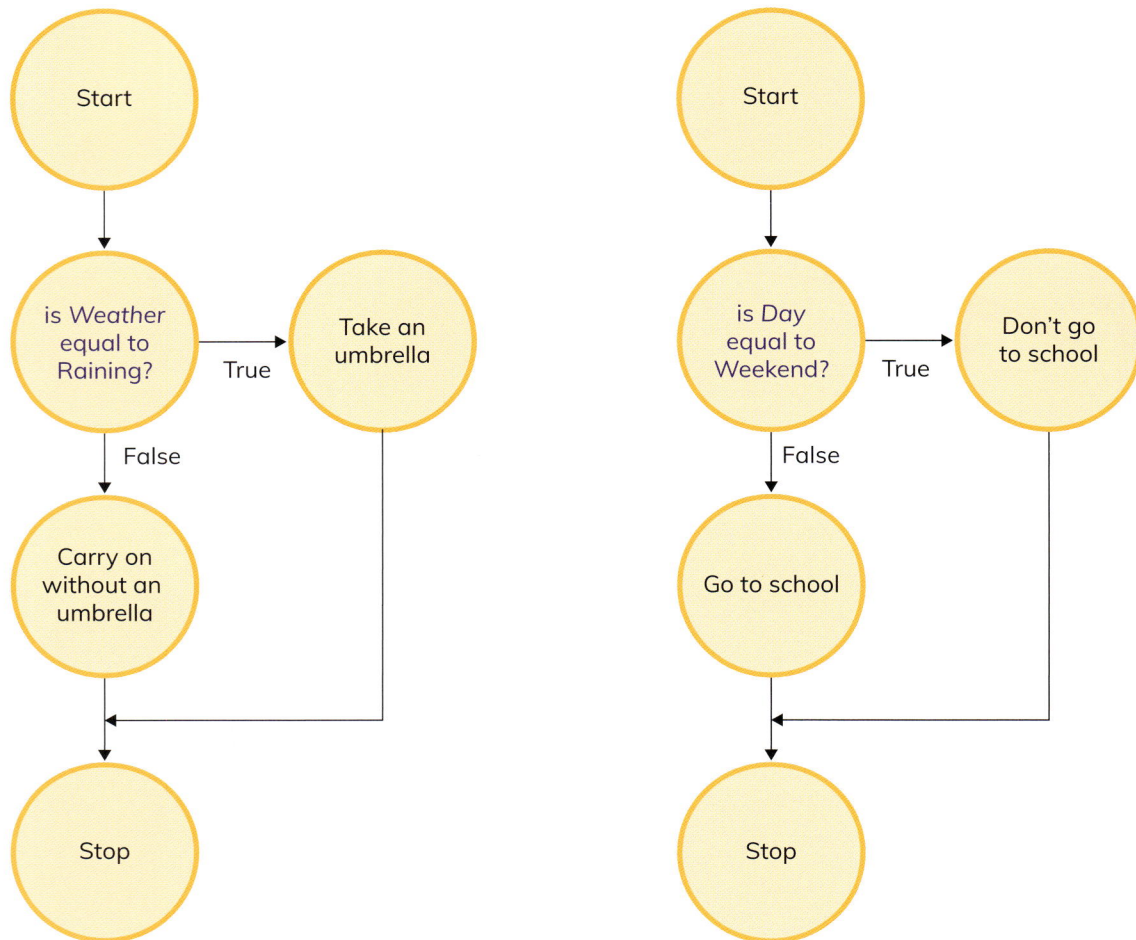

Start

is Weather equal to Raining? → True → Take an umbrella

False

Carry on without an umbrella

Stop

Start

is Day equal to Weekend? → True → Don't go to school

False

Go to school

Stop

Activity 1

You will need: a desktop computer, laptop or tablet with presentation software

Write a simple algorithm for an activity you do in your daily life that depends on a condition being True or False. Use presentation software to create a diagram of the algorithm.

Unplugged activity 2

You will need: a pen and paper

Part A

Part of an algorithm using selection has been drawn for controlling a video game. You need to correct the algorithm:

- Draw the diagram on your paper.

- Add arrows connecting the instructions in the correct order using sequence and selection.

- Label the arrows coming out of the condition as True or False.

Start

is UpArrow equal to pressed?

Move player up

Do not move player

Stop

Ask a partner to follow your algorithm with their finger and check whether it makes sense if the condition is True or False.

Continued

Part B

Modify your algorithm to control a different part of the video game.

You will need instructions for:

- start and stop
- a condition that can be either True or False
- an outcome if the condition is True
- an outcome if the condition is False
- arrows connecting the instructions in the correct order.

Writing selection statements using IF THEN ELSE

We can use selection statements to make our programs or algorithms branch. IF statements are a type of selection statement. We are going to use IF statements to make our algorithms execute different instructions depending on whether a condition is True or False.

We write an IF statement by writing IF and then the condition we want to check. Remember, the condition must be either True or False. We write the instruction we want the program to carry out if the condition is True after the word THEN, underneath the IF statement.

1	IF *condition*
2	THEN *instructions if condition is True*
3	*Continue with algorithm*

The IF statement checks the condition and provides an instruction for when that condition is True. If the condition is False, the program will just continue, ignoring the instructions under the IF statement.

For example:

1	IF Temperature equal to very cold
2	THEN Take a jacket
3	*Continue with algorithm*

If the condition is False, we might want our algorithm to do something different before continuing. For example, what do you wear if it is *not* very cold? To do this we use an IF THEN ELSE statement.

Like before, we write the condition we want to check after the word IF, and we write the instruction for if the condition is True after THEN underneath. We write ELSE after the instructions inside IF. The instructions inside ELSE are only carried out if the condition is False.

1	IF condition
2	THEN instructions if condition is True
3	ELSE
4	instructions if condition is False
5	*Continue with algorithm*

For example:

1	IF Temperature equal to very cold
2	THEN Take a jacket
3	ELSE
4	Take a jumper
5	*Continue with algorithm*

Questions

Read the following IF THEN ELSE statement.

1	IF Time equal to morning
2	THEN Say "Good morning"
3	ELSE
4	Say "Good afternoon"
5	Say "How are you?"

1 What will you say if the condition is True?

2 What will you say if the condition is False?

3 What will you say regardless of whether the condition is True or False?

Let's compare a linear algorithm for our morning routine with one that uses selection. Which algorithm would work best for most people? Which algorithm will work every day of the week?

Morning routine – Linear		Morning routine – Selection	
1	Wake up	1	Wake up
2	Take a shower	2	IF *ShoweredLastNight* equal to YES
3	Get dressed	3	THEN Get dressed
4	Eat breakfast	4	ELSE
5	Brush your teeth	5	Take a shower
6	Go to school	6	Get dressed
		7	IF *BrushTeeth* equal to Before eating
		8	THEN Brush your teeth
		9	Eat breakfast
		10	ELSE
		11	Eat your breakfast
		12	Brush your teeth
		13	IF *SchoolDay* equal to Today
		14	THEN Go to school

Unplugged activity 3

You will need: a pen and paper

In groups of three, read the selection statements that follow. Each of you has a score that is stored inside the variable *PlayerScore*. Each player's score will start at zero. Check the condition for each selection statement and follow the correct instruction to calculate your new score.

Round one

1	set *PlayerScore* to 0
2	IF *ShirtColour* equal to Red
3	THEN set *PlayerScore* to *PlayerScore* + 2
4	ELSE
5	set *PlayerScore* to *PlayerScore* + 1
6	WRITE DOWN *PlayerScore*

The condition is False so my score will increase by one.

The condition is True for me as my shirt is red, so my score increases by two!

Round two

Use your value in the *PlayerScore* variable from round one.

1	IF *ShoeSize* equal to 18
2	THEN set *PlayerScore* to *PlayerScore* + 1
3	ELSE
4	set *PlayerScore* to *PlayerScore* + 2
5	WRITE DOWN *PlayerScore*

Continued

Round three

The algorithm for scoring in round three has two bugs. The player's score increases by three whether the condition is True or False. Put the instructions in a selection statement so that *PlayerScore* increases by two if the condition is True and one if the condition is False.

1	is *FavouriteGame* equal to "football"
2	set *PlayerScore* to *PlayerScore* + 2
3	
4	set *PlayerScore* to *PlayerScore* + 1
5	WRITE DOWN *PlayerScore*

Use your value in the *PlayerScore* variable from round two and play round three once you have debugged it.

How did you decide what outcome occurs if the condition is True?
In the future, how can you use what you have learnt about selection?

Combining user inputs, variables and selection

You have already seen that conditions can be set within algorithms. We can use conditions when building programs within Scratch to change what a sprite does. The condition checks for a user input, then makes the sprite do a certain action.

Look at this Scratch block. This block is used as a condition in Scratch and checks for user input from the keyboard.

key left arrow ▼ pressed?

This is an example of a condition block. We can use this condition block with other blocks in Scratch to decide which instruction to carry out next. Condition blocks are all the same shape (a hexagon). The blocks that are used with them have a hexagonal space in them.

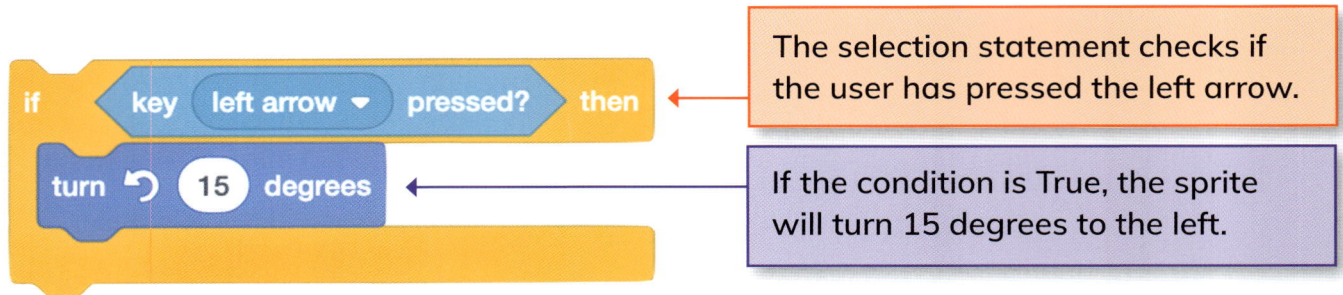

```
if   key  left arrow ▼  pressed?   then
    turn ↺  15  degrees
```

The selection statement checks if the user has pressed the left arrow.

If the condition is True, the sprite will turn 15 degrees to the left.

We can make our programs more interactive by asking the user questions.

- When the user answers questions, we can store their answers in variables.

- We can use conditions to check their answers.

- We can carry out different actions based on their response, using selection.

Look at the following example to see how these actions fit together.

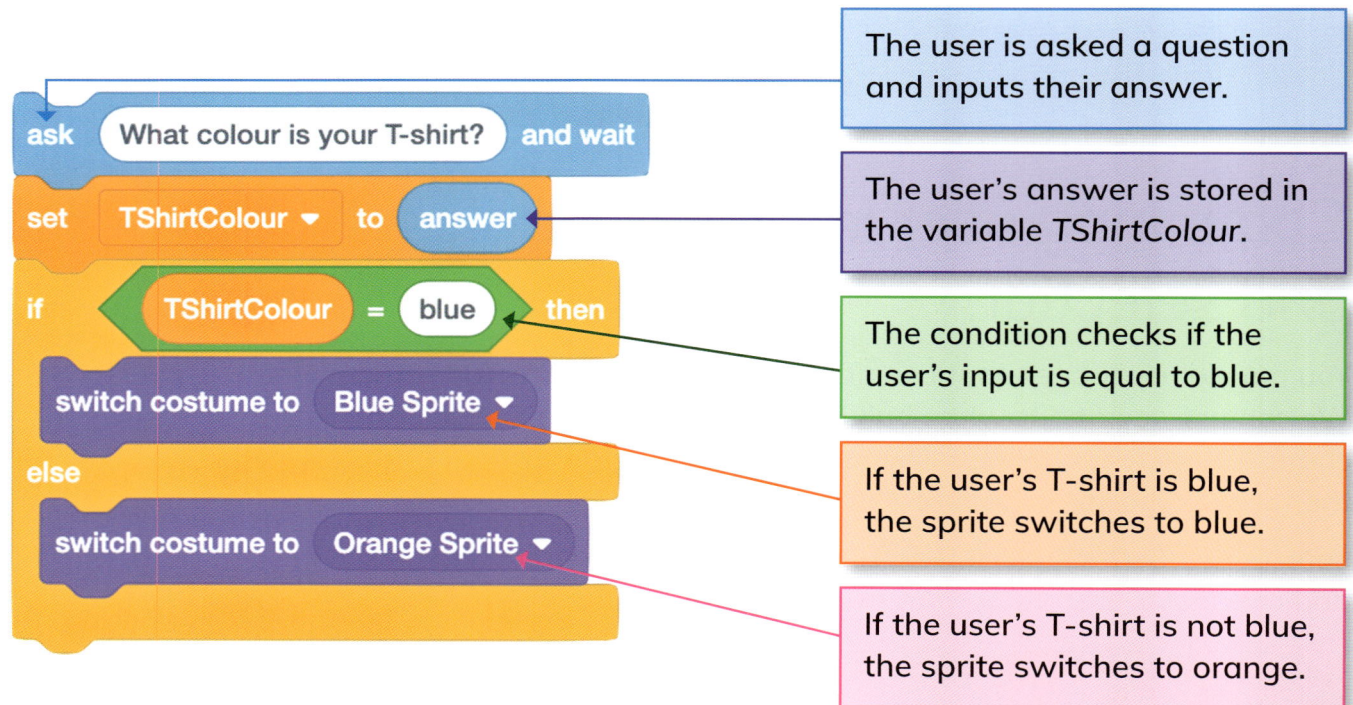

```
ask   What colour is your T-shirt?   and wait
set   TShirtColour ▼  to  answer
if    TShirtColour = blue   then
    switch costume to  Blue Sprite ▼
else
    switch costume to  Orange Sprite ▼
```

The user is asked a question and inputs their answer.

The user's answer is stored in the variable *TShirtColour*.

The condition checks if the user's input is equal to blue.

If the user's T-shirt is blue, the sprite switches to blue.

If the user's T-shirt is not blue, the sprite switches to orange.

Programming task 1

You will need: a pen and paper, and a desktop computer, laptop or tablet with access to Scratch and source file **1.4_Scratch_in_space**

Part A

With a partner, read the selection statements in the Scratch program. Discuss what will happen when the program is run.

Answer these questions about each of the selection statements.

1 What are the conditions checking in the IF statements?

2 What will happen if the condition is True?

3 What will happen if the condition is False?

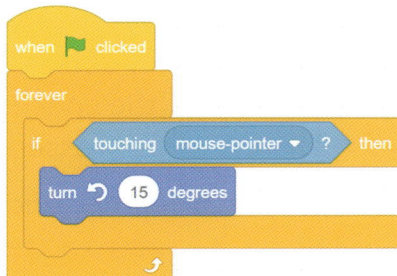

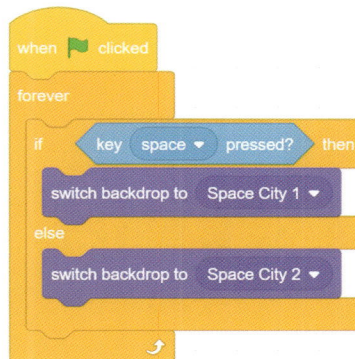

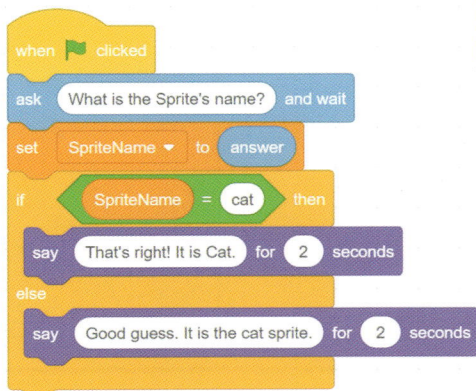

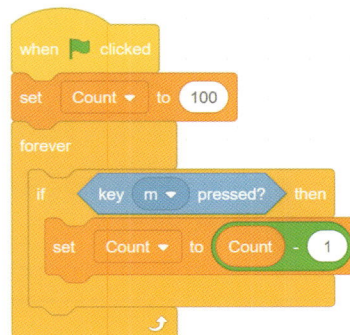

Continued

Part B

Work with a partner. Open source file **1.4_Scratch_in_space**. Click the 'See inside' button and then click the green flag to run the Scratch project to check if your predictions were correct. Discuss the following questions with your partner.

1 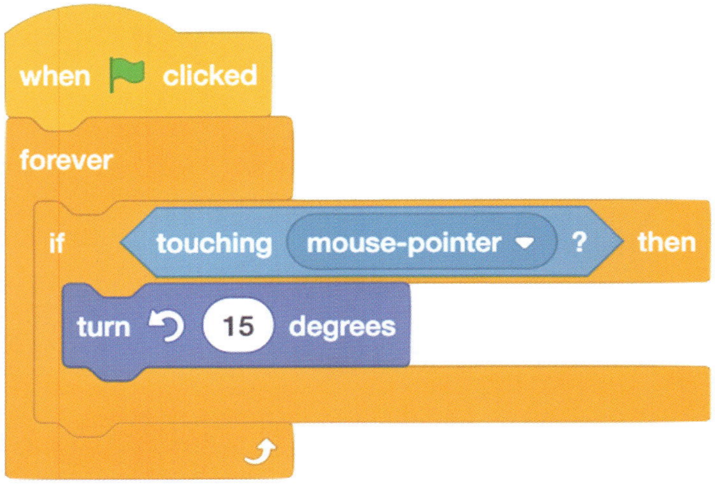	when 🚩 clicked
	forever
	  if ⟨ touching ⟨ mouse-pointer ▾ ⟩ ? ⟩ then
	    turn ↺ 15 degrees
		Which block of code runs if the mouse pointer is touching the cat?

2	when 🚩 clicked
	forever
	  if ⟨ key ⟨ space ▾ ⟩ pressed? ⟩ then
	    switch backdrop to Space City 1 ▾
	  else
	    switch backdrop to Space City 2 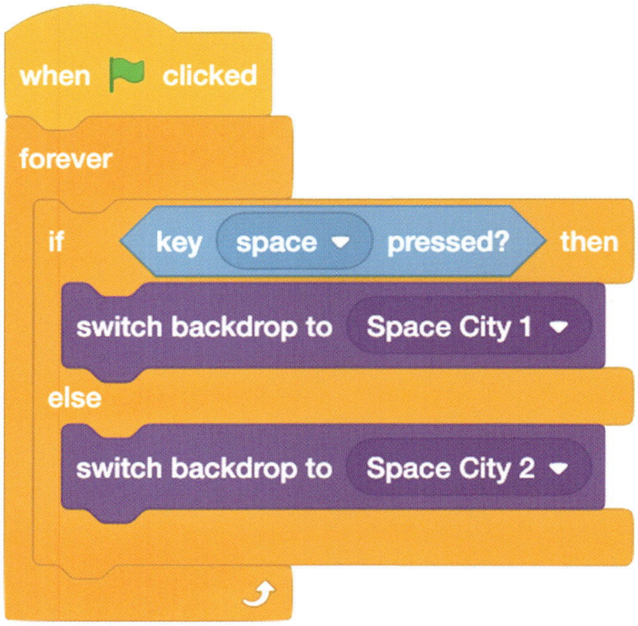 ▾
		a Which block of code runs if the space bar is pressed?
		
		b What backdrop is used if the space bar is not pressed?

Continued

3	
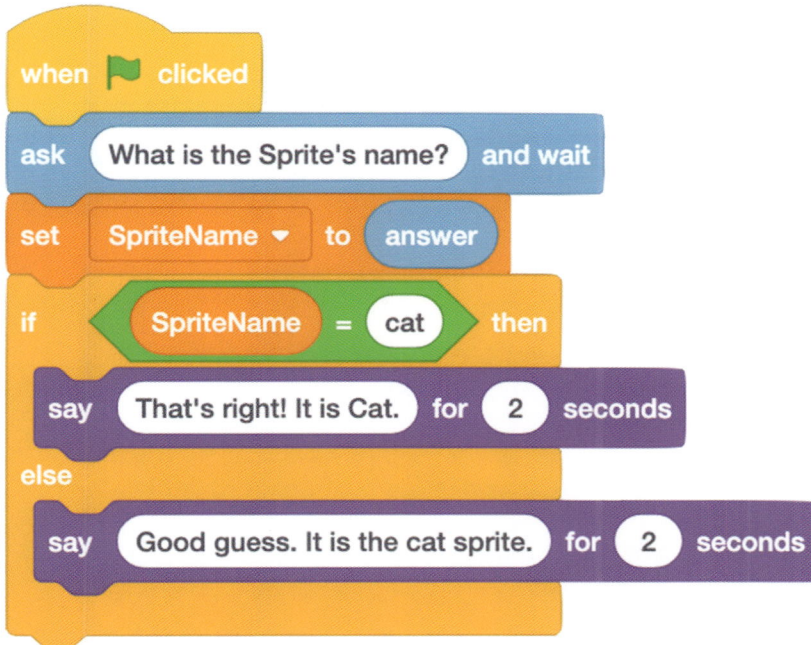	**a** What happens if the user inputs 'cat'? **b** What happens if the user does not input 'cat'?

4	
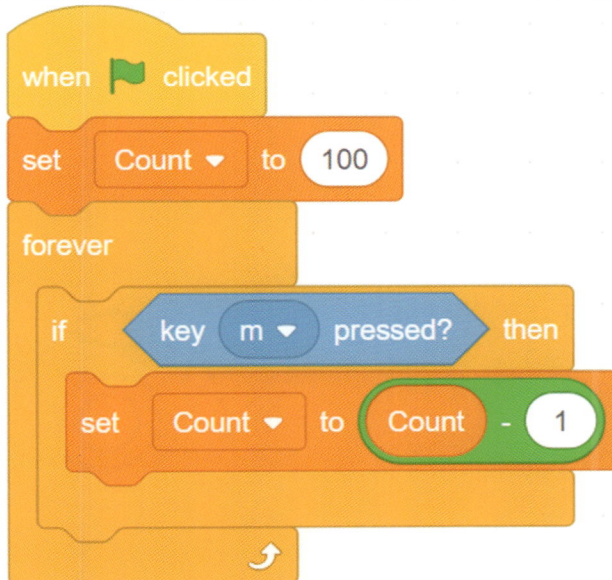	**a** What is the first value stored in the Count variable? **b** What happens if you press the 'm' key? **c** What happens if you hold the 'm' key down?

Programming task 2

You will need: a desktop computer, laptop or tablet with access to Scratch and source file **1.5_space_pilot**

Open source file **1.5_space_pilot**. Write code to control the rocket ship in Scratch using the up, down, left and right arrows on the keyboard. The rocket ship will go into space if it leaves the city. The rockets will turn on when the arrows are pressed.

Use the following algorithm to help you. The words written after the // are comments. Remember, programmers use comments to help them explain what the different parts of a program do.

```
1        REPEAT FOREVER
2            IF key up arrow pressed
3                THEN point in direction 90 //This will point the rocket ship up
4                change y by 10 //This moves the rocket ship up
5            IF key down arrow pressed
6                THEN point in direction -90
7                change y by -10
8            IF key right arrow pressed
9                THEN point in direction 180
10               change x by 10
11           IF key left arrow pressed
12               THEN point in direction 0
13               change x by -10
```

Continued

Test that your rocket ship moves correctly when you press the different arrow keys.

Careful!

How am I doing?

Read the sentences below. Record your answers in a table like this. Give yourself either a smiley face to show you have achieved them, or a sad face.

Success criteria	☺	☹
My program has an IF statement for each arrow key.		
The rocket ship moves in the correct direction when I press an arrow key on the keyboard.		

Look what I can do!

- [ ] I can follow and edit selection statements in everyday algorithms.
- [ ] I can predict the outcome of algorithms using IF THEN ELSE statements.
- [ ] I can follow and correct an algorithm using selection with IF statements.
- [ ] I can develop a program using IF THEN ELSE statements and the 'equal to' comparison operator.

> 1.4 Planning solutions

We are going to:

- understand that different algorithms can be used to complete the same task

- understand that we can make algorithms more efficient by using selection to only carry out necessary instructions

- identify the purpose, inputs, processes, conditions and outputs of a problem

- decompose problems to write an outline plan for a program.

condition | iteration
decomposition | output
efficient | process
input

Getting started

What do you already know?

- We can use iteration to create efficient algorithms.

- A loop inside another loop is known as a nested loop.

Continued

- We use decomposition to break problems down into smaller parts that are easier to solve.

- We use comments to help understand the purpose of instructions.

Now try this!

> **You will need:** a pen and paper

A robot is being programmed to plant trees to make a new forest.

Three different solutions have been written to instruct the tree-planting robot. Comments are shown with a double forward slash //.

Solution 1		Solution 2		Solution 3	
1	Plant tree	1	REPEAT 2	1	REPEAT 2
2	Move forward	2	Plant tree	2	REPEAT 2
3	Plant tree	3	Move forward	3	Plant tree
4	Move forward	4	//Turn at the top	4	Move forward
5		5	Plant tree	5	//Turn at the top
6	//Turn at the top	6	Turn right	6	Plant tree
7	Plant tree	7		7	Turn right
8	Turn right	8	Move forward	8	Move forward
9	Move forward	9	Turn right	9	Turn right
10	Turn right	10		10	
11		11	REPEAT 2	11	REPEAT 2

Continued

12	Plant tree	12	Plant tree	12	Plant tree
13	Move forward	13	Move forward	13	Move forward
14	Plant tree	14	//Turn at the bottom	14	//Turn at the bottom
15	Move forward	15	Plant tree	15	Plant tree
16		16	Turn left	16	Turn left
17	//Turn at the bottom	17	Move forward	17	Move forward
18	Plant tree	18	Turn left	18	Turn left
19	Turn left	19			
20	Move forward	20	REPEAT 2		
21	Turn left	21	Plant tree		
22		22	Move forward		
23	Plant tree	23	//Turn at the top		
24	Move forward	24	Plant tree		
25	Plant tree	25	Turn right		
26	Move forward	26	Move forward		
27		27	Turn right		
28	//Turn at the top	28			
29	Plant tree	29	REPEAT 2		
30	Turn right	30	Plant tree		
31	Move forward	31	Move forward		
32	Turn right	32	//Turn at the bottom		
33		33	Plant tree		
34	Plant tree	34	Turn left		
35	Move forward	35	Move forward		
36	Plant tree	36	Turn left		
37	Move forward				
38	Plant tree				

Read and follow each solution. With your partner, discuss the following questions.

1 Which solution has the most instructions?

2 Which solution has the most loops?

3 How is iteration used to make solutions 2 and 3 more efficient?

4 Which solution is the most efficient?

5 Which solution uses nested iteration?

Creating more efficient algorithms

The same problem can often be solved in different ways. Think about how you get to the room where you eat lunch. There are different routes you can take. Some routes will be faster than others.

An algorithm is more efficient when only necessary instructions are carried out. Efficient is doing something in a careful and complete way with no waste of time.

There are different ways to make algorithms more efficient. We can use iteration by removing instructions that repeat. We can also use selection. You already know that selection means we set conditions to only carry out an instruction if needed.

Remember, selection helps choose which instructions or code to follow based on whether a condition is True or False.

We use selection in our morning routine to check a condition before performing an activity that we may have already done. For example, if we took a shower the night before then it is not necessary to take a shower in the morning.

Morning routine – Linear	
1	Wake up
2	Get out of bed
3	Take a shower
4	Get dressed
5	Eat breakfast
6	Brush your teeth
7	Go to school

Morning routine – Selection	
1	Wake up
2	Get out of bed
3	IF *ShoweredLastNight* equal to YES
4	THEN Get dressed
5	ELSE
6	Take a shower
7	Get dressed
8	Eat breakfast
9	Brush your teeth
10	IF *SchoolDay* equal to YES
11	THEN Go to school

Questions

Compare the morning routine algorithms.

1   How many actions will the linear algorithm carry out when run?

2   How many actions will the algorithm with selection carry out when it is run as follows?

   a   Set *ShoweredLastNight* to NO and set *SchoolDay* to NO

   b   Set *ShoweredLastNight* to NO and set *SchoolDay* to YES

   c   Set *ShoweredLastNight* to YES and set *SchoolDay* to YES

   d   Set *ShoweredLastNight* to YES and set *SchoolDay* to NO

The linear morning routine algorithm will carry out every instruction, every day. The morning routine algorithm will only carry out certain instructions if the condition is True. This makes the algorithm more efficient as it will not carry out unnecessary instructions. Even though the algorithm is longer, it is more efficient.

Unplugged activity 1

You will need: a pen, paper and a small piece of sticky tack

Deforestation is the act of cutting down or burning the trees in an area of forest. Deforestation has a negative impact on the environment. We need trees and forests to capture the carbon that contributes to climate change.

Many people are trying to help by replanting trees. We could replant forests more quickly by using technology.

Continued

Work in a group of three to make the algorithm for the tree-planting robot more efficient.

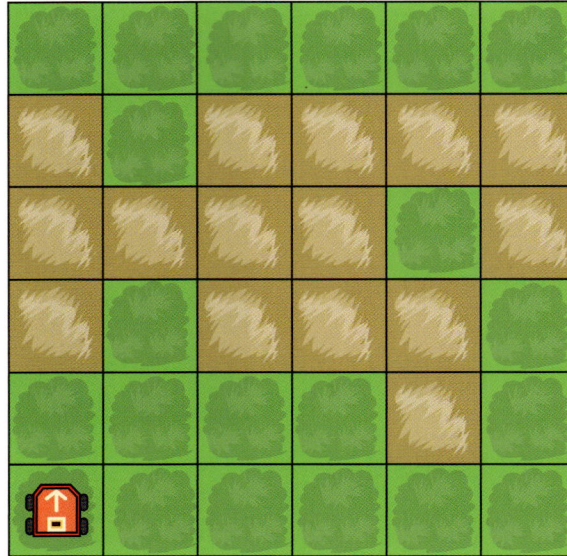

X

It looks like some trees are already planted where the squares are green.

So it would be more efficient to only plant trees where there aren't any.

Continued

Solution 1: Iteration	
1	REPEAT 3
2	REPEAT 5
3	Plant tree
4	Move forward
5	**//Turn at the top of forest**
6	Turn right
7	Move forward
8	Turn right
9	
10	REPEAT 5
11	Plant tree
12	Move forward
13	**//Turn at the bottom of forest**
14	Turn left
15	Move forward
16	Turn left

Solution 2: Iteration and Selection	
1	REPEAT 6
2	REPEAT 5
3	IF Ground equal to SOIL
4	THEN Plant tree
5	Move forward
6	**//Turn at top or bottom of forest**
7	IF *RobotPosition* equal to TOP
8	Turn right
9	Move forward
10	Turn right
11	ELSE
12	Turn left
13	Move forward
14	Turn left

In your group, assign each person one of these roles:

- Algorithm ace: Read the algorithms step by step. Make sure you follow each loop the correct number of times. Check any conditions with the Robot runner to know which instruction to carry out.

- Robot runner: Keep track of where the robot is on the grid using a small piece of sticky tack. Listen carefully to the Algorithm ace. Answer the Algorithm ace's conditions with a yes or no answer, depending on where the robot is.

Continued

- Code counter: Write down the number of times:

  - the robot moves forward

  - a tree is planted

  - a loop is repeated.

  The code counter should also help the Algorithm ace keep track of how many times a loop is repeated. Note: the robot should reach X by the end of each algorithm.

In your group, discuss the following questions.

1 How many times did the robot move forward in solution 1?
2 How many times did the robot move forward in solution 2?
3 How many trees were planted in solution 1?
4 How many trees were planted in solution 2?
5 Which solution was more efficient?
6 Could the algorithms be made more efficient?

> Remember to be positive when giving feedback so everybody can learn.

When following the tree-planting algorithms, whose role was the most helpful and why?

Activity 2

You will need: a desktop computer, laptop or tablet with access to Scratch and source file **1.6_maze_game**

Open source file **1.6_maze_game**. The aim of the maze game is to get the ball from the start to the finish while staying inside the black border of the track.

Two solutions have been written to solve the problem.

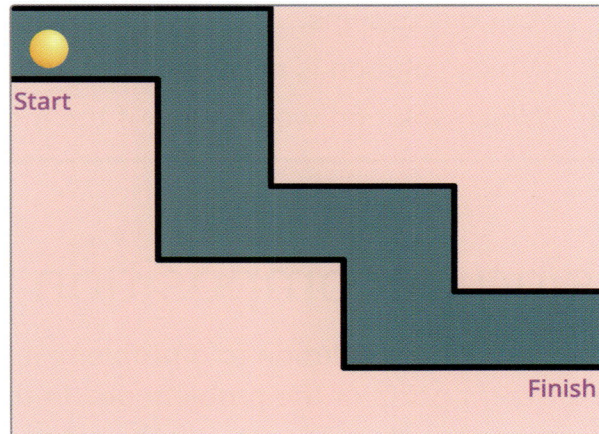

Solution 1

```
when [flag] clicked
go to x: -210 y: 145
repeat 12
  change x by 10
repeat 15
  change y by -10
repeat 15
  change x by 10
repeat 8
  change y by -10
repeat 20
  change x by 10
```

Solution 2

```
when [flag] clicked
go to x: -210 y: 145
forever
  if < touching color [black] ? > then
    change y by -10
  else
    change x by 10
```

Continued

With a partner, discuss the following questions.

1   How does each solution solve the problem of getting the ball to the finish? Try to use the words sequence, selection and iteration in your discussions.
2   Which solution is more efficient and why?
3   Which solution would work if the maze had another step added to it?

Using decomposition to plan algorithms

When planning a solution to a problem, it helps to understand what the different parts of the problem are. In the tree-planting algorithm, the different parts were moving the robot and planting trees. These small problems are called sub-problems and can be broken down even more, like this:

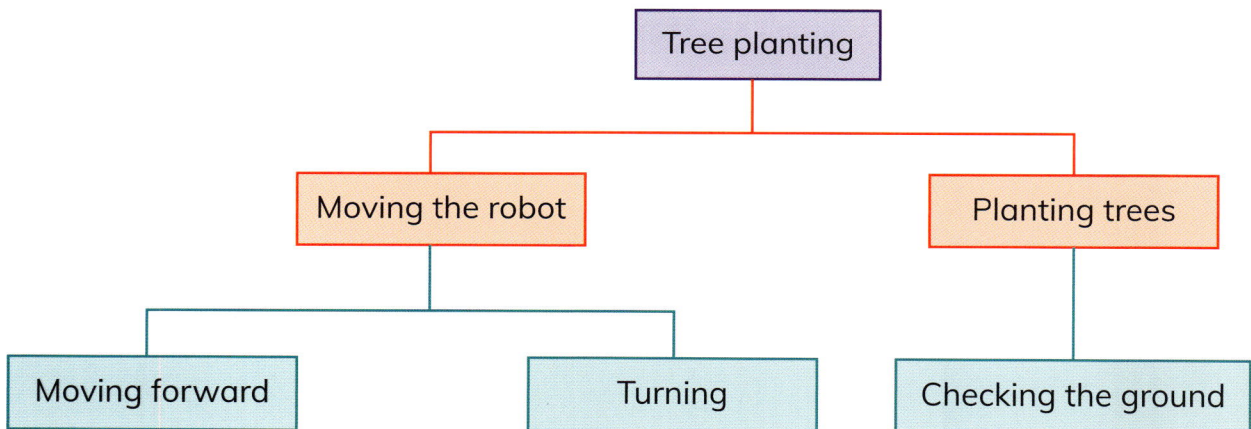

```
                        Tree planting
              ┌──────────────┴──────────────┐
        Moving the robot              Planting trees
         ┌──────┴──────┐                    │
  Moving forward    Turning       Checking the ground
```

Decomposition is when we break a problem down into smaller parts that are easier to understand and simpler to solve. When solving a problem using computers, it helps to decompose the problem into inputs, processes, conditions and outputs.

Here is a quick reminder of what the key terms mean.

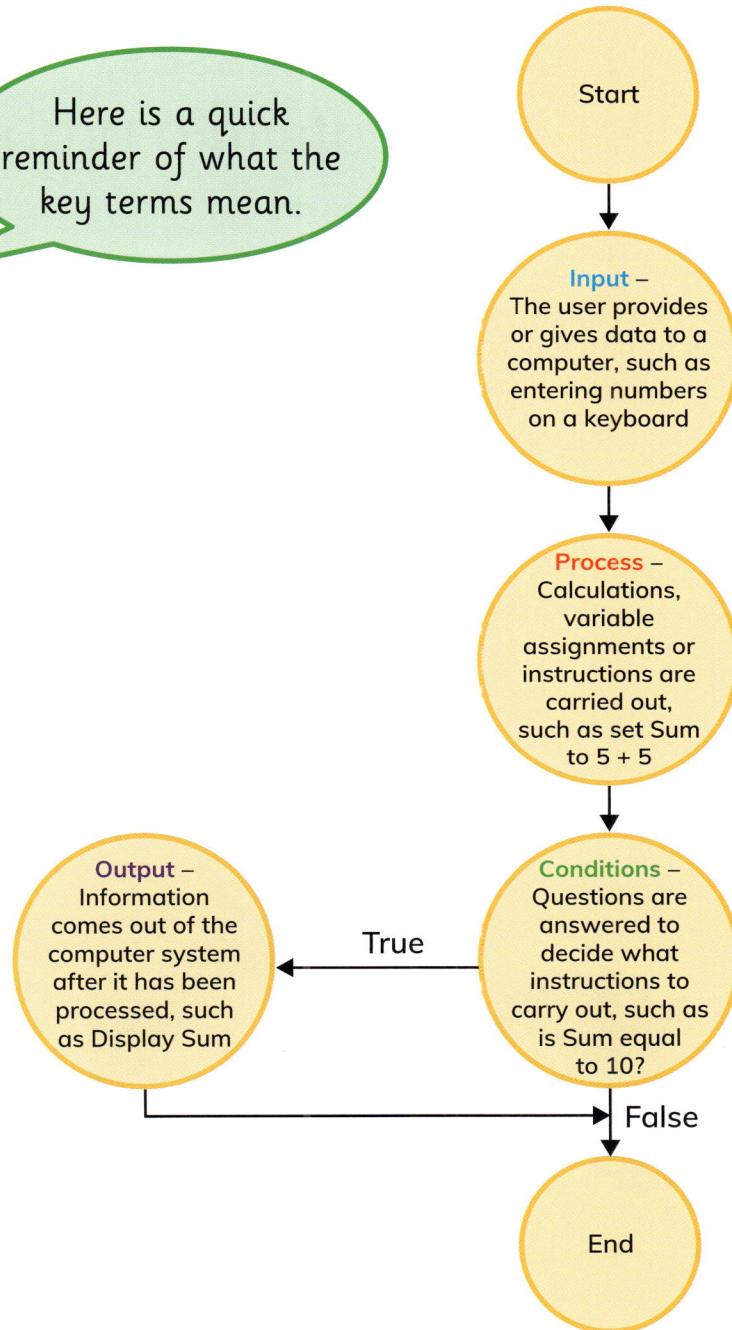

Start

Input – The user provides or gives data to a computer, such as entering numbers on a keyboard

Process – Calculations, variable assignments or instructions are carried out, such as set Sum to 5 + 5

Conditions – Questions are answered to decide what instructions to carry out, such as is Sum equal to 10?

True

Output – Information comes out of the computer system after it has been processed, such as Display Sum

False

End

Activity 3

You will need: a desktop computer, laptop or tablet and word-processing software

Use a computer to create vocabulary cards to define the following key terms: input, process, conditions, output. Share your cards with other learners.

Identifying inputs, processes, conditions and outputs in a problem

Let's look at the simple problem of setting an alarm on your digital alarm clock or phone.

We can decompose this everyday problem into terms a computer can follow by identifying the input, process, conditions, and output.

The user enters the wake-up time when they want the alarm clock to ring. The wake-up time is set and then checked against the current time. If the current time is the same as the wake-up time set, the alarm will ring.

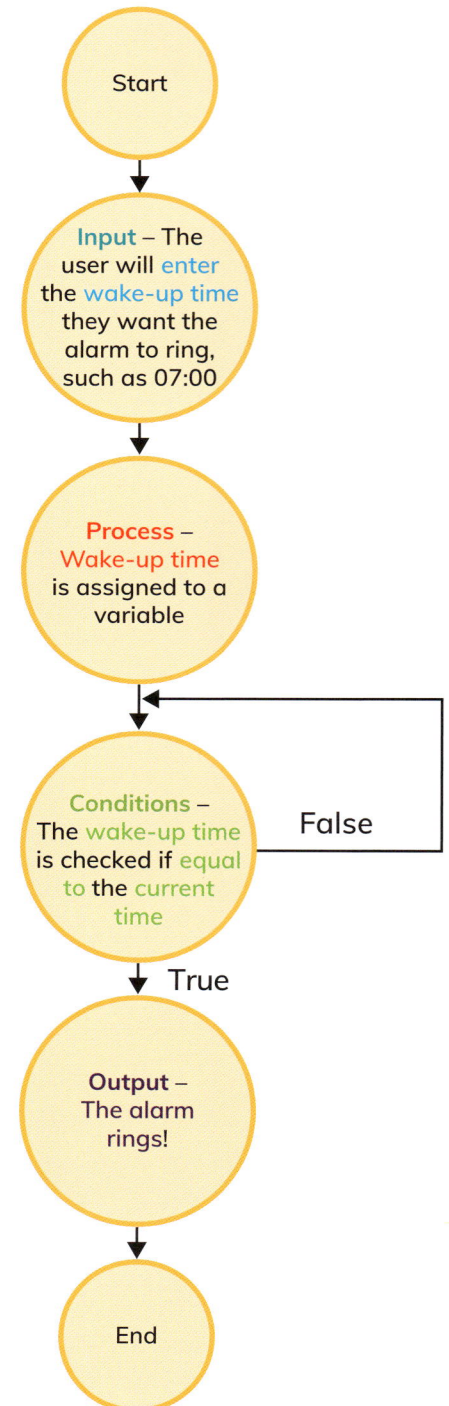

Start

Input – The user will enter the wake-up time they want the alarm to ring, such as 07:00

Process – Wake-up time is assigned to a variable

Conditions – The wake-up time is checked if equal to the current time

False

True

Output – The alarm rings!

End

Unplugged activity 4

> You will need: a pen and paper

Part A

You are going to identify inputs, outputs, processes and conditions for a chatbot. The chatbot will ask a question and allow a user to type an answer. The chatbot will check the user's answer and respond differently depending on what the user enters.

The problem has been decomposed into different parts. For each statement, discuss with a partner whether it is an input, process, condition or output.

	Statement	Input, process, condition or output
1	The chatbot asks a question.	
2	The user types their answer to the question.	
3	The user's answer is assigned to a variable.	
4	The variable answer is checked by the chatbot.	
5	The chatbot responds to the user's answer.	

Part B

The chatbot asks the user: 'What is your favourite animal?' If the user replies with 'panda', the chatbot will reply 'Mine too!' If the user enters anything else, the chatbot will respond with: 'Oh, that's a cool animal but pandas are the best!'

Continued

The problem has been decomposed into different parts. Discuss with a partner whether each statement is an input, process, condition or output.

	Statement	Input, process, condition or output
1	The chatbot asks the user: 'What is your favourite animal?'	
2	The user types their answer to the question.	
3	The user's reply is set to the variable *FavouriteAnimal*.	
4	The variable *FavouriteAnimal* is checked to see if it is equal to 'panda'.	
5	The chatbot says: 'Mine too!'	
6	The chatbot says: 'Oh, that's a cool animal but pandas are the best.'	

Part C

The chatbot asks the user: 'Do you like sport?' If the user replies with 'yes', the chatbot replies: 'Great, exercise is good for your mental and physical health!' If the user enters anything else, the chatbot will respond with: 'Maybe you have not found the right sport yet.'

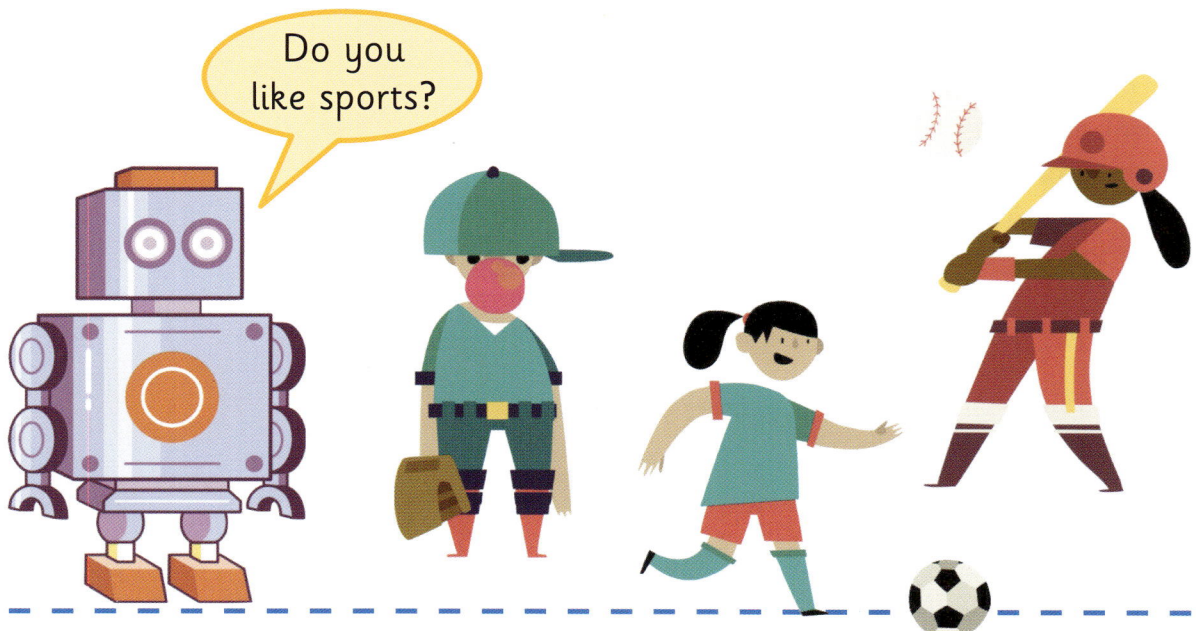

Continued

You are going to plan an algorithm for this chatbot. Decompose the problem into the input, processes, conditions and outputs. You can use a table like the ones in Parts A and B to break down the problem.

Part D

Using the plan you wrote in Part C, write each decomposed part of the problem as an algorithm using the following structure.

INPUT: set *VariableName* to USER INPUT

PROCESS: set *VariableName* to Value or *AnotherVariable*

CONDITION: IF *VariableName* equal to Value, THEN command, ELSE command

OUTPUT: say, followed by output message

How am I doing?

Look at your partner's chatbot algorithm. Copy and complete the algorithm checklist here to assess it.

Does the algorithm have the following?	☺	☹
A question asked by the chatbot as an output.		
The user's answer as an input.		
A comparison of the user's answer to another value as a condition.		
An output for if the condition is True.		
An output for if the condition is False.		

Look what I can do!

- [ ] I can follow different algorithms that solve the same problem.
- [ ] I understand that we can make algorithms more efficient by using selection to only carry out necessary instructions.
- [ ] I can identify the inputs, processes, conditions and outputs of a problem to plan programs.
- [ ] I can decompose problems to write an outline plan for a program.

› 1.5 Object interaction

We are going to:

- develop algorithms where two or more objects relate to each other
- identify different objects in programs and how they behave
- identify how different objects can affect each other
- plan instructions, outcomes and data for a game where different objects affect each other
- develop a computer game where two or more objects interact with each other.

broadcast
interaction
interrelated
object

Getting started

What do you already know?

- A script is a set of joined blocks of code that make one complete section of a Scratch program.
- Triggers tell different scripts when to run.
- A sub-routine is a set of instructions that describes how to perform one particular task.
- A sub-routine has to be defined in an algorithm and will not run unless it is called.

Continued

Now try this!

You will need: a pen and paper

Work with a partner. Look at the program and then answer the questions.

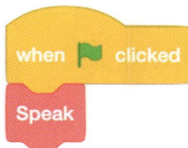

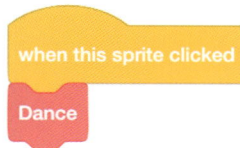

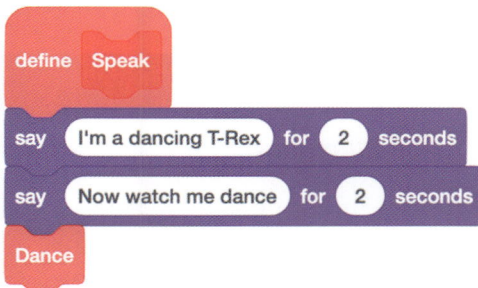

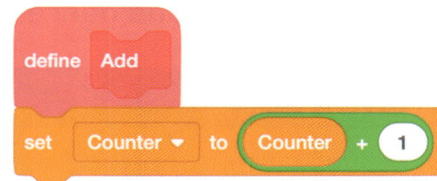

when 🏳 clicked
Speak

when this sprite clicked
Dance

define Speak
say I'm a dancing T-Rex for 2 seconds
say Now watch me dance for 2 seconds
Dance

define Dance
repeat 20
next costume
Add

define Add
set Counter ▾ to Counter + 1

1   What are the two triggers in the program?
2   What are the names of the sub-routines?
3   Which trigger(s) will make the T-Rex dance?
4   What will happen to the counter variable when you click the green flag?
5   What will happen to the counter variable when you click the sprite?

Identifying objects in everyday problems and how they behave

If you look around the room, you will notice lots of different objects. In computing, an object is a thing or person that has its own shape and has different behaviours.

An object in the room could be a learner who wears a school uniform and can read and write. Another object could be a book. It is made of paper, has text in it and can be opened and closed.

In Scratch, the objects are the sprites and stages. The sprites have different shapes and can change the way they look using costumes.

We can program the sprites to behave in different ways using scripts.

For example, the dinosaur sprite in the last program is an object. It can speak and dance (change costumes).

Activity 1

You will need: a desktop computer, laptop or tablet, access to the internet and word-processing software

With a partner, think about a team sport you enjoy.

Use a computer to make a poster. Import an image of your sport. Add text labels to show:

- the different objects (things or people) that exist in the game
- what the object(s) in the game can do.

Object interactions

Imagine a relay race with a team of runners. Each runner is an object with their own appearance and behaviours, and they need to work together to win the race.

In programming, an interaction is when two or more objects communicate or work together. Object interactions are like the way the runners pass the baton to each other during the race. Interactions are the ways in which two or more objects combine and have an effect on each other.

When objects are interrelated, it means they are connected or have a relationship with each other. In the relay race, the runners are interrelated because their actions and performance affect the overall success of the team. The next runner can only catch the baton if the previous runner passes it.

In programming, objects can be interrelated too. They depend on each other to work together effectively. The actions of one object can affect the behaviour or outcome of another object.

Using sub-routines with objects

Imagine a football game with robots. There are at least two objects: a robot football player and the football. The robot football player can move left and right, shoot and pass. The ball can also move in different directions. The player and the ball are interrelated and will interact with each other.

We can plan what different objects do and how they interact with each other in an algorithm using sub-routines. We can use sub-routines to write instructions for a particular object, like a sub-routine for a player passing the ball.

```
1    //Instructions for Player object
2    DEFINE PlayerMovement
3       REPEAT FOREVER
4          IF Keypress equal to P
5             THEN Player pass ball
```

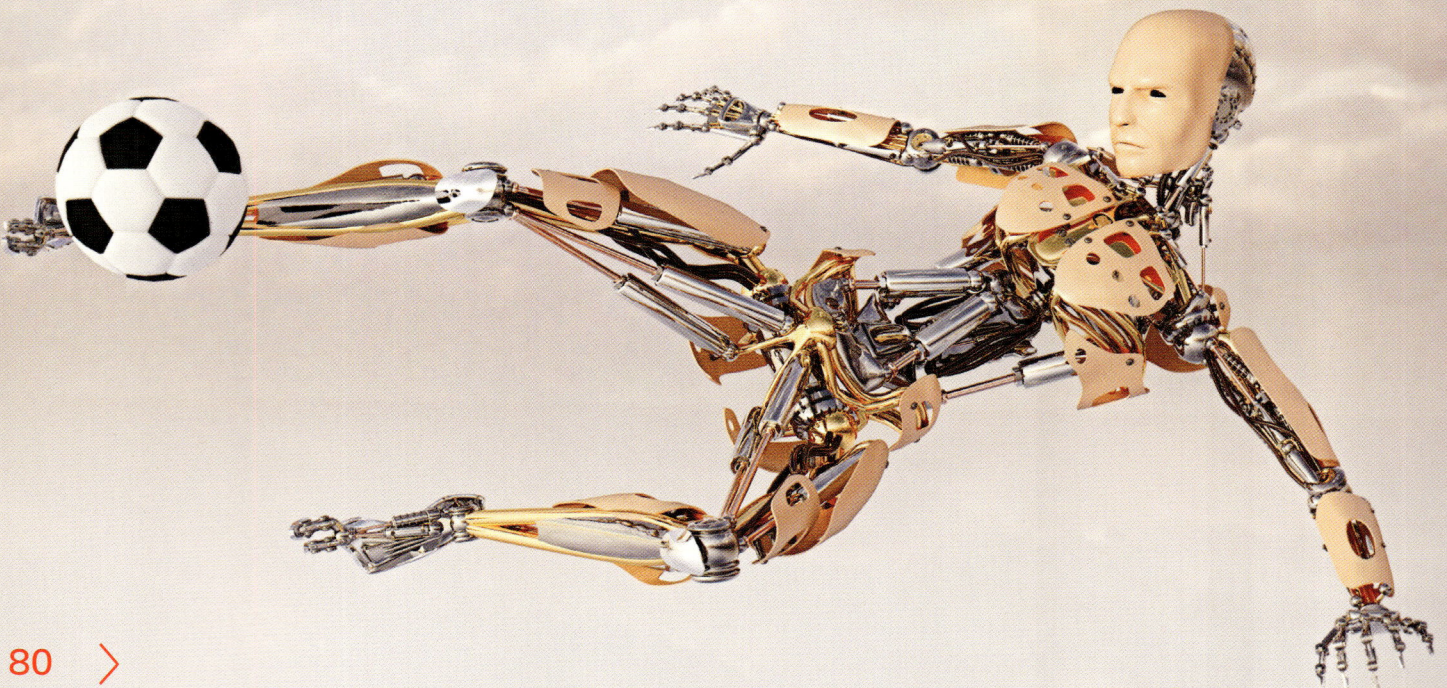

We know the player and the ball are interrelated objects because if the player passes the ball, the ball will move. This means we need another sub-routine to instruct the ball when it is passed.

```
1       //Instructions for Ball object
2       DEFINE PassBall
3               Move ball from one player to another player
```

We can make the player and ball objects interact with each other by calling the *PassBall* sub-routine in line 8 of the *PlayerMovement* sub-routine.

```
1       //Instructions for Ball object
2       DEFINE PassBall
3               Move ball from one player to another player


4       //Instructions for Player object
5       DEFINE PlayerMovement
6               IF Keypress equal to P
7                       THEN Player pass ball
8                       CALL PassBall
```

Questions

1   What instruction will run if the P key is pressed?
2   What other actions made by the player will affect the ball?

Did you know?

To make objects in computer games behave realistically, programmers need to have a good understanding of maths and physics. Variables, conditions and mathematical operations are part of every great game!

Unplugged activity 2

You will need: a pen and paper

Plan another interaction between the ball and the player. When the player moves, they should dribble the ball. You will also need to check if the player is touching the ball before you can move the player.

This is the 2021 RoboCup China Open in Tianjin, where computer scientists like you would have programmed the robots to play football.

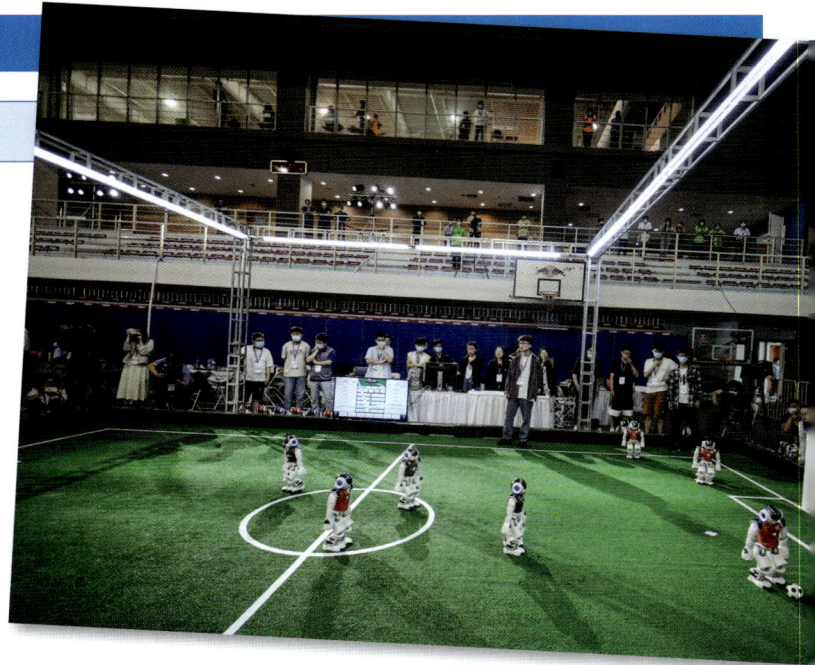

Look at the following instructions. With a partner, decide which of the instructions belong to the ball, the player and the main game.

a	DEFINE *DribbleBall*	c	IF player touching ball
b	Move ball in front of player	d	CALL *DribbleBall*

Using the instructions in the box above, complete the following algorithm. You should use all of the instructions, and some of them may be used more than once.

1	**//Instructions for ball**
2	DEFINE *PassBall*
3	Move ball from one player to another player

Continued

```
4        //Instructions for ball
5        _____
6            _____
7        //Instructions for player
8        DEFINE PlayerMovement
9            REPEAT FOREVER
10            IF keypress equal to left arrow
11                THEN Move player left
12                CALL DribbleBall
13            IF keypress equal to right arrow
14                THEN Move player right
15                _____
16            IF keypress equal to P
17                THEN Player pass ball
18                CALL PassBall
19        //Instructions for game
20        WHEN Game starts
21            _____
22            CALL PlayerMovement
```

How am I doing?

Read the success criteria and check if you are happy that you have achieved them. Record your answers in a table like this.

Success criteria	☺	☹
The instructions for moving the ball in front of the player belong to the Ball object.		
The DribbleBall sub-routine is called in the Player object sub-routine.		
The instruction for checking if the player is touching the ball is checked before calling the PlayerMovement sub-routine.		

Unplugged activity 3

You will need: a pen and paper

You are going to create a game where a rocket ship flies through an asteroid field. The goal of the game is to avoid the asteroids for as long as possible. The asteroids move from the right to the left. The rocket ship can move up and down to avoid the asteroids.

With a partner, look at the picture showing what the game might look like.

Decompose the task into smaller parts that are easier to solve. Discuss the following questions with your partner. Remember that there are different ways to solve the same problem.

1   What different objects will you include in the game?
2   What keys might be pressed to make the rocket ship go up or down?
3   What could the rocket ship output if an asteroid hits it?
4   What value would the variable *Lives* need to equal for the game to end?
5   What should happen to the variable *Score* for each asteroid that the rocket ship avoids?
6   What could happen to the rocket ship if it runs out of lives?

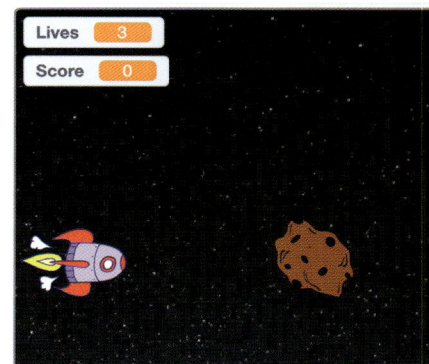

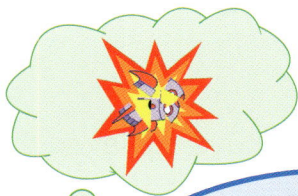

I think the rocket ship will be destroyed if an asteroid hits it, and lives will equal 0.

I think the rocket ship will output a message if it's hit by an asteroid, and change colour if there are lives left.

Programming task 1

You will need: a desktop computer, laptop or tablet with access to Scratch, source file **1.7_asteroid_dodger** and your plan from the previous activity

The Asteroid dodger game is almost complete.

The following script is for the rocket ship sprite. With a partner, read the code and the comments that explain what it does.

```
when [flag] clicked

go to x: -200 y: 0

set Lives ▼ to 3

set Score ▼ to 0

repeat until < Lives = 0 >

    switch costume to rocketship-forward ▼

    if < > then

        switch costume to rocketship-up ▼

        change y by 5

    if < > then

        switch costume to rocketship-down ▼

        change y by -5
```

- This group of blocks controls how the spaceship moves.
- The variables for holding the number of lives and the score are set at the start of the game.
- Control of the spaceship stops when there are no more lives.
- **1** If this condition is True the sprite should go up.
- **2** If this condition is True the sprite should go down.

Some parts of the code are missing. Use your plan from Unplugged activity 3 to complete the code:

1   Add a suitable key-pressed condition from the Sensing block palette to the IF statement to make the rocket ship go up.

2   Add a suitable key-pressed condition from the Sensing block palette to the IF statement to make the rocket ship go down.

Click the green flag and use your chosen buttons to see if the rocket ship moves up and down.

Programming task 2

You will need: a desktop computer, laptop or tablet with access to Scratch and source file **1.7_asteroid_dodger** updated from Programming task 1

We already know there are three objects in the game: the rocket ship, the asteroid and the stage.

The rocket ship script has two other scripts. These are a type of sub-routine called broadcasts that can be called by another object in the game (either the asteroid or the stage). The sub-routines control the rocket ship but are only called if a condition is met in the asteroid or stage script.

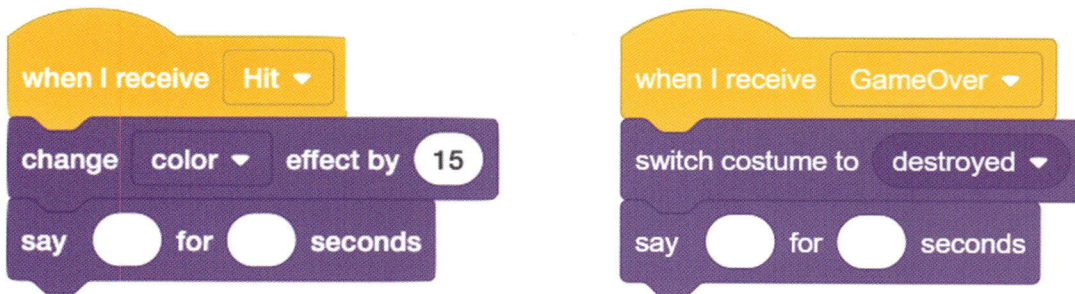

```
when I receive  Hit ▾
change   color ▾   effect by   15
say  ⬭  for  ⬭  seconds
```

```
when I receive  GameOver ▾
switch costume to   destroyed ▾
say  ⬭  for  ⬭  seconds
```

These sub-routines are called using the broadcast blocks in Scratch. You will see these in the stage and asteroid scripts:

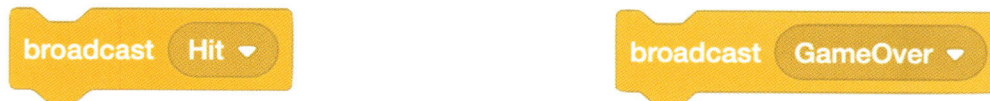

```
broadcast  Hit ▾
```

```
broadcast  GameOver ▾
```

The *Hit* and *GameOver* sub-routines are missing suitable outputs in the rocket ship script.

With a partner:

1   Complete the *Hit* sub-routine by adding a suitable output message and number of seconds for it to be displayed if the rocket ship is hit by an asteroid.

2   Complete the *GameOver* sub-routine by adding a suitable output and number of seconds for it to be displayed if the rocket ship is hit by an asteroid.

Programming task 3

You will need: a desktop computer, laptop or tablet with access to Scratch and source file **1.7_asteroid_dodger** updated from Programming task 2

The following script controls how the asteroid sprite moves across the screen. The script also controls the Score and Lives in the game. Some parts of the code are missing.

```
when [flag] clicked
go to x: 246 y: 0
forever
    if < x position < -240 > then
        go to x: 240 y: pick random -180 to 180
        change Score by ( )
    turn pick random 1 to 5 degrees
    change x by -5
    if < > then
        change Lives by ( )
        go to x: 246 y: 0
        go to x: 240 y: pick random -180 to 180
    broadcast Hit
```

Comments:
- This script instructs the asteroid to move across the screen from right to left.
- This condition checks if the asteroid has reached the left side of the screen. If this condition is True, the score should increase.
- If this condition is True, Lives should decrease. It will also affect the rocket ship as the objects are interrelated.
- This will call the sub-routine in the rocket ship script if the asteroid is touching the rocket ship.

With a partner, read the script and comments and answer the questions to complete the code.

1   Add a suitable value that the Score should increase by when the rocket ship avoids an asteroid.

2   Add a suitable condition that checks if an asteroid is touching the rocket ship.

3   Add a suitable value that Lives should decrease by if the asteroid is touching the rocket ship.

Continued

4 Place the broadcast Hit block into the correct selection statement. This will call the earlier sub-routine for how the rocket ship will behave when hit.

5 Press the green flag to run and test your changes.

   a Does the Score increase when the rocket ship misses an asteroid?

   b Do the Lives decrease when the rocket ship is hit by an asteroid?

   c Does the rocket ship's costume change when hit by an asteroid?

Programming task 4

You will need: a desktop computer, laptop or tablet with access to Scratch and source file **1.7_asteroid_dodger** updated from Programming task 3

The final part of our game is the end. The script below is for the third object, the stage. The Stars backdrop will switch to the Gameover backdrop when the Lives in the rocket ship script run out. The stage script should also call the *GameOver* sub-routine in the rocket ship script. Some parts of the code are missing.

```
when [flag] clicked
forever
    switch backdrop to Stars
    if < Lives = ( ) > then
        switch backdrop to Gameover
        stop all
broadcast GameOver and wait
```

This script will end the game and display the Gameover backdrop when there are no Lives.

If this condition is True, the game will stop. This condition will also have an effect on the rocket ship as these two objects are interrelated.

This block makes all the scripts stop running as the game is over.

This will call the GameOver sub-routine written in the rocket ship script for when there are no Lives left.

Continued

With a partner, read the code and comments and answer the questions to complete the code.

1   Add a suitable value to the condition that when True, will end the game.

2   Put the broadcast GameOver block into the correct place. This will call the sub-routine for how the rocket ship will behave when the game is over.

How are we doing?

Read the following points and discuss with a partner if you are a red, amber or green for each part of the game.

Part of the game	Red	Amber	Green
Controlling the rocket ship	The rocket ship did not move up and down.	The rocket ship moved, but not as planned.	The rocket ship moved up and down as planned.
Displaying messages	No messages were displayed.	A message displayed every time the rocket ship was hit by an asteroid.	A message displayed that the rocket ship was hit by an asteroid and there were still Lives left.
Scoring points	The Score did not increase during the game.	The Score increased during the game.	The Score only increased when the rocket ship avoided an asteroid.
Ending the game	The game never ended.	The game ended, but not when expected.	The game ended when Lives reached 0 and the GameOver stage showed.
The rocket ship's appearance	The costume stayed the same throughout the game.	The costume changed when it was hit.	The costume changed when it was hit and exploded when the game was over.

How did planning your algorithms first help you when completing the asteroid dodger program?

Look what I can do!

☐ I can develop algorithms where two or more objects relate to each other.

☐ I can identify different objects in programs and how they behave.

☐ I can identify how different objects can affect each other.

☐ I can plan instructions, outcomes and data for a game where different objects affect each other.

☐ I can develop a computer game where two or more objects interact with each other.

> 1.6 Creating user-friendly programs

We are going to:

- identify the different roles and skills of people involved in creating a program
- understand the different stages of the project life cycle
- understand the importance of creating clear criteria at the start of a project
- judge how good a final program is based on criteria.

analysis   design   evaluation
content   development   project life cycle
criteria   end user   testing

Getting started

What do you already know?

- Before writing programs, it is good practice to break down the problem into smaller parts that are easier to solve.
- Programmers use comments to make their code easier to understand.
- Programmers use meaningful variable names to make their code easier to understand.

Continued

Now try this!

In pairs, read and compare the two algorithms that follow.
Discuss these questions.

1 What do the algorithms do?

2 How are the algorithms different?

3 Name two things that make Algorithm B easier to understand.

Algorithm A		Algorithm B	
1	set X to USER INPUT	1	//Gets two user inputs of different numbers and assigns them to variables
2	set Y to USER INPUT	2	set Number1 to USER INPUT
3	IF X is equal to Y	3	set Number2 to USER INPUT
4	THEN set Z to X + Y	4	//Checks if the numbers input by the user are the same
5	ELSE	5	IF Number1 is equal to Number2
6	set Z to X – Y	6	//If the numbers input are equal, they are added together
7	DISPLAY Z	7	THEN set Result to Number1 + Number2
		8	ELSE
		9	//If the numbers are not equal, they are subtracted from each other
		10	set Result to Number1 – Number2
		11	//The result is displayed to the user
		12	DISPLAY Result

Roles involved in making computer programs

We use computer programs every day. There are programs for almost everything and everyone – from searching the World Wide Web on a web browser to playing games on a tablet.

Most programs start with an idea about how to solve a problem. Having a good idea is a small part of a bigger project. To turn that idea into a final program requires input from people with a range of skills. Some programs are made by teams with hundreds of people in them.

Here are some examples of the roles involved in making computer programs:

End user

Programs are made with an end user in mind. The end users are the people who use your program when it is finished, like a teacher, parent, learner or teenager. It is important to know who the end user is and to understand their needs.

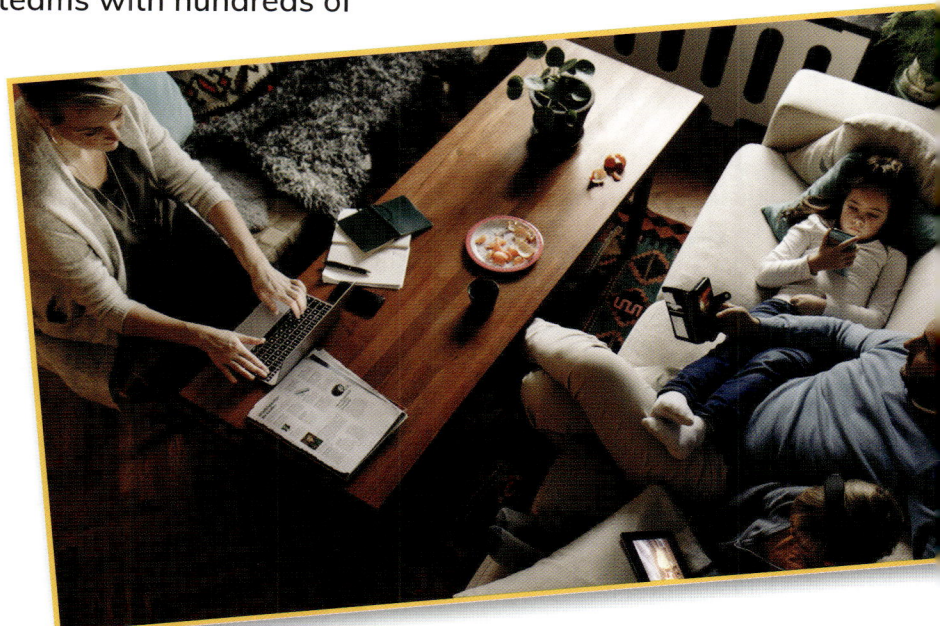

Analyst

Analysts gather information that helps to turn an idea into a great program. They interview the end user to understand what they need and like.

Criteria are standards used to judge if a project or program is successful. Analysts help to create criteria for the program. Criteria need to be specific and measurable so people can check if they have been met when the final program is created.

User experience (UX) designer

UX designers make sure programs are user-friendly. They start by drawing designs for the menus, buttons and positioning of content. They use these designs to understand how the end user will use the program. If you can use a program without reading the instructions, it means the UX designer did a good job.

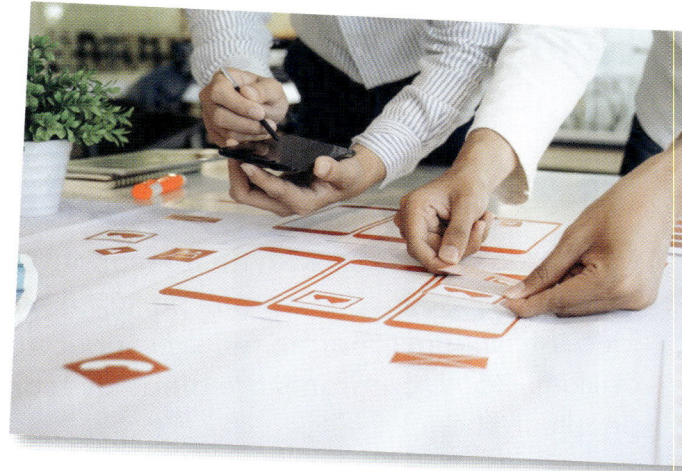

Content creator

Content is the information in a program, such as text, images, videos, sounds or music. For example, the description of a website, or the sound effects for a video game. There are lots of different types of content creator.

Graphic designer

Graphic designers communicate the ideas and content for a program in a visual way. They create a digital version of the images using design software.

Software developer

Development is the making part of a program. Software developers plan a solution to the problem using algorithms. Developers then create the program by writing code.

Product testers

Programs need to be tested thoroughly both during and after development. Product testers use the programs a lot to make sure that they work. Testers report any problems so they can be fixed before the final program is released.

Project manager

The project manager keeps track of all the work to be completed. They set deadlines and give tasks to different team members, depending on their role. The project manager sets the success criteria with the analyst at the start of the project. They must then ensure that the program meets the success criteria when it is finished.

Activity 1

You will need: a desktop computer, laptop or tablet with presentation software

Create a simple digital presentation to explain the different roles involved in creating a program. Include a title with each role, an image and a short description.

Unplugged activity 2

Imagine you are creating a new app and need to find team members to help you.

Part A

With a partner, take it in turns to interview each other by asking and discussing the following questions.

1   Are you really organised, and do you get on well with people?

2   Are you good at paying attention to details?

3   Do you love programming?

4   Are you good at drawing, writing or making music?

5   Do you like finding simpler ways to do things? Can you give an example of when you have done this?

6   Do you like asking questions and solving problems? Give an example of a problem you solved recently.

Part B

Compare your partner's answers to the different job descriptions. Write two to three sentences on what role you think your partner would be best suited to and why. Try to include what they are good at or what they enjoy doing to help make your point.

The stages of making a program

We can decompose the process of making a program into different stages. This is called the project life cycle. You do not have to know about the project life cycle at this stage, but it is really useful knowledge to have for computer science, and for other subjects and professions.

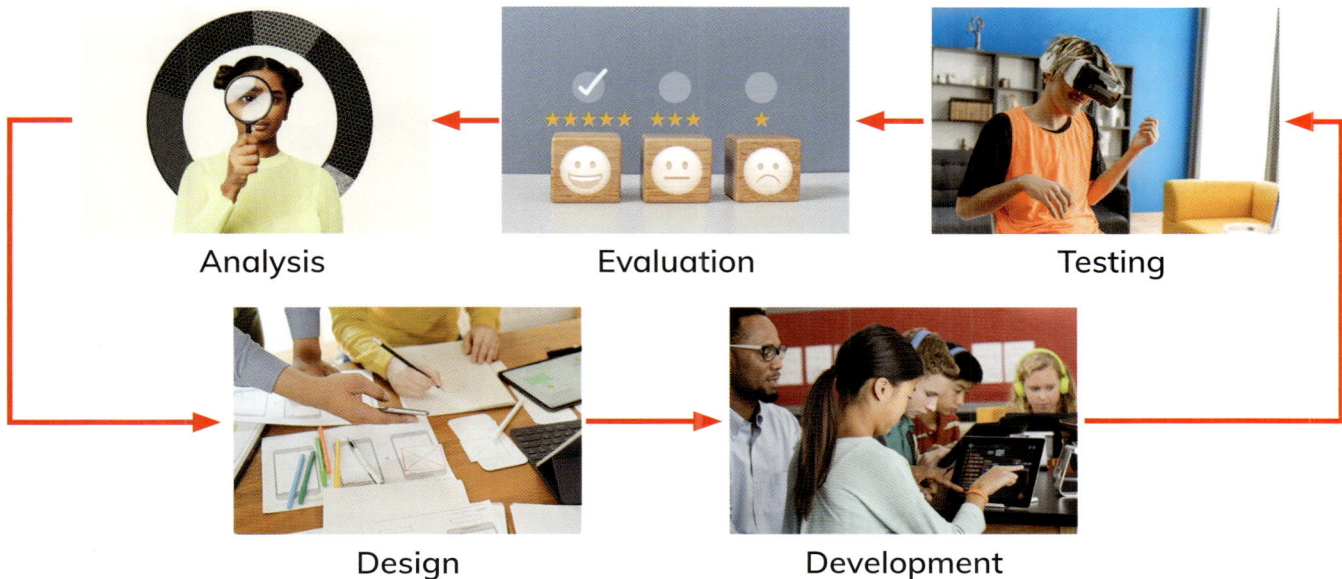

Analysis

Evaluation

Testing

Design

Development

Analysis: This is the act of studying something in detail to understand more about it. Coming up with an idea to solve a problem is the first step in making a good computer program. The criteria and main features of the program are decided at this stage.

Design: A plan for what the program will look like and how it will work is created at the design stage. Drawings of different parts of the program are created. Algorithms are written to plan how the program will work.

Development: The program and contents are made at this stage. The program is written in code based on the algorithms planned at the design stage. Any content such as text, images or sounds is created based on the program requirements.

Testing: This involves running the program and checking that it works based on the original success criteria. If something does not work it can be redeveloped.

Evaluation: This is when the quality of the program is judged. The program is evaluated by checking its features against the original criteria.

This is called a cycle because there is no set end point. For example, even if the program meets all the original criteria, it might still be possible to improve it after the evaluation, or to develop new features. There might be original criteria that seemed like a good idea at the start but do not make sense later. There might also be criteria that were not thought about until testing the program. This means that the cycle is continued by analysing the problem again and updating or creating new criteria.

Unplugged activity 3

Imagine you have an idea for an app that teaches your classmates how to recycle more.

Read the tasks for each stage of the project life cycle for creating the app. With a partner, discuss and decide which roles should be involved at each stage.

Roles: analyst, UX designer, content creator, software developer, project manager, end user, graphic designer, tester.

Stage	Tasks
Analysis	Carry out research on recycling to understand it better. Interview classmates about how they recycle and what features they think the app should have. Create success criteria for the recycling app. Decide who should do what in the project.
Design	Design the menus, buttons, layout and navigation for the app. Analyse how the end user will be able to use the app easily. Plan algorithms for how the app will work.
Development	Create the program with code using the algorithms. Create video tutorials on how to recycle. Make designs for the different pages in the app.
Testing	Use the app and try all the different features to see if they work. Fix any bugs the app might have.
Evaluation	Check that the app meets the original success criteria. Decide if any improvements could be made to the app.

Did you know?

E-waste is waste from electronic devices. According to the World Economic Forum, there will be 74.7 million tonnes of e-waste by 2030. That is the same as 10 million elephants. To prevent this, we need to recycle, reuse and drastically reduce buying new electronic devices.

Setting clear criteria

Setting clear criteria at the start of a project is essential for planning the project life cycle. These criteria are used to evaluate the final program. If the program meets these criteria, it shows that it is fit for purpose.

Imagine being told to create a quiz program in Scratch. You know how to output questions and take user answers as inputs. You also know how to check if the user input is equal to the correct answer. So you have all the skills to build a quiz program.

Imagine that you have written the script below. With a partner, discuss whether you think it is a good quiz program.

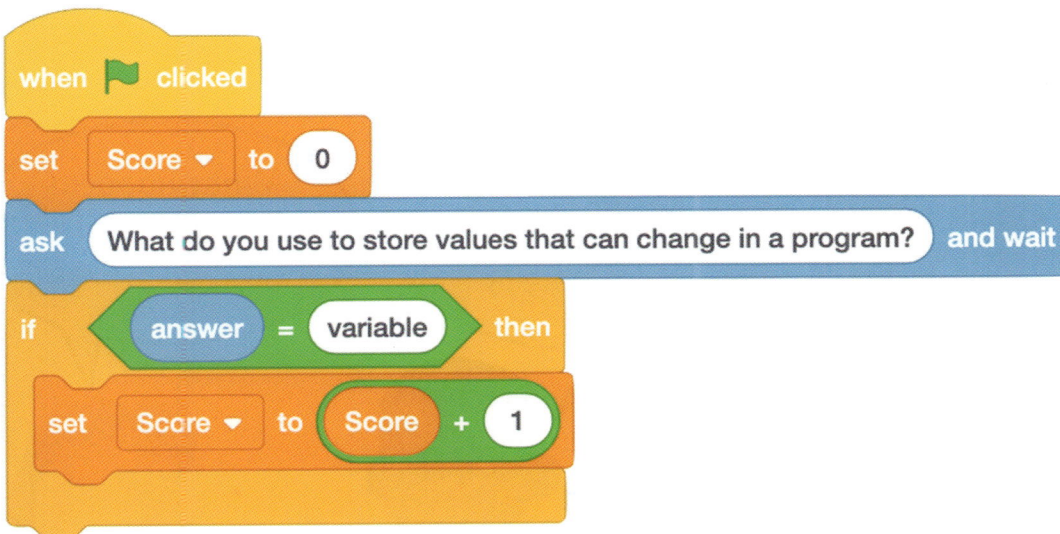

```
when [flag] clicked
set Score to 0
ask What do you use to store values that can change in a program? and wait
if < answer = variable > then
    set Score to Score + 1
```

I think the quiz is good. It will ask the user a question and check if they got it right, just like a real quiz.

You are right. The program will work like a quiz but it is not very user-friendly. I think it could be better.

It is difficult to decide if the program is good because there were no clear criteria. It would have been much better to create criteria at the start.

At the analysis stage of a project life cycle, we should always ask lots of questions and involve different people to help create the criteria for a program.

Is there a score?

How many questions should the quiz have?

What happens if the user gets a question right?

What happens if the user gets a question wrong?

Programming task 1

You will need: a pen and paper, a desktop computer, laptop or tablet with access to Scratch and source file **1.8_quiz_master_Toco**

An analyst wrote the criteria for a quiz program called Quiz Master Toco. The design and development team created the program in Scratch and it is now ready to be evaluated.

Run and evaluate the program against the following criteria. Write the numbers 1–12 on a piece of paper. Draw a tick or a cross next to each number to show whether the criteria have been met.

Score 0

Hello! I'm Quiz Master Toco and welcome to my Computer Science Quiz!

Criteria	
1	A sprite welcomes the user at the start of the quiz.
2	The sprite is a character most of your classmates would like.
3	A sprite displays the question to the user for 5 seconds.
4	There is a score set to 0 at the start of the quiz.
5	The sprite asks the user a question and waits for an answer to be input.
6	The question is about programming.
7	The question has a one-word answer.
8	An appropriate message is displayed if the answer is correct.
9	The score increases by one if the user answers correctly.
10	An appropriate message is displayed if the user answers incorrectly.
11	The quiz has four computer science questions.
12	At the end of the program, the user's score and an appropriate message are displayed.

Unplugged activity 4

You will need: a pen and paper

The program did not meet criterion 11 as it only has one question and should have four.

Plan three more questions for the quiz. Follow the original criteria from Programming task 1, especially numbers 6–8. Remember, this would be the job of the content creator.

Copy the table and add content for Q2–Q4.

Structure	Q1	Q2	Q3	Q4
Ask Question	What do you use to store values that can change in a program?			
IF answer equal to	variable			
THEN Say	Yes! That is correct. You get a point.			
ELSE Say	Oh, no. The correct answer is: variable.			

How am I doing?

Before you modify the code, check that your new questions meet criteria 6–11. Record your answers in a table like this.

Criteria	☺	☹
6 The question is about programming.		
7 The question has a one-word answer.		
8 An appropriate message is displayed if the answer is correct.		
10 An appropriate message is displayed if the user answers incorrectly.		
11 The quiz has four computer science questions.		

Programming task 2

You will need: questions from Programming task 2, a desktop computer, laptop or tablet with access to Scratch and source file **1.8_quiz_master_Toco**

Add your new questions to your quiz program. Do this by duplicating the IF ELSE block and editing the question, answer and messages. Make sure you insert the block into the correct sequence.

How are we doing?

Even your learning is checked against criteria! Swap your quiz program with your partner and evaluate your partner's program against the criteria here. Record your answers in a table like this.

Criteria	☺	☹
1 The sprite asks four or more questions about programming.		
2 An appropriate response is displayed if the user gets the question right or wrong.		
3 The correct score is displayed at the end of the program.		

How can you use what you have learnt in this topic to make your future Scratch programs better?

Look what I can do!

☐ I can identify the different roles and skills of people involved in creating a program.

☐ I understand the five stages of the project life cycle.

☐ I understand why creating clear criteria at the start of a project is important.

☐ I can evaluate how successful a final program is based on criteria.

> 1.7 Using selection with a physical device

We are going to:

- use conditions to check if a micro:bit has received an input
- use selection to change the flow of a program based on a user input
- use IF THEN ELSE selection statements to change the flow of a program based on variable values
- create a two-player game that produces different outputs using selection statements.

condition
logic
selection

Getting started

What do you already know?

- How to create programs that use loops for a micro:bit.
- How to use the micro:bit buttons and accelerometer as inputs for a program.
- How to create programs that produce an output from a micro:bit when you use the input devices on a micro:bit.

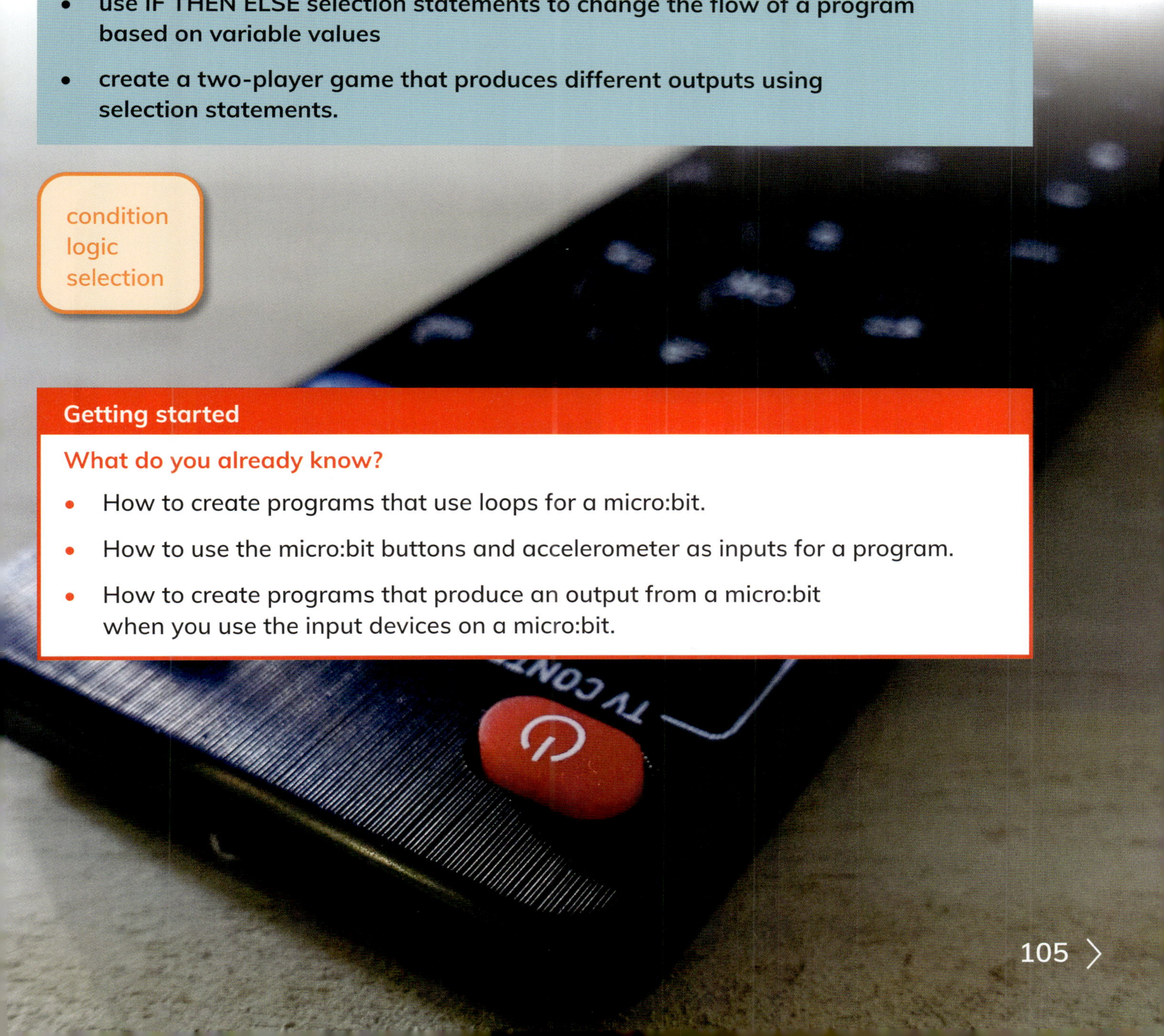

Continued

Now try this!

You will need: a pen and paper, a desktop computer or laptop, a micro:bit, a mini USB cable and access to the MakeCode website; or a tablet, a micro:bit, a battery pack and access to the MakeCode app

1   With a partner, read the BBC micro:bit script and discuss what it will do.

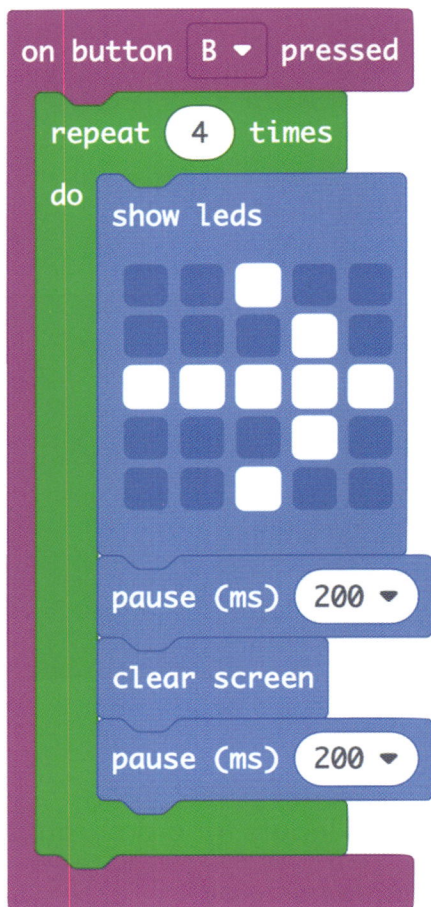

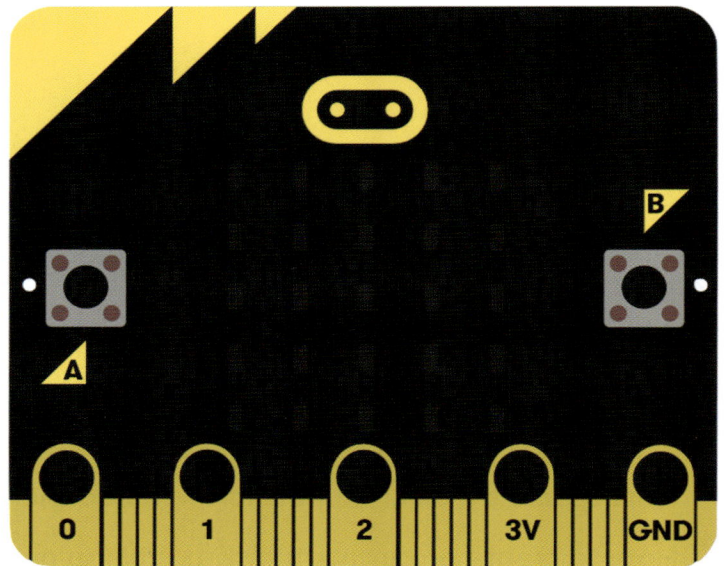

```
on button B ▼ pressed
    repeat 4 times
    do
        show leds

        pause (ms) 200 ▼
        clear screen
        pause (ms) 200 ▼
```

2   Now make the program using MakeCode. Download it to the micro:bit to test it.

Using variables and conditions with micro:bits

We can create variables for the micro:bit to store values that can change using the Variables script in MakeCode.

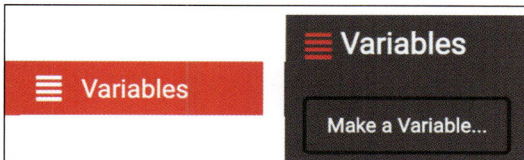

The variable *CountB* is assigned the value 0.

We could use a variable in a micro:bit to store the number of times someone presses a button, shakes or tilts the micro:bit.

Once we have created a variable, we can assign values to it through variable assignments and arithmetic operations using the Variables and Maths scripts.

1 is added to the value stored in the variable *CountB*.

Remember, a condition is a statement that can be either true or false. You can think of a condition like a question that can only be answered with yes or no. Physical devices use conditions to check user inputs. For example, a television remote control could have a condition to check if the power button has been pressed in order to turn on the TV.

Questions

Which of the following questions could be conditions?

1   What colour is your T-shirt?
2   Is dinner time at 6.00 p.m.?
3   Which button are you pressing?
4   Is the volume on?

The micro:bit has ready-made conditions for checking if an input is true or false. You can find them in the Input scripts. The conditional statements to check inputs are in hexagonal shapes.

Logic

Logic is a way of thinking or explaining in a sensible way. In computing, we use logic so that programs can make decisions based on a set of rules or conditions. Computers do not think for themselves but they can follow instructions that use logic.

We can create conditions for the micro:bit using the Logic blocks in MakeCode. We can create conditions with the 'equal to' comparison operator. Remember, the 'equal to' comparison operator compares two values or variables and checks if they are the same, just like in Scratch.

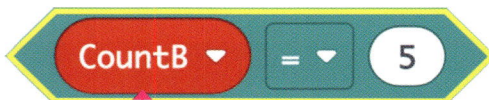

The variable *CountB* is compared to the value 5. If the value stored inside *CountB* is equal to 5 then the condition is True.

Questions

5 What inputs could you check with a micro:bit?

6 Look at the picture of a block in MakeCode.

CountA ▼ = ▼ 2

What should the variable CountA store for the condition to be True?

Using selection with micro:bits

When we want to carry out one set of actions if a condition is True and a different set of actions when a condition is False, we use selection and IF THEN ELSE statements.

Imagine you want to program your television remote control to switch on when you press the power button once. When you press the button again, the television switches off. We can write this as an algorithm using a condition and IF THEN ELSE statement:

1	IF *PowerButton* equal to Pressed once
2	THEN Turn on TV
3	ELSE
4	Turn off TV

We can use selection statements with our micro:bits to only carry out actions if a condition has been met. To create selection statements we need a conditional statement from the Logic scripts and an if true then block. We can then add conditions from either the Input or Logic sections of MakeCode.

Logic

Conditionals

```
if   true ▼   then

⊕

if   true ▼   then

else            ⊖

⊕
```

Logic

Comparison

```
0   = ▼   0
```

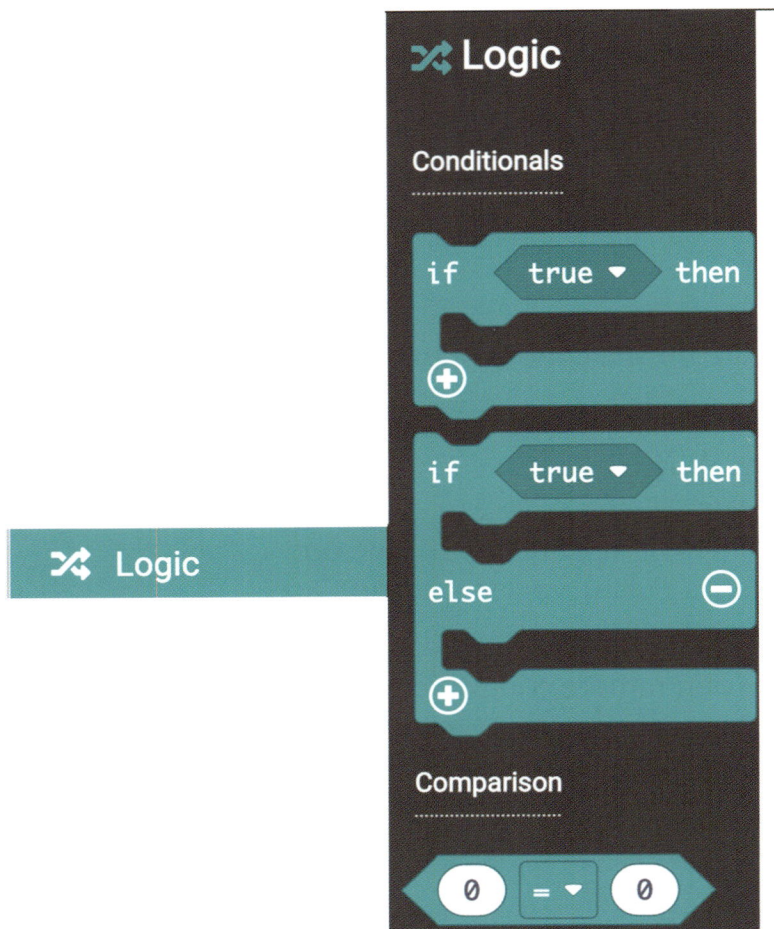

This is what the if true then block looks like when placed in the MakeCode script:

```
forever
  if   is shake ▼ gesture   then
    show icon ▦ ▼
  else                        ⊖
    show icon ▦ ▼
  ⊕
```

The selection statement is put in a forever loop so the condition is continuously checked.

The selection block has a condition checking if micro:bit is being shaken.

If the condition is True, a sad face is displayed.

If the condition is False, a happy face is displayed.

Question

7   Look at the micro:bit code. This is the output on the micro:bit:

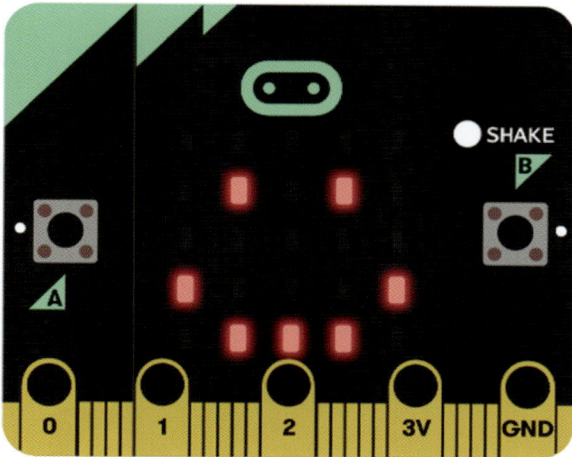

Is the condition 'is shake gesture' True or False when this icon is shown?

Activity 1

You will need: a desktop computer, laptop or tablet with voice/video recording software

Record a short screencast or video to explain which MakeCode scripts can be used to code for variables, conditions and selection.

Programming task 1

You will need: a desktop computer or laptop, a micro:bit, a mini USB cable and access to the MakeCode website; or a tablet, a micro:bit, a battery pack and access to the MakeCode app

Part A

Work with a partner. Talk about what this program will do.

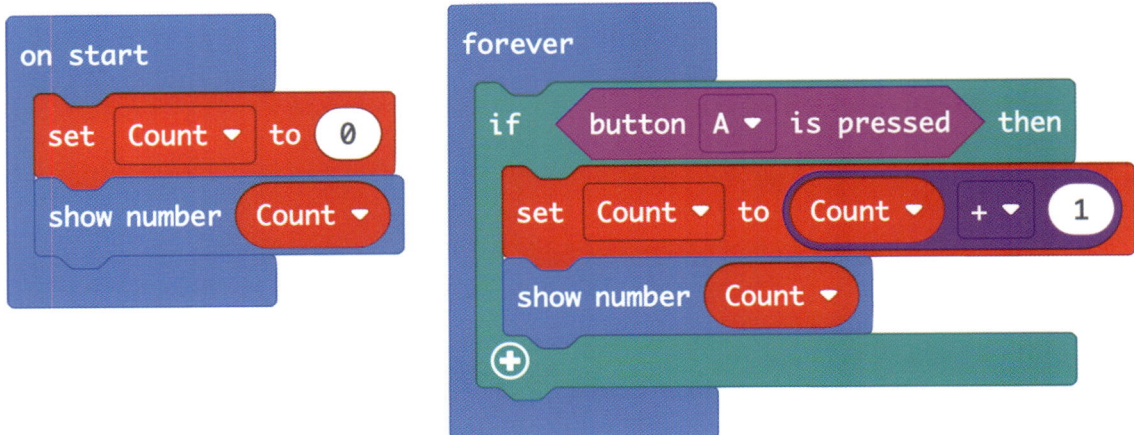

Use these questions to check your understanding of the code.

1 What input is being checked?
2 What is the name of the variable?
3 What happens to the variable when button A is pressed?
4 What will be displayed if you press button A three times?

Part B

With a partner, make the program in Part A using MakeCode and run it. Check if your predictions in Part A were correct.

Remember, you will need to create the variable *Count* by clicking on the Variables section and Make a Variable.

Download your program to the micro:bit to test it.

To stop the program, unplug the micro:bit from the USB cable or unplug the battery pack as this will stop the power.

Plug the battery pack back in to see if the program is stored on the micro:bit.

Programming task 2

You will need: a desktop computer or laptop, a micro:bit, a mini USB cable and access to the MakeCode website; or a tablet, a micro:bit, a battery pack and access to the MakeCode app

Part A

The micro:bit should add one to the variable *Count* each time button A is pressed and display the new number on the LED screen. Add to the code from Programming task 1, so if button B is pressed, 1 is subtracted from the variable *Count*.

To do this, you can duplicate the existing IF block and modify it. Remember to place the new IF block into the forever loop so the condition keeps being checked.

Use this algorithm to help you:

1	FOREVER
2	IF button A is pressed THEN
3	THEN set *Count* to *Count* + 1
4	Show *Count*
5	IF button B is press THEN
6	THEN set *Count* to *Count* − 1
7	Show *Count*

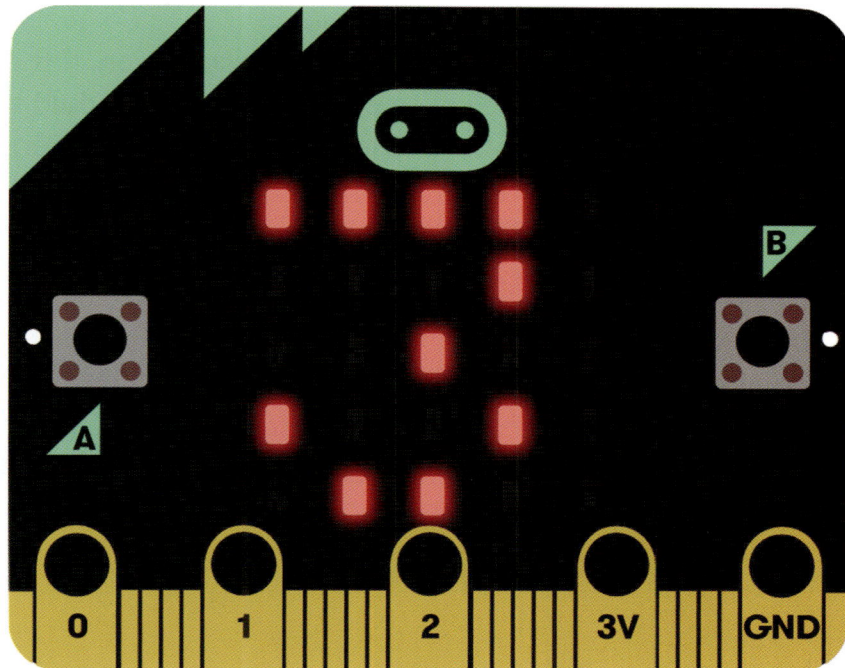

Continued

Download the file onto your micro:bit to test that it works correctly.

To run the program again, press the 'Reset' button on the back of the micro:bit.

Part B

Work with your partner to add one more condition. If the micro:bit is shaken, Count should be set to zero. The screen should be cleared at the end of each loop. Part of the algorithm has been written to help you.

```
1        FOREVER
2             IF button A is pressed THEN
3                  Set Count to Count + 1
4                  Show Count
5             IF button B is pressed THEN
6                  Set Count to Count – 1
7                  Show Count
8             IF _____
9                  Set Count to _____
10                 Show Count
11
```

After making the changes, download the file onto your micro:bit to test it works correctly.

To run the program again, press the 'Reset' button on the back of the micro:bit.

Continued

How am I doing?

Read the statements below and tell your teacher whether you are red, amber or green.

Red	Amber	Green
The micro:bit displays a number that increases by 1 every time I press button A.	The micro:bit displays a number that increases by one every time I press button A and decreases by 1 every time I press button B.	The micro:bit displays a number that increases by 1 every time I press button A and decreases by 1 every time I press button B. The number shown on the screen goes back to zero after I shake the micro:bit.

Programming task 3

You will need: a pen and paper; a desktop computer or laptop, a micro:bit, a mini USB cable and access to the MakeCode website; ar a tablet, a micro:bit, a battery pack and access to the MakeCode app

Part A

Work with a partner to plan and then make a 'Guess the Press' game.

The game will be for two players. Player one will press button A on the micro:bit a secret number of times. Player two will then have to guess the number of times button A has been pressed by using button B.

Read the criteria for this game:

1   When button A is pressed, 1 will be added to player one's number.
2   When button B is pressed, 1 will be added to player two's number.
3   When the micro:bit is shaken, player one's number will be compared to player two's number.
4   If both numbers are equal, a smiley face will be displayed.
5   If the numbers are not equal, a sad face will be displayed.
6   At the end, the screen should be cleared and both players' numbers will reset to zero.

Continued

Write an algorithm for this game for criteria 1 and 2.

- You will need two variables: one variable to store the number of presses for player one, and one variable to store the number of presses for player two.

- You can use the On Input blocks to set the number of presses for each variable.

Follow the diagram Arun drew for criteria 3–6.

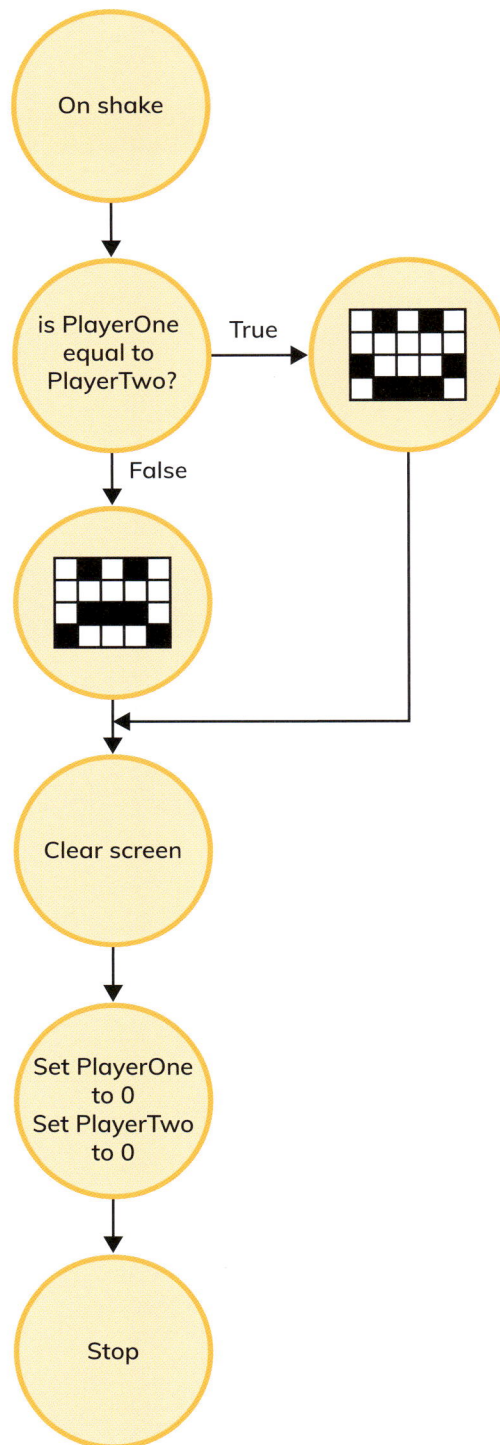

On shake

is PlayerOne equal to PlayerTwo? — True

False

Clear screen

Set PlayerOne to 0
Set PlayerTwo to 0

Stop

Write out Arun's algorithm on a piece of paper.

Continued

Part B

Using your algorithm from Part A, create the program in MakeCode.

Download the file to your micro:bit to test it is working correctly.

How are we doing?

Play the game with your partner. Start by telling each other how many presses you have done to test the outputs are correct.
Did your algorithm work correctly and could you run your program?

How did using criteria and planning your algorithm make creating the program easier?

Look what I can do!

☐   I can use conditions to check if a micro:bit has received an input.

☐   I can use selection to change the flow of a program based on a user input.

☐   I can use IF THEN ELSE selection statements to change the flow of a program based on variable values.

☐   I can create a two-player game that produces different outputs using selection.

Project

You will need: a pen and paper, a desktop computer, laptop or tablet, with access to Scratch

Did you know that, sometimes, to make your password even more secure it is run through an algorithm that changes it using different calculations?

Create a Scratch program to make a secret number using variables, arithmetic operators and selection. The program asks you to enter two or more numbers. The program performs a calculation on them and another person has to try to guess what the final secret number is.

The program should meet the following criteria.

Criteria	
1	A sprite welcomes the users to the password program.
2	The user inputs two or more numbers in two or more meaningfully named variables.
3	The numbers input are added to or subtracted from each other, one at a time, and stored in a new variable called *SecretNumber*.
4	The numbers the user input can be visible on the screen, but the *SecretNumber* variable should be hidden.
5	A second user should be asked to input a guess of the secret number based on the two or more numbers input by the user.
6	The guess should be compared to the secret number.
7	If the guess is correct, an appropriate message is output.
8	If the guess is incorrect, a message saying: 'Secret number not guessed' is output.

1 Plan your algorithm first. You can either write the algorithm or draw a diagram to represent the algorithm.
2 Create your program using Scratch.
3 Add comments to your program to explain how it works.
4 Finally, evaluate the different parts of your program against the success criteria.

Check your progress

Look at the program.

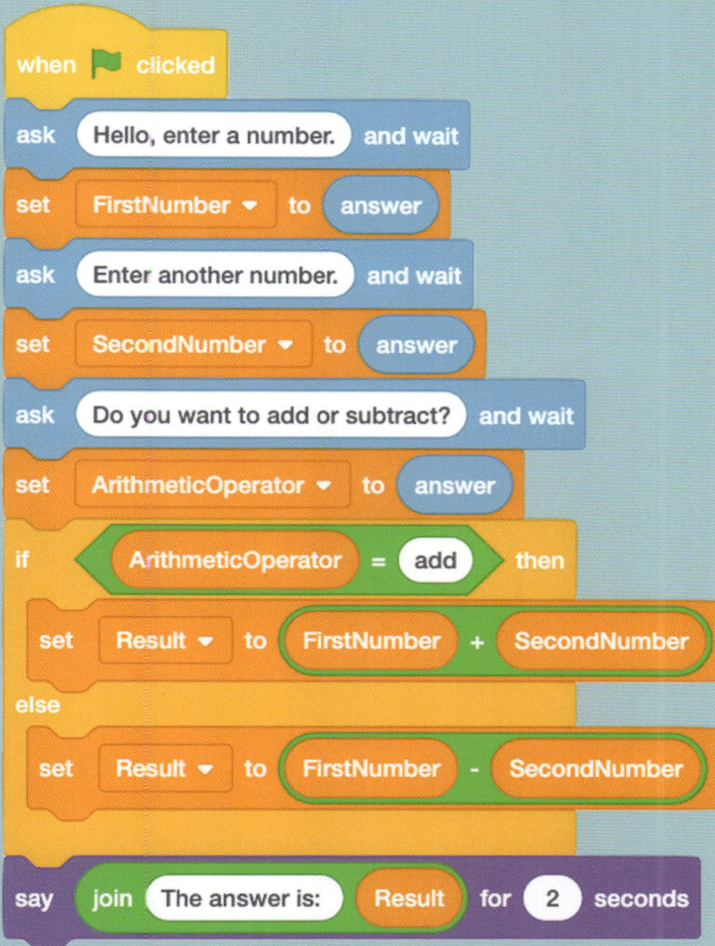

```
when 🏳 clicked
ask  Hello, enter a number.  and wait
set  FirstNumber ▼  to  answer
ask  Enter another number.  and wait
set  SecondNumber ▼  to  answer
ask  Do you want to add or subtract?  and wait
set  ArithmeticOperator ▼  to  answer
if   ArithmeticOperator = add  then
     set  Result ▼  to  FirstNumber + SecondNumber
else
     set  Result ▼  to  FirstNumber - SecondNumber

say  join  The answer is:  Result  for  2  seconds
```

1   Which of the following does the program contain?
    You can pick more than one answer.

    A   Sequence   B   Selection   C   Iteration

2   List the names of all the variables that are used in the program.

3   What is the condition checking in the program?

Continued

4 What does the user need to input so that their numbers are subtracted? Pick the best answer.

A add

B +

C –

D subtract

E anything that is not 'add'

5 The program asks the user for three inputs. If they enter 15, 5 and –, what will be the last output? Pick the correct answer.

A 20

B The answer is: –10

C The answer is: 10

D The answer is: 20

This picture is from a game called 'The Floor is Lava'. The character has to get across the screen, only stepping on the stones. If the character touches the hot lava then they lose.

6 Study the picture. What are the different objects in the game?

7 Write or draw an algorithm that checks if the character is touching the lava. If they are touching the lava, then output a suitable message.

Managing data

> 2.1 Collecting and storing data

We are going to:

- investigate the computing tools we use in a statistical investigation

- understand how to use questions to collect different types of data

- find out how to make rules in spreadsheet cells to help avoid mistakes in data.

analyse	data logger	statistical investigation
automatically	form	statistics
average	information	validation
continuously	numerical data	
database	spreadsheet	

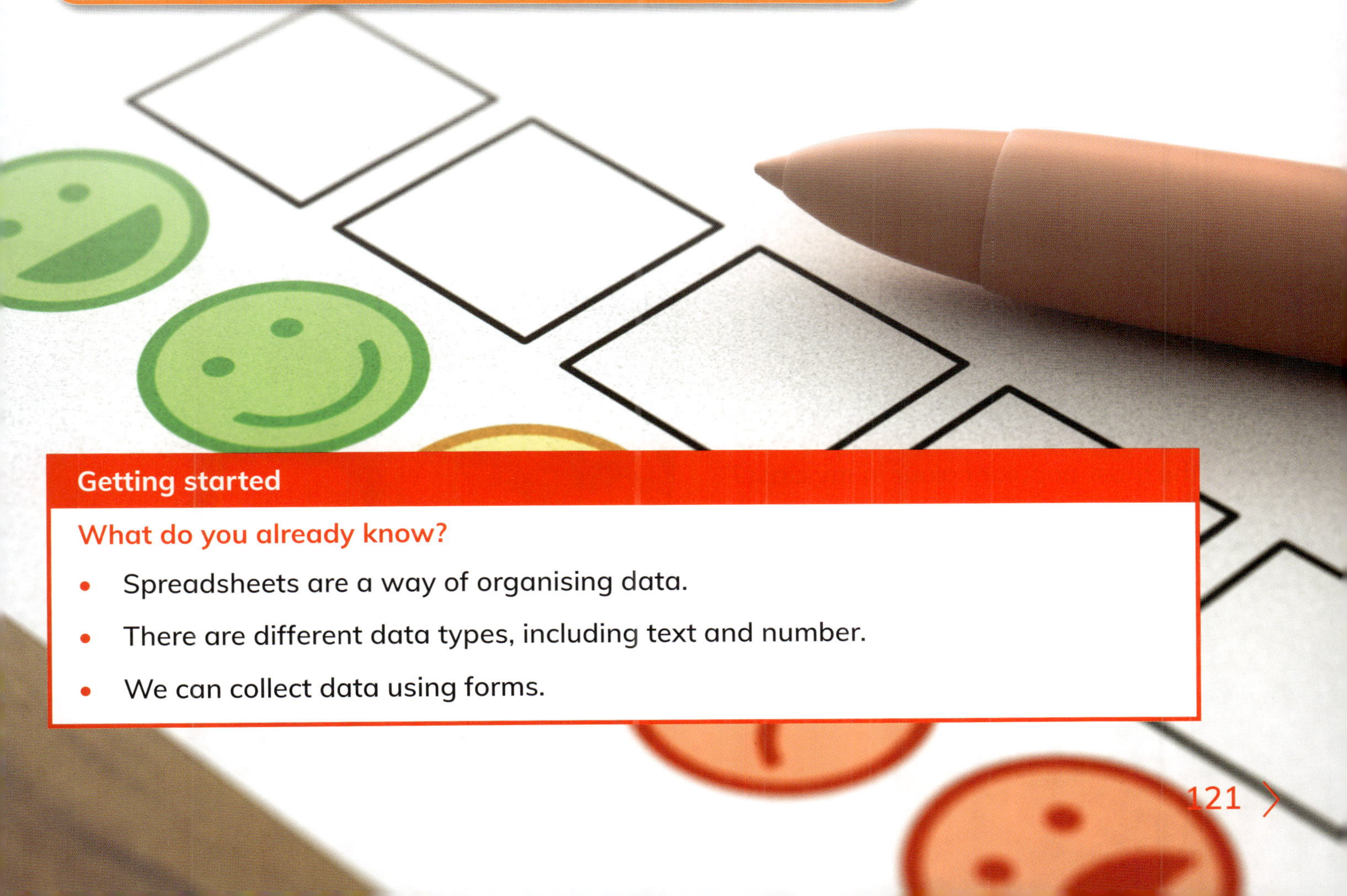

Getting started

What do you already know?

- Spreadsheets are a way of organising data.

- There are different data types, including text and number.

- We can collect data using forms.

Continued

Now try this!

You will need: a pen and paper

> I have three cats called Snowflake, Pickles and Mungo. I wonder what type of pet is the most popular in my class.

Make a list of different pets that the children in your class might own. Think about ways that you can categorise the pets. For example, the number of legs they have or where they live.

- How would you collect this data?

- How would you record this data?

Statistical investigations

In many areas of life, it is useful to collect data about the world so that we can learn things. In a statistical investigation we collect data to answer questions, such as: 'Which is the most popular colour in my class?' The data is called statistics.

For example, imagine that an ice-cream shop wants to find out the most popular flavour of ice cream. To do this, the manager counts the number of scoops of each flavour of

ice cream that they sell. Then, they analyse this numerical data. Numerical data is data with a number data type, for example 2, 14, 3.6 or −60.87. To analyse data means to look closely at the data, find patterns in it and think carefully about what it means.

Many businesses, like this ice-cream shop, analyse data about what they sell. This is useful because it helps the manager to know which items are more popular. They can then buy more of these items to make sure they do not run out.

> Remember, data is meaningless facts or figures, like '7' or 'green'. Information is data with meaning, like 'green is the most popular colour in the class'.

In a statistical investigation we can collect different kinds of data. Data can be categorical, discrete or continuous.

Categorical data is data that can be grouped into categories. It is often made up of words. Examples include colours, people's names and book titles.

Discrete data is numerical data that can only have certain values (such as whole numbers only). Examples include the number of customer reviews received for a product, or a number of people.

Continuous data is numerical data that can have any value in a certain range. Examples include time, weight and length.

Before you start a statistical investigation, you have to decide:

- what data you want to collect
- how you will collect the data
- how you will organise the data you collect
- how you will use the data to get information.

Unplugged activity 1

You will need: a pen and paper

The school kitchen cooks lunch every day, but lots of food gets thrown away because not everybody likes it.

Write down how a statistical investigation could help with this problem.

Tools we use when working with data

Humans are not very good at collecting, recording and organising data by ourselves. If we just talked to people to gather data, it would take a lot of time and effort. We would probably make mistakes and forget things. It would also be difficult to put all the data together in an organised way so that we could analyse it.

Computers are much better at collecting and organising data. They do not forget, and they can take measurements and do calculations very quickly. There are lots of computer-based tools we can use to help us with a statistical investigation. The most useful tools are:

- data loggers
- spreadsheets
- databases and forms
- document production tools.

Data loggers

A data logger is a device that can read and record data from the world automatically (by itself without any human input) and continuously (carrying on until someone tells it to stop). Some data loggers can be set up to take data readings all day and night at regular times. For example, a data logger could take the temperature of a fish tank every five minutes.

Examples of data that data loggers can record include:

*   the temperature in a house

*   the level of light in a certain place

*   someone's pulse.

Data loggers are also used in some control systems, where certain data makes something happen automatically. For example, hotels use automatic systems to keep the building at a comfortable temperature. When the temperature reaches a set value, such as 23 degrees, a cooling system is switched on. If the temperature falls to 18 degrees, the heating turns on.

Unplugged activity 2

> **You will need:** a pen and paper

Can you think of a statistical investigation that you could use a data logger for? It might be helpful to think of a question that a data logger could help to answer.

Spreadsheets

A spreadsheet is a document that contains lots of boxes, called cells, arranged in rows (lines of cells from side to side) and columns (lines of cells from top to bottom). You can type data into the cells and easily organise and analyse your data.

Spreadsheets are designed to make it easier to work with numerical data. For example, spreadsheet software allows you to easily and quickly add together all the numbers in a row or column. You can also do lots of other calculations very easily.

Spreadsheets also make it easy to show data in different ways using charts and graphs. This makes it much easier to view and understand the data you have collected. This is called representing data.

> **Did you know?**
>
> A Microsoft Excel spreadsheet can contain up to 1 048 576 rows and 16 384 columns (over 17 billion cells!). That is a lot of data. However, digital databases can handle even more data than that!

Databases

Databases are used to store data in an organised way. They can be paper-based, such as a diary or calendar, or digital, a bit like a spreadsheet. Understanding the difference between a spreadsheet and a digital database can be tricky.

Spreadsheets are best for working with numbers and doing calculations, and they cannot store much more than 1 million rows of data. Most database software programs have no problem storing 10 million rows of data!

Databases are good for storing pieces of data of different types (not just numbers), that are related in some way. Databases make it really easy to find the exact data you are looking for, and to sort and analyse the data. Database data is also very easy to change, even if the same piece of data is in lots of different places. Some examples of databases include:

- a diary or journal
- a family's calendar

- IMDb, which is an online database that stores information about films, TV shows, and actors

- a shop's catalogue (a digital or physical book which lists all of its products, the price, its ID number, and more)

- trading cards like Pokémon or Top Trumps (the same data is collected for each character, and is represented on a card. Lots of cards together form a database)

- medical records, either digital or physical.

Forms

An easy way to collect data to store in a database is by using a form. A form is a list of questions with spaces for people to mark or write their responses. Forms can be on paper or on a screen. A good form will make sure that people enter their data in a specific way, so that the data is easy to organise and analyse.

Forms collect data on related questions, like your most favourite and least favourite kind of food, and how often you eat it. These are related questions because they are about the same topic. Other examples include:

- filling in a form to register with a doctor

- registering for a library card

- applying for secondary school

- registering for an account on a website.

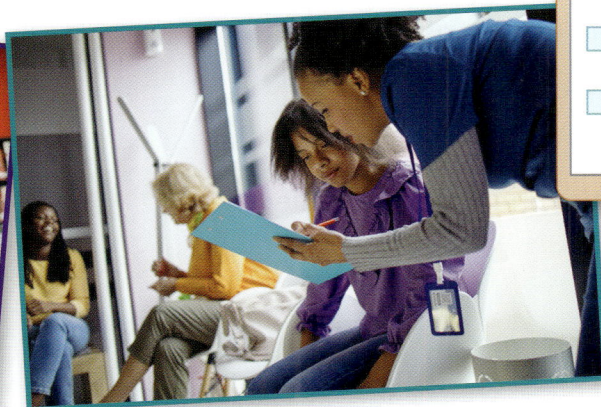

Document production tools

Document production tools are programs that allow us to put text and pictures together to create a report or presentation. Reports and presentations can be very useful for sharing the results of statistical investigations because they show information in a way that is easy to understand. Examples of this kind of software include word-processing and presentation software.

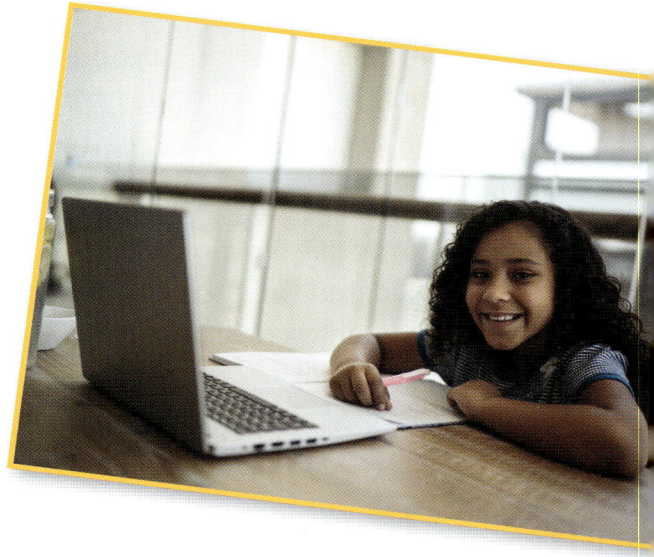

Using tools to collect data

Collecting data with a form and spreadsheet

Think about Sofia's statistical investigation from the Getting started activity.

Which type of pet is the most popular in my class?

To complete her investigation, Sofia needs to begin by answering the following questions:

- What data do you want to collect?
- How will you collect the data?
- How will you organise the data you collect?

Sofia might answer:

- I want to find out all the different types of pet the people in my class have, and how many people have each type of pet.

- I will collect the data using an online form.

- I will organise the data by downloading it into a spreadsheet and sorting the pets in order, from most popular to least popular.

Sofia creates the following form:

Pet survey

Which is the most popular pet in our class?

*Indicates required question

What kind of pet do you have? You can select more than one box. *

- ☐ Bearded dragon
- ☐ Budgie
- ☐ Cat
- ☐ Chicken
- ☐ Fish
- ☐ Gecko
- ☐ Gerbil
- ☐ Goat
- ☐ Guinea pig
- ☐ Hamster
- ☐ Horse
- ☐ Llama
- ☐ Mouse
- ☐ Parrot
- ☐ Rabbit
- ☐ Rat
- ☐ Stick insects
- ☐ Terrapin
- ☐ Tortoise
- ☐ I don't have any pets.
- ☐ Other:

Submit   Clear form

Sofia makes sure that she includes lots of different pets that people might have, and there is an option to type in a different kind of pet in case she has missed anything out. She also includes an option to tick if someone has no pets. Sofia checks her form carefully then saves it. Next, she emails the link to the form to all her classmates and asks them to complete it.

After everyone has filled in the form and submitted their answers, Sofia looks at the results. She downloads a spreadsheet of the data. The spreadsheet looks like this:

	A	B
1	Timestamp	What kind of pet do you have?
2	8/30/2022 13:23:49	Cat
3	8/30/2022 13:34:04	I don't have any pets.
4	8/30/2022 13:40:12	Tortoise, Mouse, Chicken
5	8/30/2022 13:44:21	Cat, Rabbit
6	8/30/2022 13:47:24	Guinea pig
7	8/30/2022 13:51:00	Cat
8	8/30/2022 13:55:09	Fish
9	8/30/2022 13:56:18	Terrapin
10	8/30/2022 13:56:26	Budgie
11	8/30/2022 13:57:32	Hamster
12	8/30/2022 13:59:42	Fish, Gerbil
13	8/30/2022 14:00:57	Cat, Horse, Rat, Gecko
14	8/31/2022 14:01:02	I don't have any pets.
15	8/31/2022 14:01:23	I don't have any pets.
16	8/31/2022 14:01:55	Bearded dragon
17	8/31/2022 14:02:16	Stick insects
18	9/1/2022 14:03:33	Rabbit, Hamster
19	9/2/2022 14:03:47	Budgie, Parrot, Cat
20	9/3/2022 14:04:56	Chicken, Goat, Llama
21	9/4/2022 14:05:02	Fish
22	9/4/2022 14:07:11	Cat
23	9/4/2022 14:07:36	I don't have any pets.
24	9/4/2022 14:08:10	I don't have any pets.
25	9/4/2022 14:08:27	Cat, Guinea pig, Terrapin, Rat

Sofia could also enter the data into a spreadsheet herself, in a way that makes the most sense and does not have extra information, like whether they filled in the form at 14:00 or 14:01!

	A	B
1	Type of pet	Number
2	Cat	7
3	I don't have any pets.	5
4	Fish	3
5	Budgie	2
6	Chicken	2
7	Guinea pig	2
8	Hamster	2
9	Rabbit	2
10	Rat	2
11	Terrapin	2
12	Bearded dragon	1
13	Gecko	1
14	Gerbil	1
15	Goat	1
16	Horse	1
17	Llama	1
18	Mouse	1
19	Parrot	1
20	Stick insects	1
21	Tortoise	1

Stay safe!

If a form asks you for personal data like your name, make sure that you trust the person you are giving it to. If you are not sure, ask an adult.

Sofia has now collected data on the types of pets owned by her classmates.

Questions

1 What is the most popular pet in Sofia's class?

2 If you added any pets that you have, would the most common pet change?

The number of people who own each type of pet is an example of discrete data.

Collecting data with a data logger and spreadsheet

How warm does our classroom get in the afternoon?

Arun wants to find out how the temperature in the classroom changes during the day. He sets up a data logger to capture the temperature every hour between 9 a.m. and 6 p.m. At the end of the day, he connects the data logger to a computer and downloads the data into a spreadsheet. The spreadsheet looks like this:

	A	B
1	Time	Temperature in °C
2	9:00 AM	16
3	10:00 AM	17
4	11:00 AM	19
5	12:00 PM	20
6	1:00 PM	21
7	2:00 PM	21
8	3:00 PM	21
9	4:00 PM	21
10	5:00 PM	20
11	6:00 PM	20
12		

Arun collected this data continuously (he kept on collecting data) over time. Arun could have used the data logger to collect more data over days, weeks or even months to see how the temperature changed. This temperature data is an example of continuous data.

Unplugged activity 3

You will need: a pen and paper

Which tools would be best for collecting and storing each type of data? Copy the table below. Work with a partner and tick the correct box or boxes in each row. You might want to look back at the information about the different tools earlier in this topic.

Type of data	Data logger	Spreadsheet	Form
1 How the amount of light in a garden changes over 24 hours			
2 How many children in a school can swim			
3 How popular different free time activities are among 6–10-year-olds in the local area			
4 How much rain falls in a week in April			
5 How tall the children in each class in a school are			

How are we doing?

Share your answers with another pair. Were the answers the same? If not, why not? As a group of four, talk about each kind of tool and why you ticked the boxes you did. Make sure you all understand the advantages of each tool.

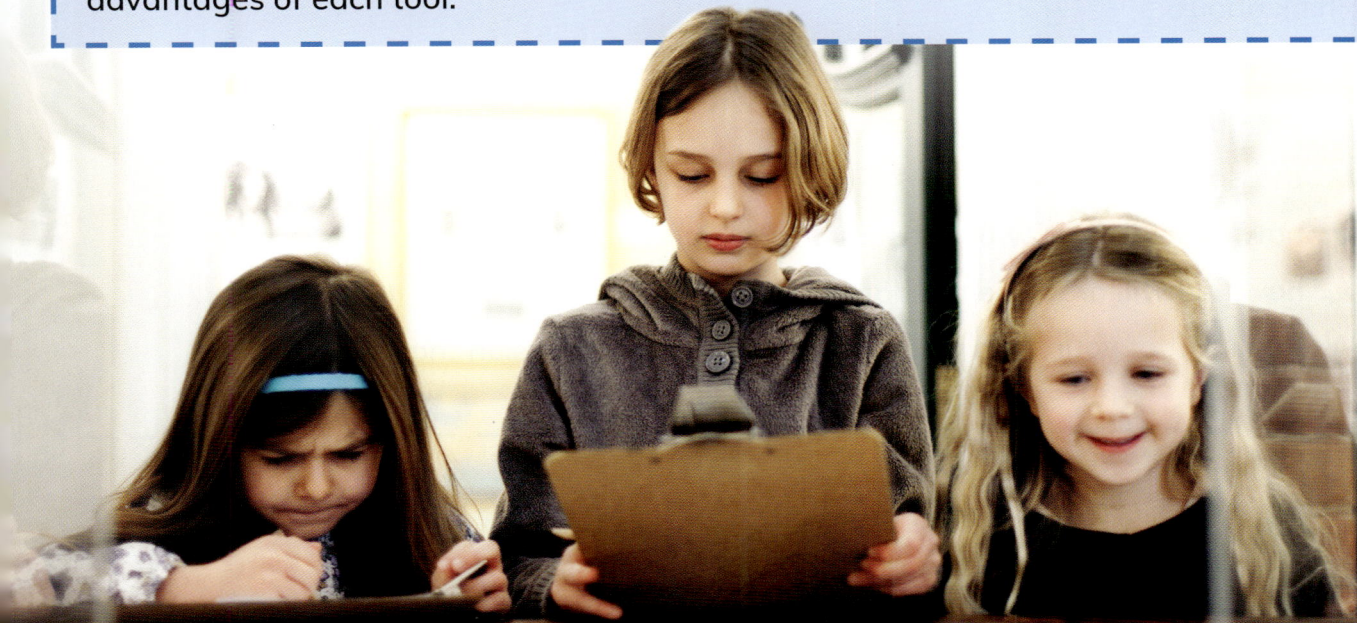

Unplugged activity 4

You will need: a pen and paper

Work in a group of five or six. On paper, plan a simple digital form to find out:

- how your group members travel to school each day

- the average amount of time it takes the class to get to school. An average is a value in the middle of a set of values. It is a way of representing the pattern of the whole set in one value. You can calculate the average by adding all the values together, then dividing by the number of values.

Think about:

- what data you need to collect

- the questions you need to ask

- the data types you need

- how you will deal with unusual answers

- how you will organise the data you collect.

Write a draft of your form on paper (a draft is a first version that you might make changes to later).

Unplugged activity 5

You will need: your form from Unplugged activity 4, a pen and paper

How will you organise the data you collect using this form? Will you use a digital or a paper database? What kinds of categories will you include in your database? Draw what it might look like.

Practical task 1

You will need: a desktop computer, laptop or tablet with internet access, a Google account

In your groups, you are now going to create the real version of your form using Google forms. Then you will all fill it in to collect your data.

1 Log in to a Google account and go to Google Forms. Ask your teacher if you are not sure how to do this.

2 Under 'Start a new form' press 'Blank'.

3 Create your form, working from your paper plan.

When all of your group members are happy with the form, use it to collect your data.
Let each person in your group complete the form. To view your results:

1 Make sure you are logged in to the same Google account you used to create the form.

2 Go to Google Forms/Google Drive and open your form.

3 Press 'Responses' at the top.

If you are all using the same computer, you can all fill in the form one after the other. Just press 'Submit another response' after each person submits their answers.

135 >

Restricting cells

It is easy to enter data incorrectly. If Zara wanted to keep a spreadsheet of all her friends' birthdays, she might accidentally type '32/12' or '3112' instead of '31/12'. If she searched to find out which friend had a birthday on 31 December, she would not find the birthday.

Another example could be a spelling mistake. If Zara was collecting data on her friends' favourite games, she might type 'ouzzle' instead of 'puzzle'.

Some spreadsheets limit the kind of data you can add to a cell. This is called data validation and helps you to enter data correctly. Some cells might only allow numbers, some allow dates, and some allow text.

Some cells might only let you enter text from a set list, and will reject text that is not from the list. An example of this is a cell that lets you enter 'Yes' or 'No', but rejects any other words or numbers.

This can happen with numbers too. Imagine you are giving something a score out of 5, so the only numbers you can give are 1, 2, 3, 4 or 5. A cell with a validation rule would reject 6 as a number.

How can I make sure my data is entered correctly?

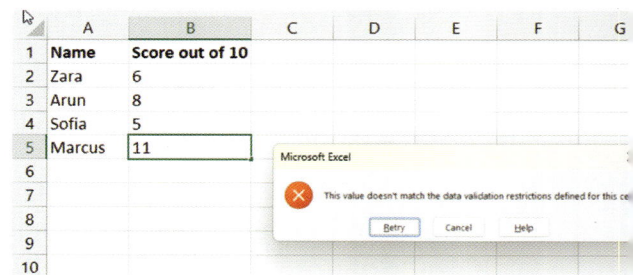

Error!

Data validation in forms

When you create an online form, you can usually add data validation rules. For example, you might want to restrict answers to 'Yes' or 'No' rather than letting people type in their own answers. You might want people to rank their favourite foods, so you could restrict the form so that it won't let people move on until they have ranked all of the options.

Can you think of an example of how you might want to add data validation to a form?

I could restrict a form to only let people enter their birthday in a DD/MM/YYYY format to keep my data consistent.

Practical task 2

You will need: a desktop computer, laptop or tablet with spreadsheet software (such as Microsoft Excel), source file **2.1_Marcus_game_data**

You are going to see what happens when you try to enter data into a cell which has validation rules.

Open source file **2.1_Marcus_game_data**.

Try to enter the word 'cheese' in cell B2 (the cell next to Marcus's name).

You will get an error message! This is because you have entered data that is not accepted by the cell.

Instead, select the little arrow on the right side of the cell.

You will see a list of game types that the cell accepts. Choose one. The cell will accept the data.

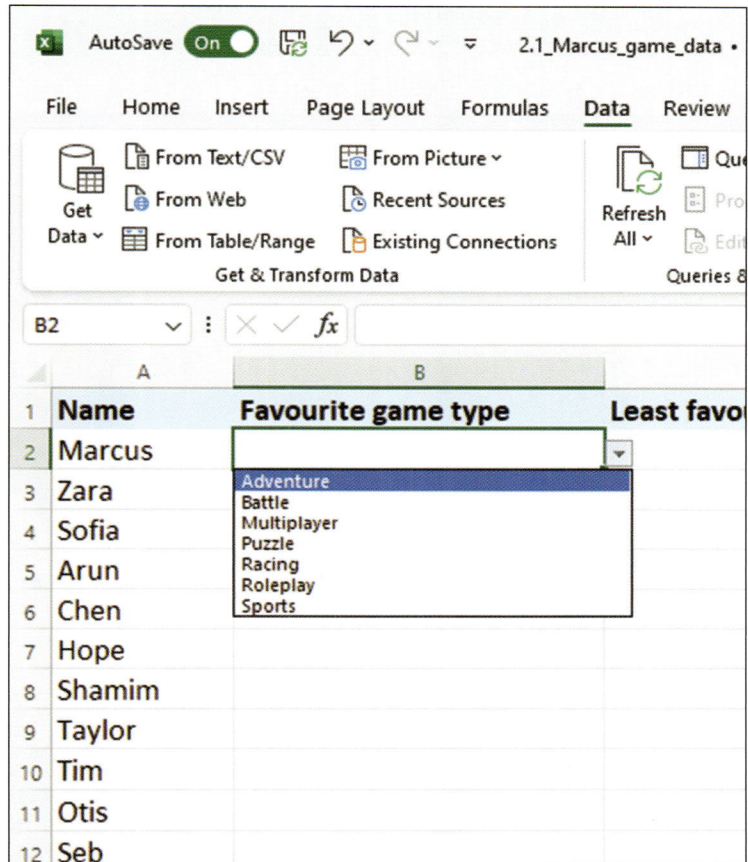

Now:

1 Try typing 'ouzzle' into cell B3 (next to Zara's name). What happens? Why?

2 Choose a game to enter into cell B4 – try to avoid an error message!

3 Try to enter a written number like 'one' or 'two' in cell D2. What happens?

4 What happens when you type '2' into cell D2 instead?
    Why do you think this happens?

Look what I can do!

☐ I can use computing tools to carry out a statistical investigation.

☐ I can create questions to collect different types of data.

☐ I know that rules can be added in spreadsheet cells to help avoid mistakes in data.

> 2.2 Representing data

We are going to:

- look at different ways of representing data
- find out how to change representations of data for different reasons
- investigate how arithmetic operators such as + and − are used in spreadsheet calculations
- explore simple functions that are built into spreadsheet programs.

average	horizontal
bar chart	legend
cell reference	line graph
chart	operator
formula	range
function	vertical

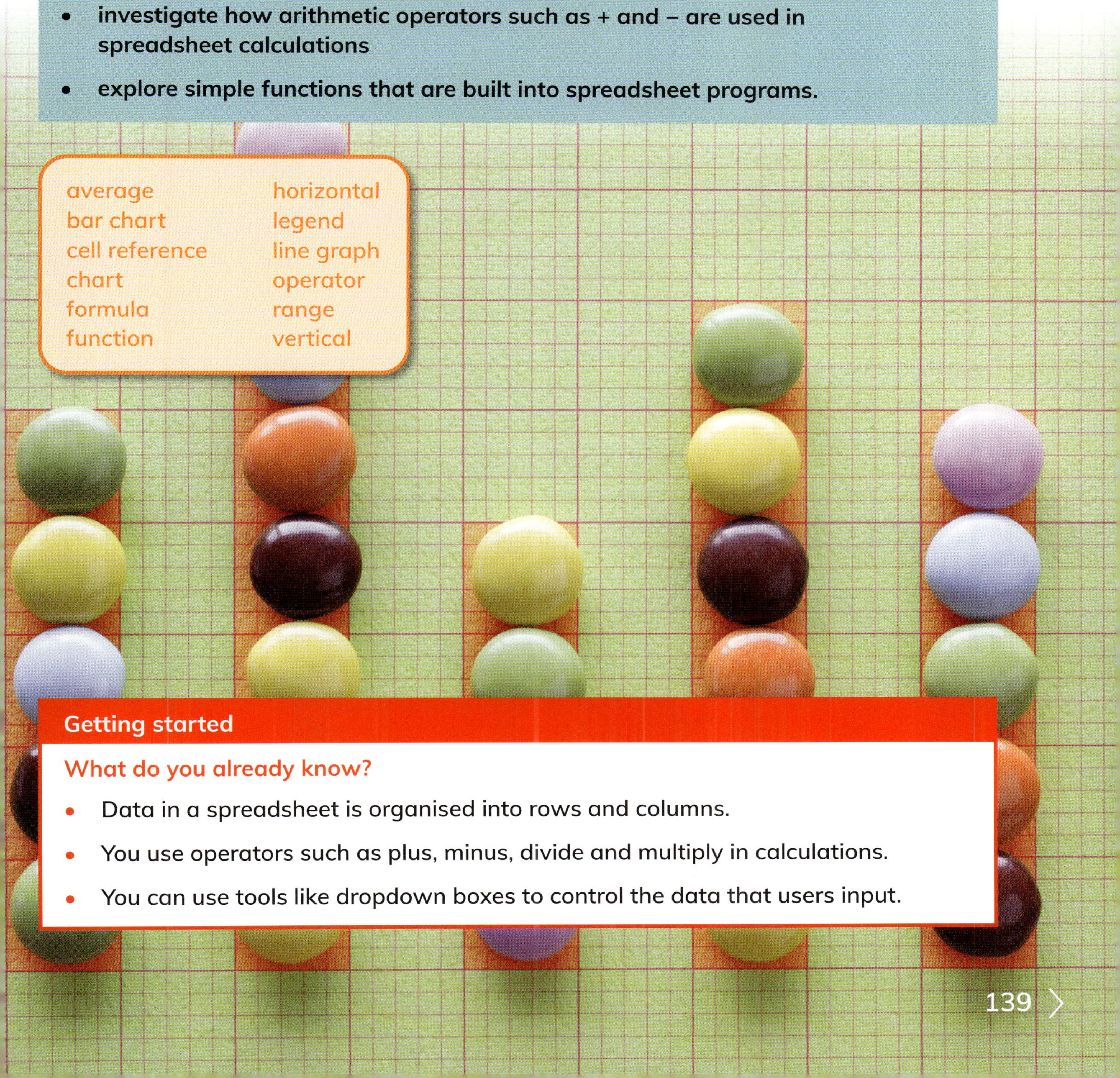

Getting started

What do you already know?

- Data in a spreadsheet is organised into rows and columns.
- You use operators such as plus, minus, divide and multiply in calculations.
- You can use tools like dropdown boxes to control the data that users input.

Continued

Now try this!

You will need: a pen and squared or lined paper, a coin

Using a pen and squared or lined paper, create a table with ten rows and two columns. Under the first column write 'Heads' and under the second column write 'Tails'. Your table should look like this:

Now flip a coin. Did it land on heads or tails? Colour in a cell in the correct column, starting with the bottom cell. Flip the coin ten times and colour a cell in the correct column each time, working up the column so that the coloured cells are always touching each other.

Which did you flip more – heads or tails? What type of chart have you created?

Heads　　　　Tails

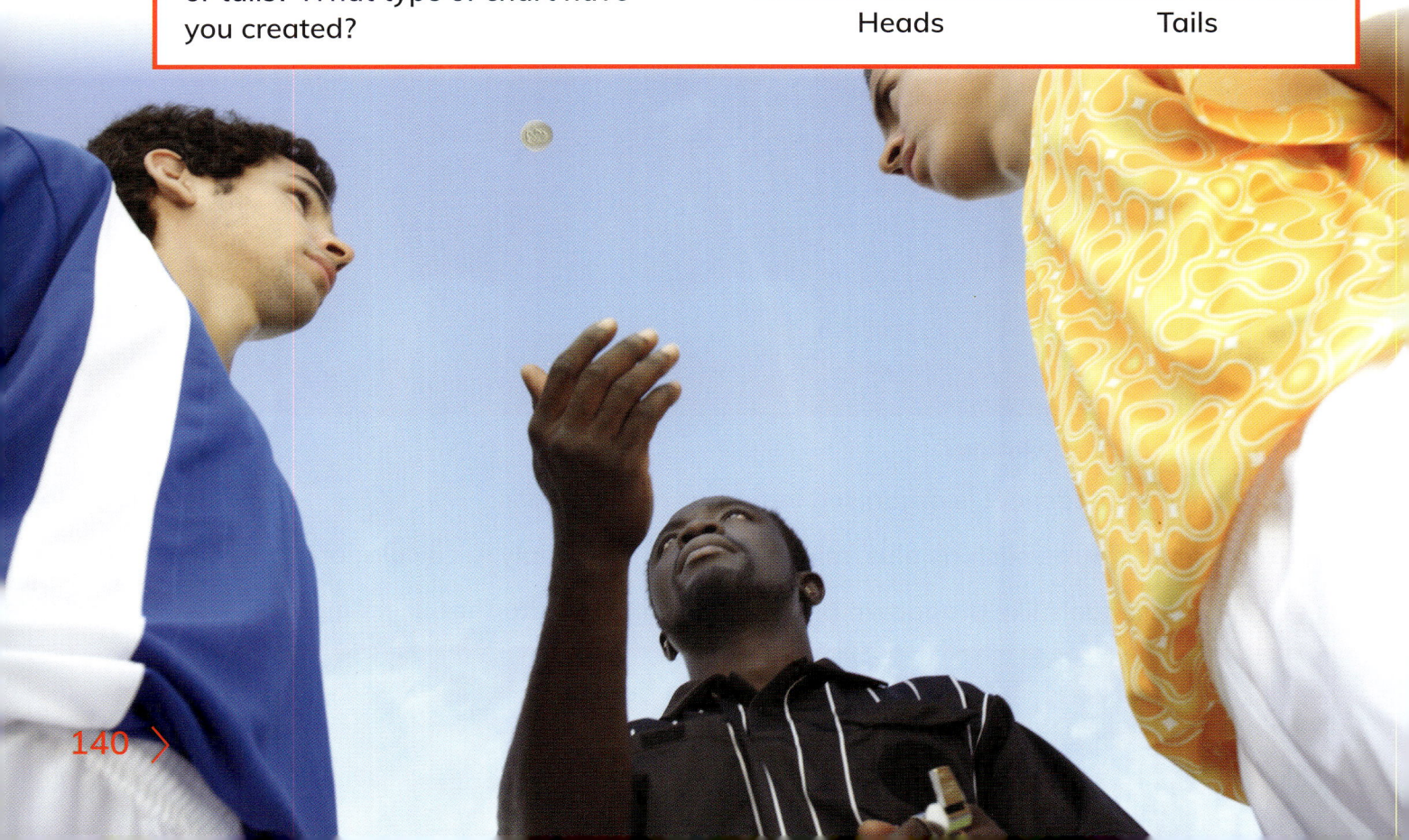

Different ways to represent data

Tables

Once we have collected some data, we can represent (show) it in different ways. We have looked at representing it in a spreadsheet. A spreadsheet or database uses a table to organise data in rows or columns, making it easy to see which bits of data go together. By representing the data in a table, we can get information from the data.

For example, Zara has collected data about the eye colour of all the children in her class. She puts the data into this table.

Eye colour	Number of children
Brown	12
Green	3
Blue	9

By looking at the table we can see that 12 children have brown eyes, 3 children have green eyes and 9 children have blue eyes. This means the most common eye colour in the class is brown, and quite a lot of people have blue eyes. Not many people have green eyes.

If we add up the numbers, we can work out that there are 24 children in the class. So half of the children have brown eyes, as 12 is half of 24. Putting the data in a table makes it easier to read and analyse this information than just writing it in a sentence.

But sometimes, putting data in a table is not enough to make it easy to get information.

Look at this table. It shows eye colour data for all the people who live in a city (the city's population).

Eye colour	Number of people
Brown	252 780
Green	344 700
Blue	574 500

Because the numbers are much bigger, it is not as easy to get a clear idea of what percentage of the population have each eye colour. This is when it becomes useful to use a chart to represent the data.

Charts and graphs

A chart or graph is like a picture or diagram that shows the data. Charts make it much quicker and easier to see patterns in the data and summarise the information.

There are different types of chart. These include bar charts, line graphs, tally charts and frequency diagrams. When you use charts you have to choose the type that is best at displaying the information you want to share.

Here is a bar chart of the data in the table about the eye colour of people in a city.

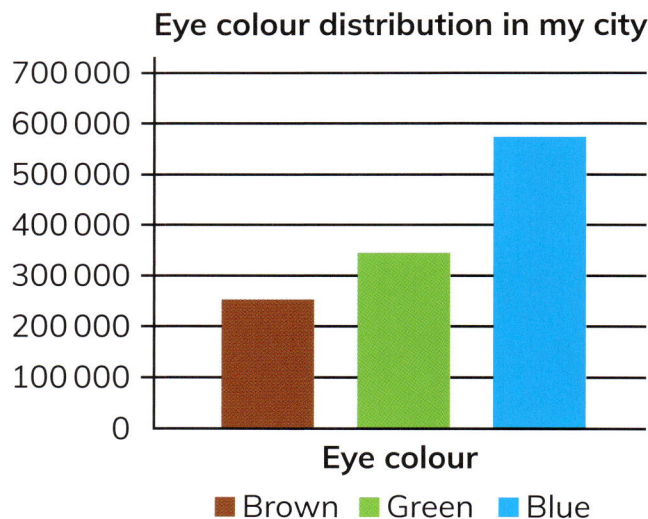

Eye colour distribution in my city

Eye colour

■ Brown ■ Green ■ Blue

A bar chart has a coloured bar for each category. The longer the bar, the greater the value.

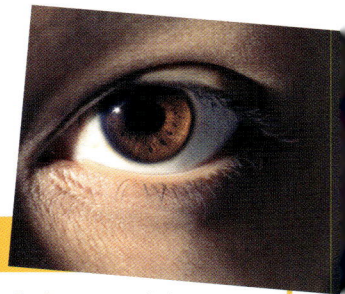

Did you know?

More than half of the world's population has brown eyes – that is around 4 billion people. Different countries have very different distributions of eye colour, so not every country has half of its population with brown eyes. But on average, half of the people in the world have brown eyes. Do you?

It is much easier to see which is the most common eye colour in the city by just looking at the bars instead of the numbers in the table.

Bar charts can be useful for smaller numbers too. Marcus wanted to find out which game type was the most popular in his class. Using a form, he asked his classmates what their most favourite and least favourite game types were.

Game type	Votes up
adventure	2
battle	2
multiplayer	1
puzzle	4
racing	2
roleplay	1
sports	3

I have reorganised the data in my spreadsheet to count how many votes each game type got for favourite game. Let's call these 'votes up'.

Marcus has made a bar chart of the data.

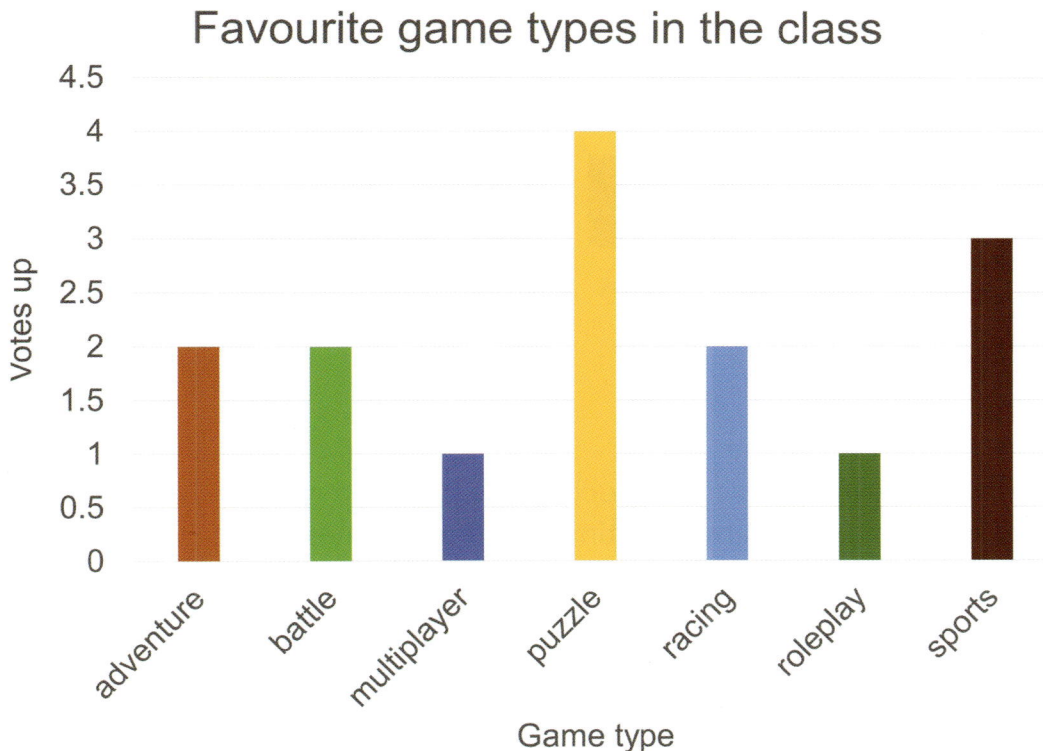

Favourite game types in the class

143

Questions

1 What does this chart tell Marcus about how popular each game type is?

2 How easily can you identify which game type got the most votes up and which got the least? What makes it easy or difficult?

Representing categorical and discrete data

We can represent categorical and discrete data using bar charts. We can also use waffle diagrams or tally charts, but these are not very easy to create with spreadsheet software. Bar charts are simple to create using spreadsheets. Below is Marcus' bar chart from earlier.

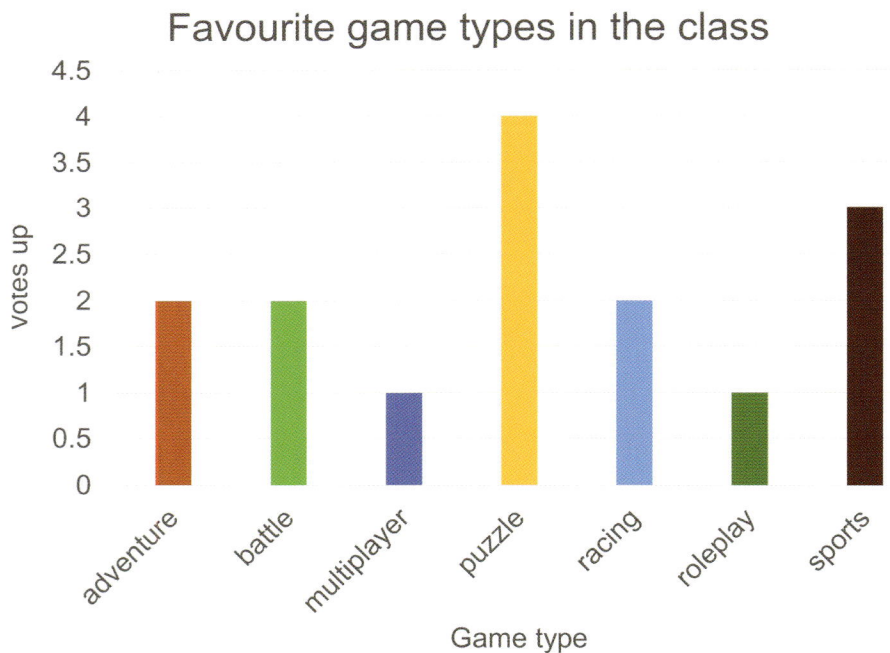

Favourite game types in the class

The bar chart shows how many learners chose each game type as their favourite. Bar charts organise data by counting how many times each option is chosen. This makes them very useful for representing categorical and discrete data.

Unplugged activity 1

You will need: a pen and paper

Make a list of five examples of data that you could collect and represent in a bar chart.

How am I doing?

Swap your list with a partner.

Take a look at their five examples of data. Can all of them be represented by a bar chart? If not, suggest a new one to your partner.

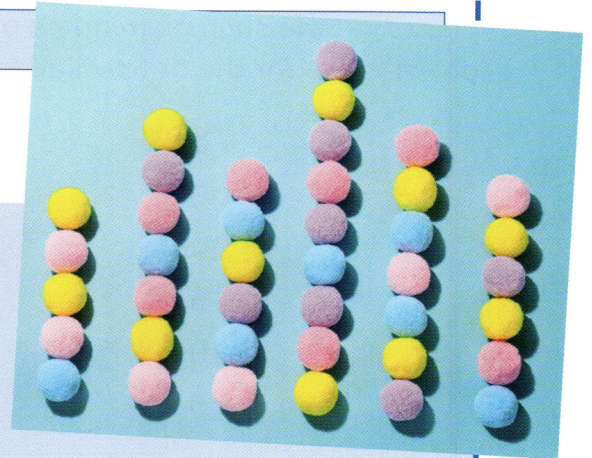

Representing continuous data

Continuous data usually records changes over time. A line graph is useful for representing continuous data because it shows the changes between the data points.

We can create a line graph by hand on grid paper. First we draw a vertical y axis (a line that goes up and down) and a horizontal x axis (a line that goes from left to right), as shown above.

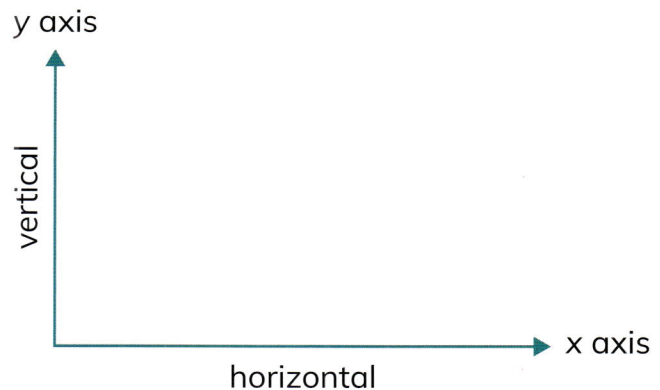

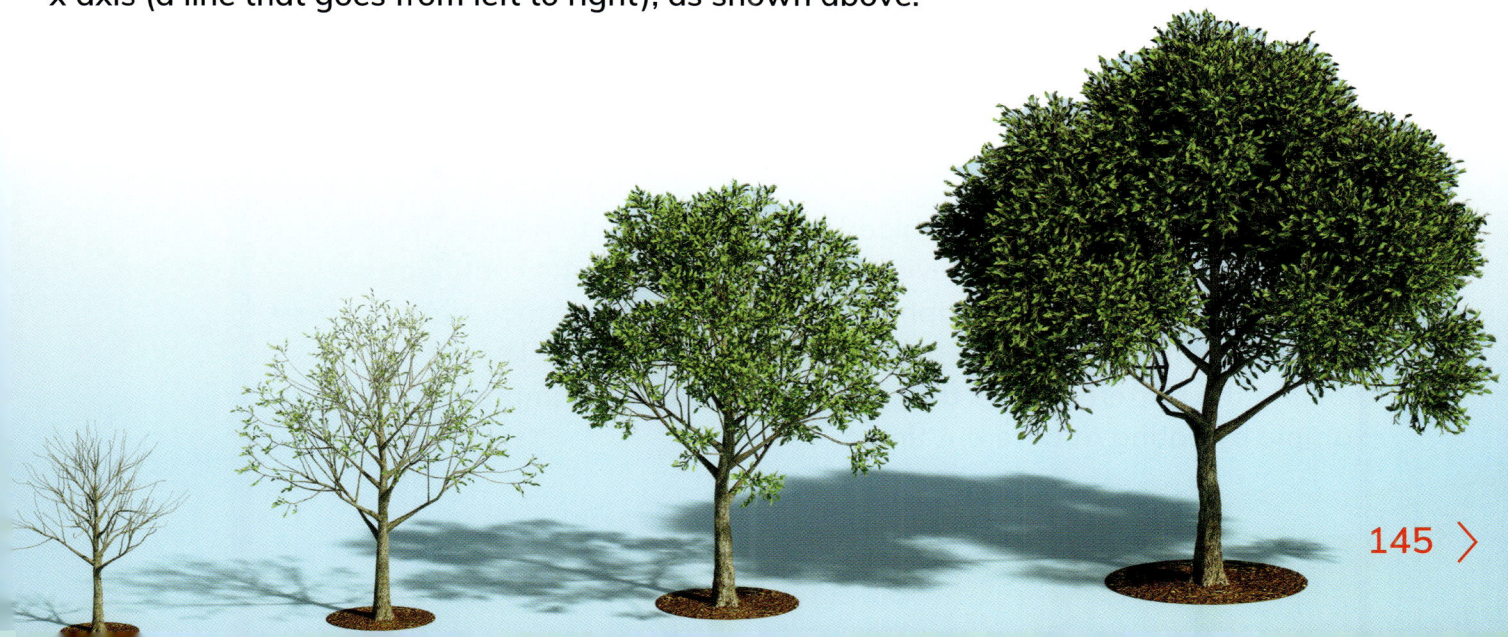

y axis

vertical

horizontal

x axis

The vertical axis will show the scale for the data values from bottom to top (for example 0 to 10), like on a bar chart. The horizontal axis will show points in time such as minutes or days, from left to right. We then mark a dot or cross for the data value for each time, at the correct height. Like this:

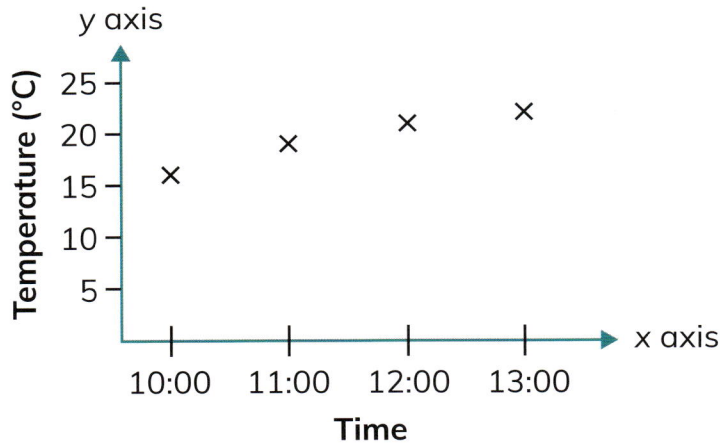

Then we draw straight lines between the data points to show the changes in the data over time.

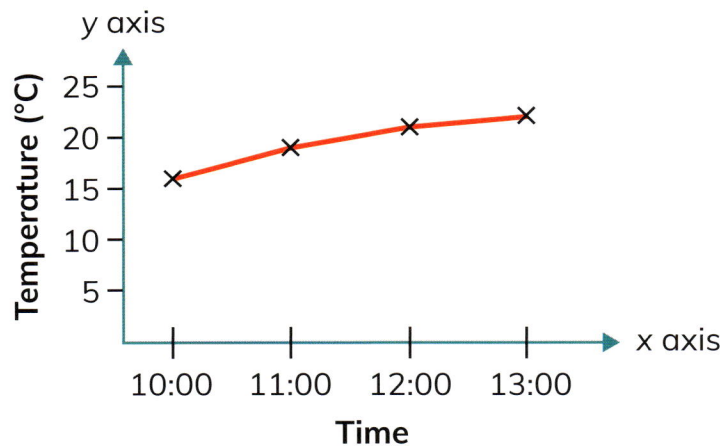

Spreadsheet software can create line graphs from data very quickly and easily.

People with diabetes test their blood sugar each day to help them stay healthy. Some people use a device or app that shows the continuous blood sugar data as a line graph. Seeing a line graph of their data means the person can easily see the pattern in their blood sugar levels. Knowing the pattern means they can make changes to improve it, for example by eating at different times.

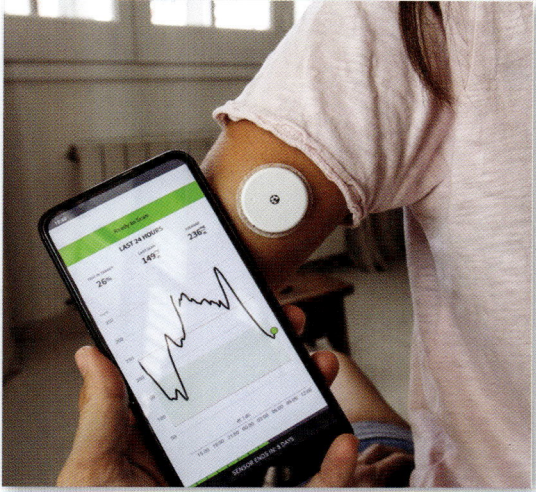

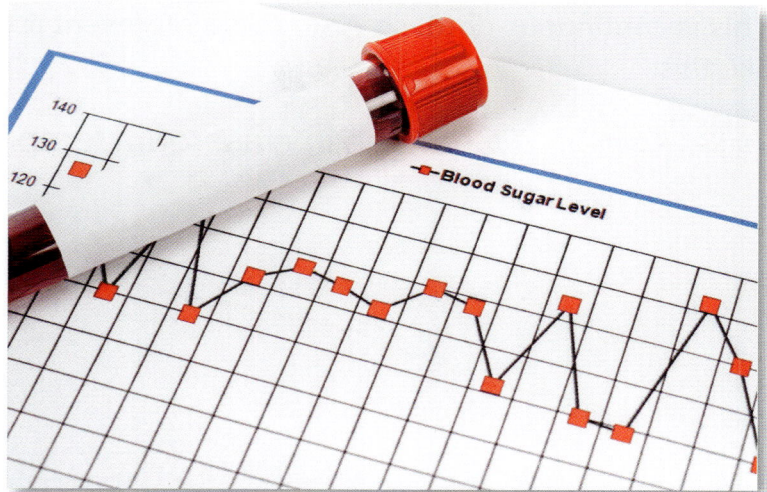

Questions

3   Why wouldn't a bar chart be a useful way of representing blood sugar data?

4   Why wouldn't a line graph be a useful way of representing your family's favourite meals?

There are also examples of continuous data in everyday life. Here is the data Arun collected. It shows how the temperature changed in the classroom over a day.

Remember my classroom temperature investigation?

Time	Temperature in °C
9:00 a.m.	16
10:00 a.m.	17
11:00 a.m.	19
12:00 p.m.	20
1:00 p.m.	21
2:00 p.m.	21
3:00 p.m.	21
4:00 p.m.	21
5:00 p.m.	20
6:00 p.m.	20

This is continuous data, so Arun could represent it using a line graph, like this:

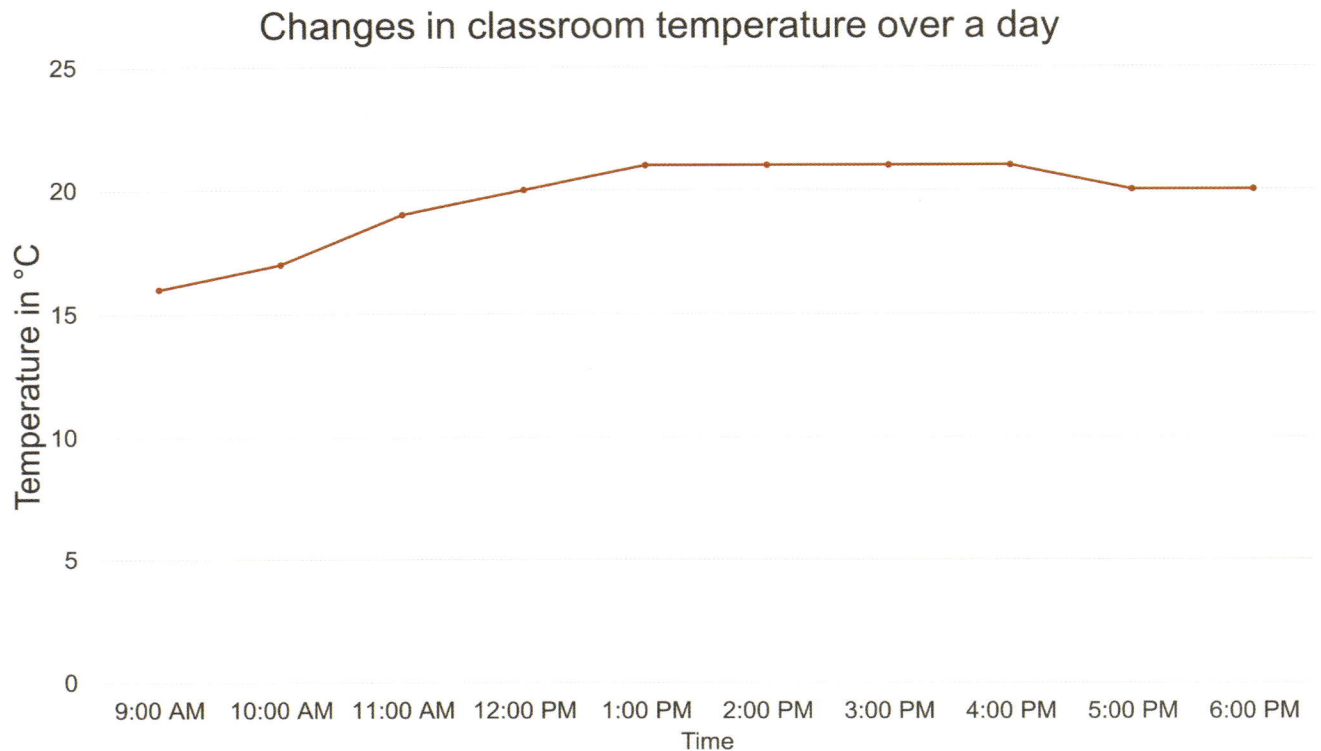

Changes in classroom temperature over a day

What programs can we use to create charts?

Spreadsheet software allows you to create lots of different charts from your data.

Bar charts and line graphs have an x axis and a y axis. The y axis is vertical. The x axis is horizontal. The title you add to each axis is called a **label**. Axis labels explain what each axis measures.

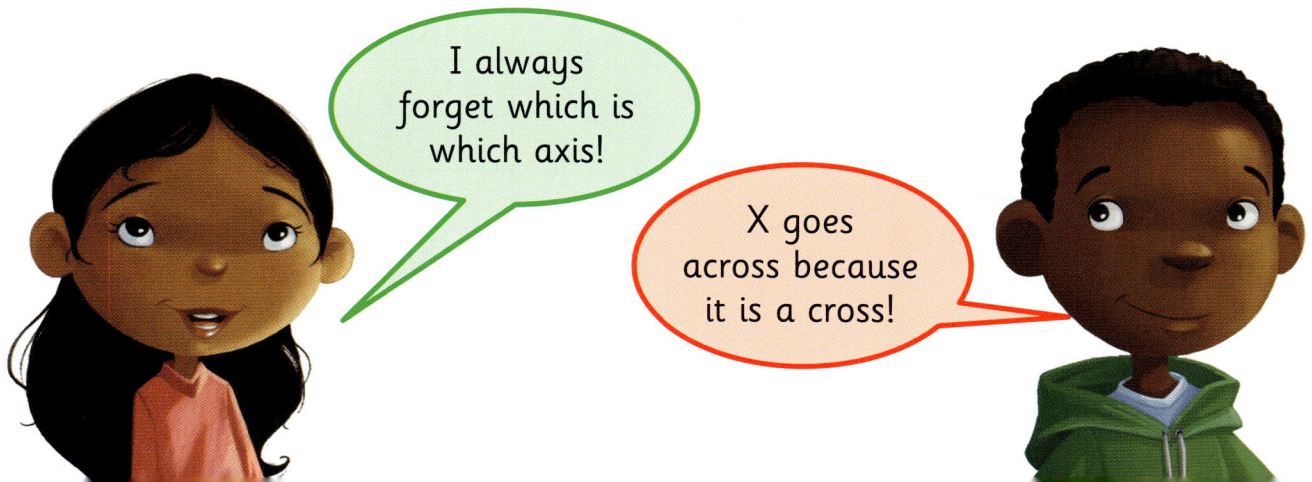

I always forget which is which axis!

X goes across because it is a cross!

Did you know?

Bar charts can be vertical (with the bars going up) or horizontal (with the bars going across).

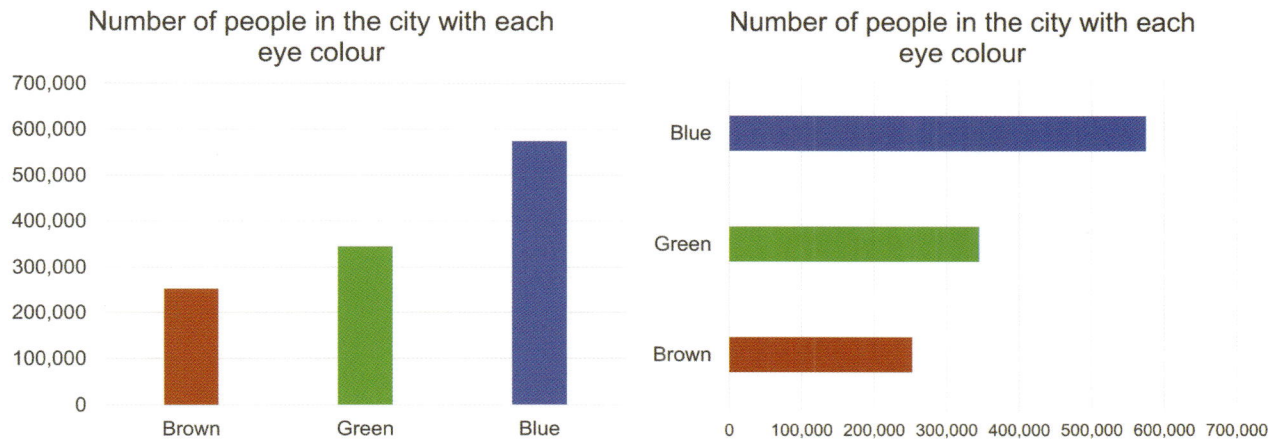

Number of people in the city with each eye colour

Number of people in the city with each eye colour

Practical task 1

You will need: a desktop computer, laptop or tablet with spreadsheet software (such as Microsoft Excel) and source file **2.2_Marcus_game_data_class**

We are going to look at the data from Marcus's computer game investigation. Marcus organised the data in his spreadsheet to count how many people said each game type was their favourite. He called these 'votes up' and made a bar chart of this data.

1   Open source file **2.2_Marcus_game_data_class**.

First, let's create a bar chart that shows the votes down next to the votes up, so that we can compare them.

Continued

2 Select cells A18 to C25 by clicking on the 'Game type' heading and dragging down and across to the last vote in the 'Votes down' column. These cells should now look grey, like this:

	A	B	C	D
	Game type	**Votes up**	**Votes down**	**Popularity score**
18				
19	adventure	2	1	1
20	battle	2	2	0
21	multiplayer	1	2	-1
22	puzzle	4	2	2
23	racing	2	2	0
24	roleplay	1	4	-3
25	sports	3	2	1

3 Click on the Insert menu, then click the little button with a picture of a bar chart. Click on the first option under 2-D Column.

A chart will appear beside your data. Notice that the chart does not have a proper title, so it will not be clear to someone else what this chart is showing.

4 To add a chart title, click on the chart. Then select the words 'Chart Title' and type your chart title in their place. Make sure the title tells us clearly what the chart shows.

5 Save your file.

The labels right at the bottom of the chart are called the legend. The legend is like a key on a map: it shows what the colours on the chart mean. So in this case, light blue means votes up and dark blue means votes down.

2-D Column

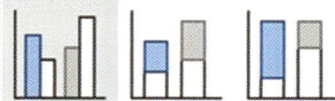

3-D Column

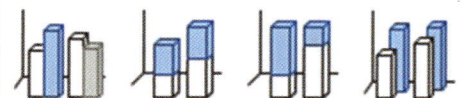

2-D Bar

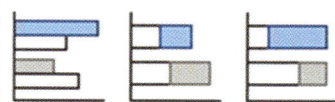

3-D Bar

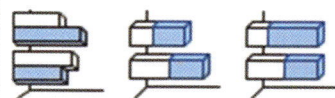

 ▮▯ More Column Charts…

Questions

Look at your chart.

5   Which game types got the same number of votes up and votes down?
6   Which game types got the highest and lowest number of votes up?
7   Which game types got the highest and lowest number of votes down?
8   Does this chart tell us which game is the most or least popular overall? Why/why not?

Practical task 2

You will need: a desktop computer, laptop or tablet with spreadsheet software (such as Microsoft Excel), source file **2.2_Marcus_game_data_class** and your chart from Practical task 1

In Practical task 1 you made a chart that compares the votes up and votes down. Now we are going to represent the data using positive and negative numbers.

Column D puts together the information about votes down and votes up.
It subtracts the votes down from the votes up to give a popularity score for each game type.

This is a measure of how popular each game type is among my classmates.

Let's make a bar chart of the popularity scores.

1   Select cells A19 to A25. Then hold down the Ctrl key on your keyboard while you select the popularity scores in cells D19 to D25 as well. The first and last columns of the table should now look grey, like this:

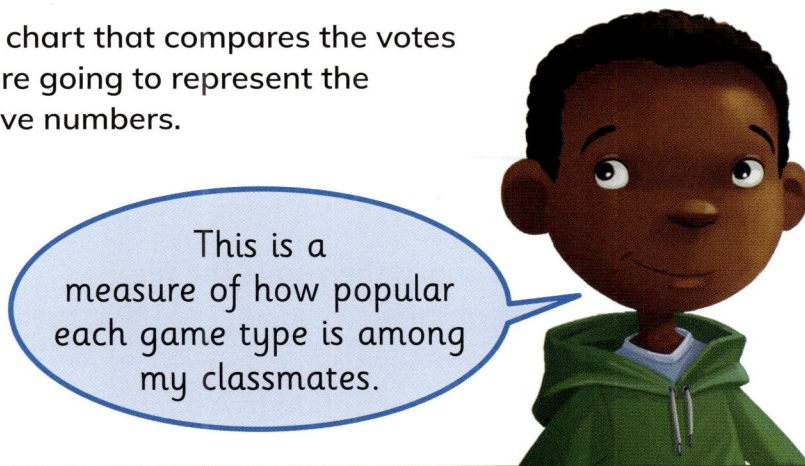

	A	Votes up	Votes down	Popularity score
	Game type	**Votes up**	**Votes down**	**Popularity score**
18	**Game type**	**Votes up**	**Votes down**	
19	adventure	2	1	1
20	battle	2	2	0
21	multiplayer	1	2	-1
22	puzzle	4	2	2
23	racing	2	2	0
24	roleplay	1	4	-3
25	sports	3	2	1

Continued

2 As before, click on Insert > Bar chart > 2-D Column chart.
Your chart should look like this:

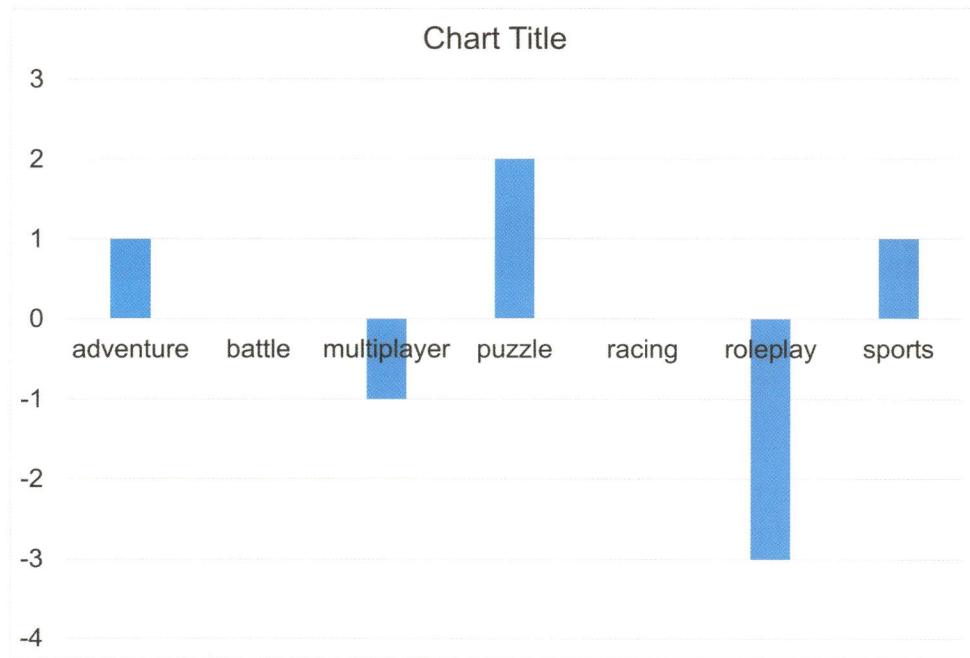

3 Add a title to your chart, then save the file.

How am I doing?

Use your body to show how confident you felt with this task.

- Stand up tall if you found this task easy and you understood it well.
- Bend your knees if you felt OK about this task but could use a little more help.
- Kneel or sit on the floor if you did not really understand the task and would struggle to do another similar one.

Questions

9 Why do some of the bars go down instead of up?

10 Why is there no bar for battle or racing games?

11 Which game type is the most popular?

12 Which type is the least popular?

Activity 2

You will need: a desktop computer, laptop or tablet with spreadsheet software

Arun is going out for dinner with his family to celebrate his brother's birthday. However, they cannot decide where to go! Arun decides to collect some data to see what the most popular option is. His data is as follows.

Family member	Favourite food
Mum	Pizza
Dad	Burger
Sister	Shawarma
Brother	Pizza
Uncle	Burger
Cousin	Shawarma and pizza
Aunt	Salad
Grandma	Pho and shawarma
Grandpa	Salad and burger
Arun	Pizza

Help Arun by creating a chart that shows the data in the best way.
Make sure you represent all of the data, and include labels.
Based on the data, which restaurant should they go to?

Continued

Arun also wants to create a graph to show his mum how much his brother has grown in recent years. He has found the following data from the kitchen height chart.

Age	Height (cm)
3	95
4	102
5	109
6	115
7	121
8	128
9	133

Create a chart for Arun that represents this data in the best way. Again, make sure you represent all of the data, and use labels.

How are we doing?

- Swap your two charts with a partner's charts.
- Did you choose the same chart types? If not, why?
  Whose charts do you think show the data in the best way?
- What is one thing your partner did really well, and one thing they could improve on?

Changing the way we display data

When creating a chart from data, the choices you make about chart type, style and labels are very important. These things can make a real difference to how easy the chart is to use and how useful it is.

Changing chart type

Sometimes it does not matter very much whether you choose a bar chart or a line graph. However, for some types of data, the kind of chart you choose will make a big difference to how useful the chart is.

Can you copy this and fill in the gaps in your exercise book?

Bar charts are good for showing _____ and _____ data.
Line graphs are best for _____ data.

Arun has collected more temperature data. This time, he has used a data logger to record the classroom temperature every two hours for a week. He has combined this with data that other students collected at other times of the year.

Arun has asked Sofia for help to analyse his data. She has made the data into a bar chart. Her chart looks like this:

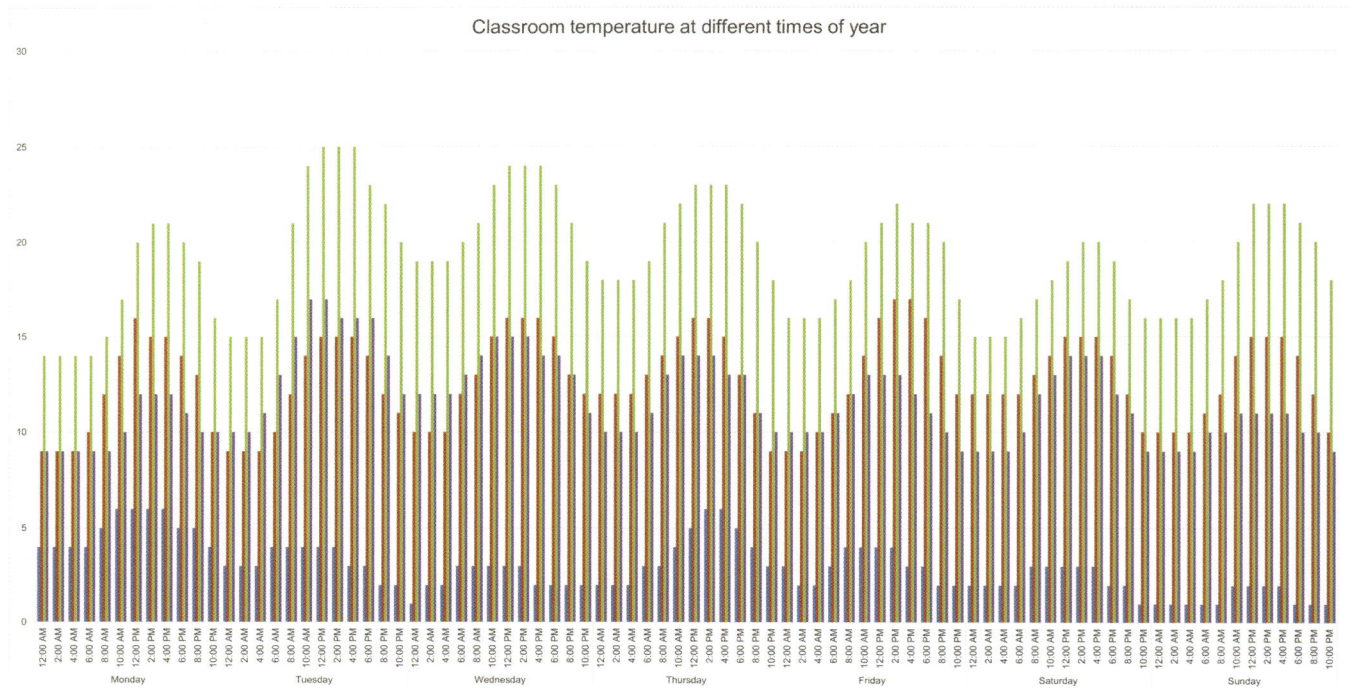

Classroom temperature at different times of year

Unplugged activity 3

You will need: a pen and paper

In your exercise book, write down the answers to these questions.

1 Why is a bar chart not the best choice for this data?

2 What kind of chart would be better?

Share your ideas with a partner. Did you agree?

Thankfully, if we make a chart and then realise it is not the best kind of chart to use, it is easy to change it to a different kind.

Practical task 3

You will need: a desktop computer, laptop or tablet with spreadsheet software (such as Microsoft Excel), source file **2.3_Arun_temp_week**

In this task you are going to change Sofia's bar chart to a line graph.

1. Open source file **2.3_Arun_temp_week.** You will see the data table and the bar chart.
2. Click on the chart, then click the right mouse button to bring up the chart menu. Click 'Change Chart Type . . . '.
3. Click on 'Line' on the left, then 'OK'.
4. Save the file.

Answer these questions about the chart.

1. Is this chart easier to understand? Why/why not?
2. Just by looking at the chart, can you tell which line gives data for which month?
3. Is anything missing from your chart that would make it easier to use?

Changing chart style and labels

When you have chosen the correct type of chart, the options you choose for how the chart looks can make a big difference to how useful the chart is.

For example, you can choose:

- exactly which information is shown
- what labels there are and where they are placed
- which gridlines are shown
- the colours used
- the size of the text.

The style and labels you use will also depend on what the chart will be used for and who will be using it. For example, the colours in some charts are not suitable for people who are colour-blind as they cannot see certain colours. One type of colour-blindness means that both red and green look grey.

Unplugged activity 4

You will need: a paper copy of your line graph from Practical task 3, pen and paper

Get into pairs and look at the table below. One person will think about Situation A; the other person will think about Situation B. What changes would make the chart as useful as possible in your situation? Write or draw ideas for changes on your chart or on a separate sheet of paper.

Situation A	Situation B
The person reading the chart is hard of hearing.	The person reading the chart is colour-blind and cannot tell the difference between red and green.
The person reading the chart is only interested in the temperature in July.	The person reading the chart wants to be able to see all of the data points with lots of detail.
It will be viewed on a small screen.	It will be viewed on a big screen.

How are we doing?

Swap notes with your partner and think about their situation.
Look at the ideas they have written.

- What have they done well?
- Do you disagree with any of their ideas? If so, why?
- Can you think of any other ideas to add to theirs?
  If so, discuss them together and add them if your partner agrees.

Practical task 4

You will need: a desktop computer, laptop or tablet with spreadsheet software (such as Microsoft Excel), source file **2.3_Arun_temp_week** with Practical task 3 completed

Make the chart changes that you wrote down in Unplugged activity 4.

Things you could change include:

- how much detail the chart shows – it could show a summary of the data or very precise data points
- which parts of the chart have labels and how big the label text is
- the colours used
- the thickness of the lines
- the title of the chart.

To change how much detail your chart shows, try:

- making the chart taller or shorter
- adding data labels to the lines
- making the axis labels bigger or smaller.

Here is how to change the colour and thickness of lines on the chart.

- Click on a line. When you see that the line is selected (there are lots of little selection points on the line), right click on it.
- Click on 'Outline' at the top of the toolbar that appears, and choose a different colour.
- Click the 'Weight' button (line thickness is also known as the line's weight) to choose a different thickness.

Continued

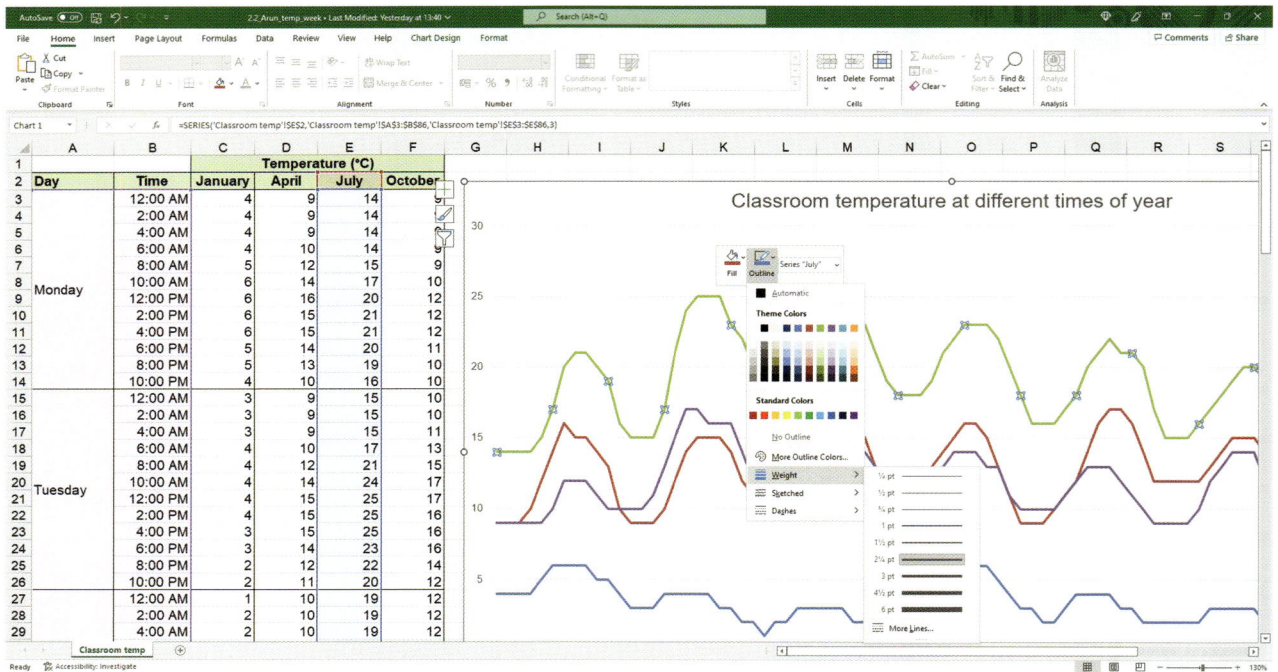

When you have finished making all your changes, save the file.

How are we doing?

Find a partner and show each other your charts. Explain why you made the changes you made.

Did you make any extra changes that you had not planned in Unplugged activity 4? If you did, explain why to your partner.

Doing calculations in spreadsheets

When we work with data in spreadsheets, we often need to do calculations on the data. For example, we might want to add up all the values in a column to find the total, or we might want to work out the average from a set of values. Remember, an average is a value in the middle of a set of values.

We can do calculations easily using tools in the software.

In maths, we use operators when we do calculations.
Some mathematical operators are:

- add +

- subtract −

- multiply ×

- divide ÷

We use these operators when we write calculations on paper.
For example: 10 − 3 + 8 ÷ 3 × 6 = 30

When you do calculations in spreadsheet software, you need to use different symbols for some of the operators.

	Maths symbol	Computer symbol
Add	+	+
Subtract	−	-
Multiply	×	*
Divide	÷	/

It can be difficult to learn new symbols for calculations.

How will you remember these new symbols?

What do you think might help you to remember?

Calculations using formulae

You already know that in spreadsheets, we can talk about each cell using a cell reference. A cell reference is a code made up of a letter and a number. The letter refers to the column and the number refers to the row. For example, cell A4 is the fourth cell down in column A.

In a spreadsheet, we can do a calculation using a formula. A formula is a sequence of operators, numbers and/or cell references. A formula is a bit like a sum you would write on paper, but a formula must always start with =. This tells the software that we are doing a calculation.

Often, when we type a formula into a spreadsheet, we use a cell reference instead of a number.

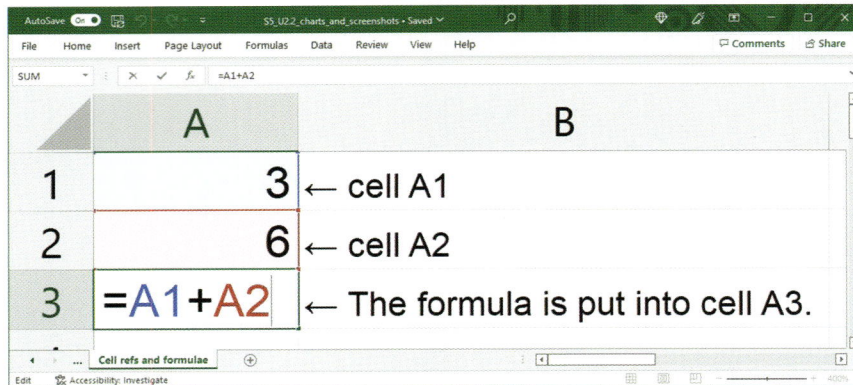

Using a cell reference instead of a number in a formula means we are telling the software to take whatever value is in that cell at the time and use that value in the calculation. So the formula in the diagram means 'the value in cell A1 + the value in cell A2'. If the value in cell A1 or cell A2 changes, the value in cell A3 will update automatically.

When we have written the formula, we press Enter and the result of the calculation shows in the cell instead of the formula, like this:

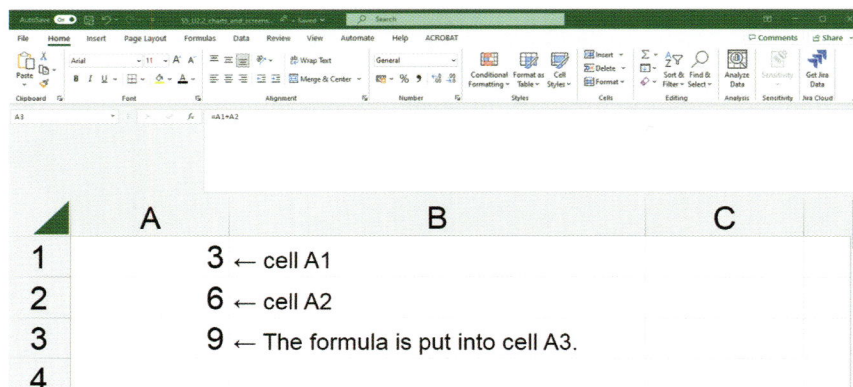

To see the formula again and make changes to it, we just double-click in the cell.

In Practical task 1, you used data Marcus had collected about the popularity of different types of computer game. He subtracted the votes down from the votes up to give a popularity score for each game type. He did this using a formula in each cell of column D of his spreadsheet.

	A	B	C	D
				Popularity
18	**Game type**	**Votes up**	**Votes down**	**score**
19	adventure	2	1	=B19-C19
20	battle	2	2	0
21	multiplayer	1	2	-1
22	puzzle	4	2	2
23	racing	2	2	0
24	roleplay	1	4	-3
25	sports	3	2	1

Questions

13 Can you predict what the formula in cell D20 is?

14 What would the formula in cell D24 be?

Practical task 5

You will need: a desktop computer, laptop or tablet with spreadsheet software (such as Microsoft Excel), source file **2.4_test_scores**

Arun, Marcus, Sofia and Zara's class have done three maths tests this term. Their teacher has a spreadsheet of their marks out of ten for each one. The teacher would like to calculate each student's total score.

You are going to do this by adding formulae to the spreadsheet. Let's do the first calculation together. This is Arun's total.

1. Open source file **2.4_test_scores**.
2. Click on cell E2.
3. Type = into E2.
4. After the =, type B2+C2+D2.
5. Press Enter. You should see the answer appear in cell E2.
6. Do this for all other learners.

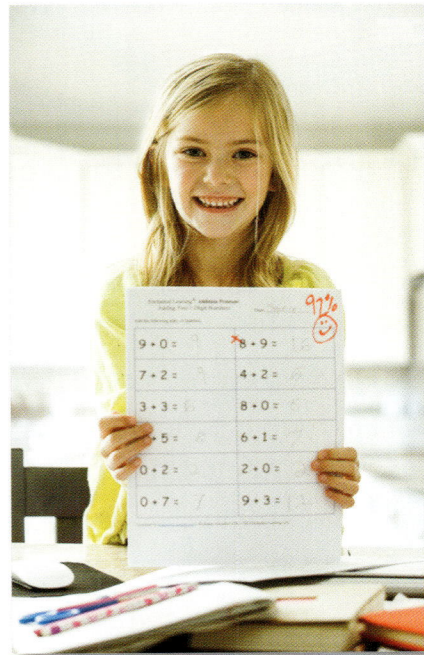

Continued

Remember, if you want to subtract, divide or multiply, you would format your formula in the same way, but changing the operator to -, /, or *.

Next, let's calculate the percentages using the operator / (divide).

1 Click on cell F2.

2 Type = and then type E2.

3 Type /30 then press Enter. This tells the spreadsheet you want to see what proportion of 30 the student's total score is (30 is the total score they would have got if they had scored 10 out of 10 on every test). You should see the result of the calculation appear in the cell. It will not look like a percentage yet. You need to change the format of the cell.

4 With cell F2 selected, click the small button that looks like a percentage symbol (%) in the Home menu at the top of the screen. The cell will now contain a percentage value.

	A	B	C	D	E	F	G
1	Name	Test 1	Test 2	Test 3	Total	Percentage	
2	Arun	8	7	8			
3	Chen	6	8	7			
4	Connor	7	9	8			

5 Repeat this with the other learners in the list. Save the file.

How am I doing?

Hold up a coloured card to show how confident you feel using formulae and operators in spreadsheets.

- Hold up a green card if you feel confident enough to teach someone else.
- Hold up a yellow card if you partly understand but are still unsure about a few things.
- Hold up a red card if you do not really understand.

Calculations using functions

Sometimes formulae can get very long and complicated.
For example, what if the class had done 20 tests throughout
the year and the teacher wanted to add all the scores together?
The formula would take a long time to write.

For this reason, spreadsheet software has **functions** to help us do
calculations more quickly. Functions are little chunks of code that
have been written into the software, ready for us to use.

To use a function, you type = then the function's name, then the cell
references in brackets. Two useful functions are SUM and AVERAGE.

The SUM function

The SUM function adds together all of the cells in a **range**. A range is a
sequence of values from start to finish. In a spreadsheet, a range is all the
cells between (and including) two cells. Ranges that we use in functions
usually just cover one row or one column. We write a cell range like this:

B3:B9

This will include data from cells B3, B4, B5, B6, B7, B8 and B9.

If we wanted to use the SUM function with this range, we would write:

=SUM(B3:B9)

This means 'add together all the values in cells B3 to B9'.

Remember our spreadsheet of test scores from Practical task 4? Instead of using a formula to calculate the total test scores, we could have used the SUM function. Let's use it now to calculate a different total in the same spreadsheet.

Practical task 6

You will need: a desktop computer, laptop or tablet with spreadsheet software (such as Microsoft Excel), source file **2.4_test_scores** (ideally with Practical task 5 completed, but this is not essential)

The teacher would now like to add up all the scores for each test to see if the class found one test easier than the others. You are going to use the SUM function to do this.

1   Open source file **2.4_test_scores**, which you used in Practical task 5.
2   Click on cell B17, type =SUM(B2:B16) and press Enter.
3   Repeat this for Test 2 and Test 3.

The AVERAGE function

Another built-in function is the AVERAGE function.

The AVERAGE function adds up all the values, then divides the total by the number of values.

For example, take this set of four values: 3, 7, 4, 6.

This is how we work out the average:

3 + 7 + 4 + 6 = 20

20 ÷ 4 = 5

So the average is 5.

To use the AVERAGE function in a spreadsheet, we type the same as when using the SUM function, but we replace 'SUM' with 'AVERAGE'. For example:

=AVERAGE(B3:B9)

I wonder what the average score on each test was.

Practical task 7

You will need: a desktop computer, laptop or tablet with spreadsheet software (such as Microsoft Excel), source file **2.4_test_scores** (ideally with Practical tasks 5 and 6 completed, but this is not essential)

You are going to use the AVERAGE function to find out what the average score was for each test.

1   Open source file **2.4_test_scores**, which you used in Practical tasks 5 and 6.
2   Click on cell B18 and type =AVERAGE(B2:B16). Press Enter.
    Repeat for Test 2 and Test 3.

Why do the average scores have decimal places?

How different is the average score for Test 2 compared to the other tests? You could use a formula to calculate this.

Activity 5

You will need: a desktop computer, laptop or tablet with spreadsheet software (such as Microsoft Excel)

Marcus collects some data on the height of the 14 people in his dance class.

Name	Height (cm)
Arun	134
Patience	127
Pavithra	139
Sangeeta	128
Brett	129
Lucas	131
Li	133

Name	Height (cm)
Mohammed	135
Julian	141
Joshi	120
Mahmood	135
Jon	114
Katrina	129
Whitney	131

Enter this data into a spreadsheet and calculate the average height of the class.

How am I doing?

Draw a face on a piece of paper or a small whiteboard and hold it up to show how confident you are using the SUM and AVERAGE functions in spreadsheets.

- Draw a ☺ face if you found it easy and could do it again by yourself.
- Draw a ☺ face if you were able to do the task but still have questions.
- Draw a ☹ face if you need someone to explain functions again.

Look what I can do!

- ☐ I can make different charts to represent data.
- ☐ I can change the style of a chart for different reasons.
- ☐ I can use arithmetic operators in spreadsheet calculations.
- ☐ I can use functions that are built into spreadsheet programs.

〉 2.3 Using data

We are going to:

- **look at what happens when we change data in a spreadsheet**

- **use search criteria to find specific data in a spreadsheet.**

criteria
search criteria

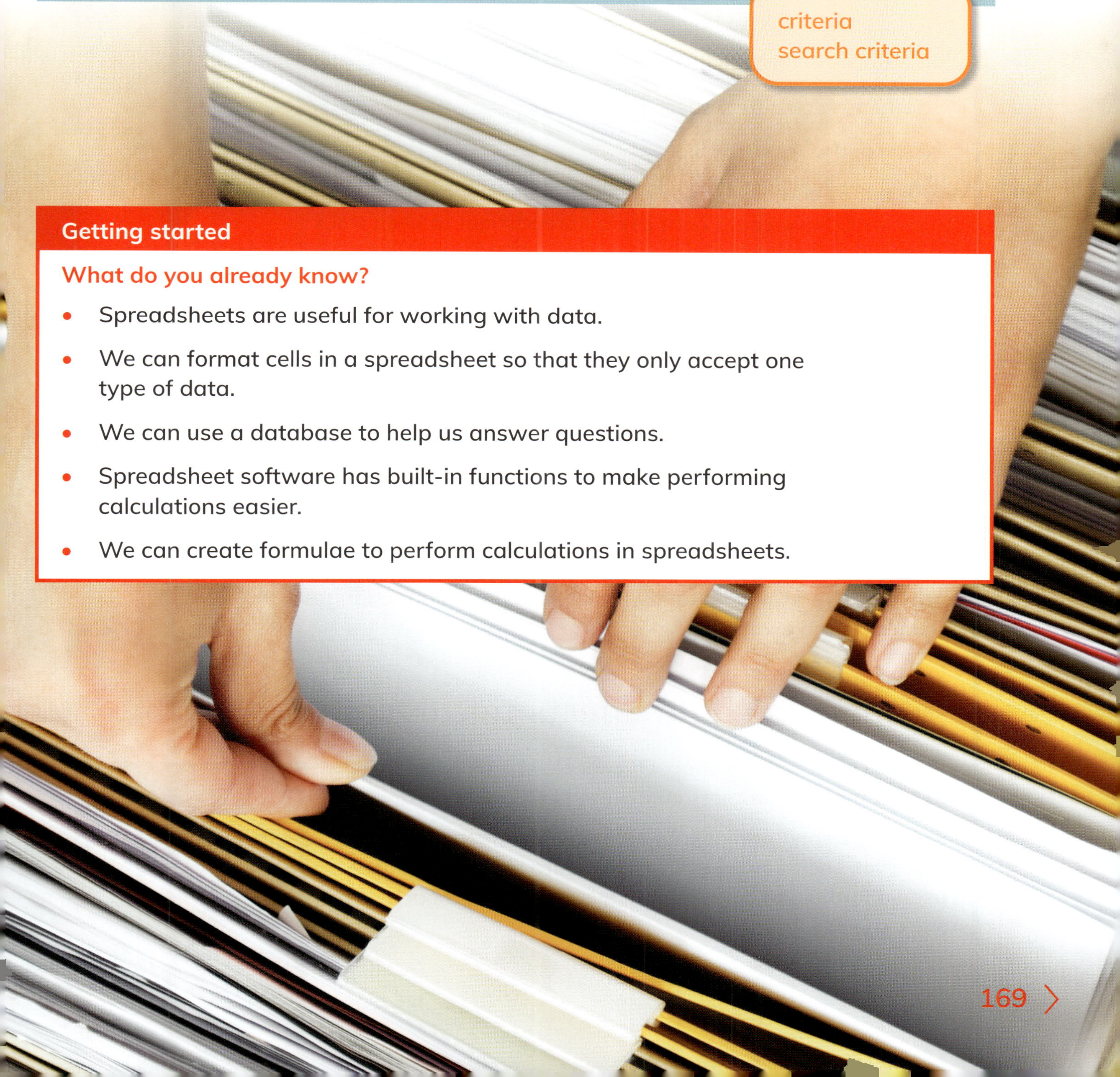

Getting started

What do you already know?

- Spreadsheets are useful for working with data.

- We can format cells in a spreadsheet so that they only accept one type of data.

- We can use a database to help us answer questions.

- Spreadsheet software has built-in functions to make performing calculations easier.

- We can create formulae to perform calculations in spreadsheets.

Continued

Now try this!

You will need: a pen and paper

Zara gets pocket money each week. She has $30 in her money box. It is Sofia's birthday soon and Zara would like to buy her a present. The present she wants to buy costs $15. Zara would also like to buy the following things:

- a magazine that costs $5
- a cinema ticket that costs $10
- a dress that costs $15.

Which things could she buy and still have money left over for the present? How could Zara use a spreadsheet to keep track of her money?

> Will I have enough money to buy my friend a birthday present?

What happens when we change data?

Sometimes we want to change the data in a spreadsheet. Maybe we realise we have made a mistake in the data and we need to correct it. Or maybe we have new information that we need to add, or something has changed, such as a price or the amount of something.

Spreadsheets are very clever. Even if we have added calculations and charts to our spreadsheet, when we change the data in the spreadsheet, everything instantly updates to match our changes. Let's look at some examples.

How changing data affects calculations

Sasha runs an ice-cream shop. One week, she decided to record how many customers came into her shop each day.

Sasha's till system automatically records how much money the shop receives each day. She put all this data in a spreadsheet and used a formula to calculate the average amount each customer spent.

Sasha's spreadsheet looked like this:

	A	B	C	D
1	Day	Customers	Income	Average spend per customer
2	Monday	50	$466.00	$9.32
3	Tuesday	82	$501.20	$6.11
4	Wednesday	97	$552.97	$5.70
5	Thursday	112	$652.25	$5.82
6	Friday	160	$1,098.00	$6.86
7	Saturday	255	$1,669.72	$6.55
8	Sunday	222	$1,324.25	$5.97

Sasha has realised she forgot to ask her assistant to count customers while she was out for a while on Monday. Her assistant says there were about 25 customers while Sasha was out, so Sasha updates the data in cell B2.

	A	B	C	D
1	Day	Customers	Income	Average spend per customer
2	Monday	75	$466.00	$6.21
3	Tuesday	82	$501.20	$6.11
4	Wednesday	97	$552.97	$5.70
5	Thursday	112	$652.25	$5.82
6	Friday	160	$1,098.00	$6.86
7	Saturday	255	$1,669.72	$6.55
8	Sunday	222	$1,324.25	$5.97

Questions

Look at the two spreadsheet images.

1 What has changed in the spreadsheet, apart from the number of customers on Monday?

2 Why has this happened?

3 Why has the value in cell C2 stayed the same?

How changing data affects charts

Any charts will also change when the data is changed. The spreadsheet updates your charts automatically when you change the data.

Sasha made a bar chart from her data before she corrected the data. As soon as she changed the value in cell B2, the bar for Monday became longer to show the change.

Before:

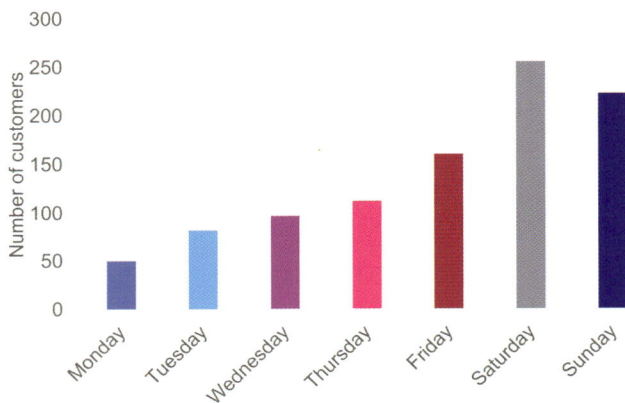

After:

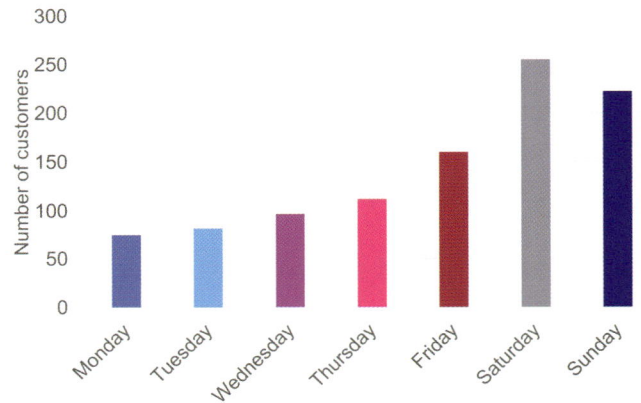

Let's look at another example.

Sofia enjoys swimming and is in the advanced class. To move up to the master class, she needs to be able to swim underwater for up to 30 seconds. She is practising staying underwater every day (under her teacher's supervision), and tracks her progress.

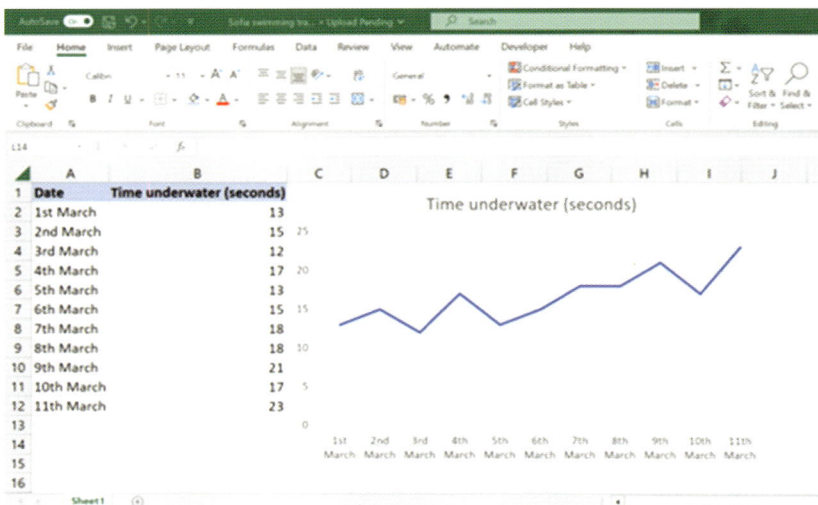

Wow, Sofia, you are really brave!

Unplugged activity 1

You will need: a pen and paper

For the five days after Sofia makes her chart, she records:

- 25 seconds on 12th March
- 21 seconds on 13th March
- 22 seconds on 14th March
- 27 seconds on 15th March
- 21 seconds on 16th March

Working with a partner, predict how the graph will look after Sofia updates her spreadsheet. How will the shape change? Will the y and x axis labels change?

How are we doing?

Compare your predictions with those of another pair. Did you predict the same changes? Why or why not?

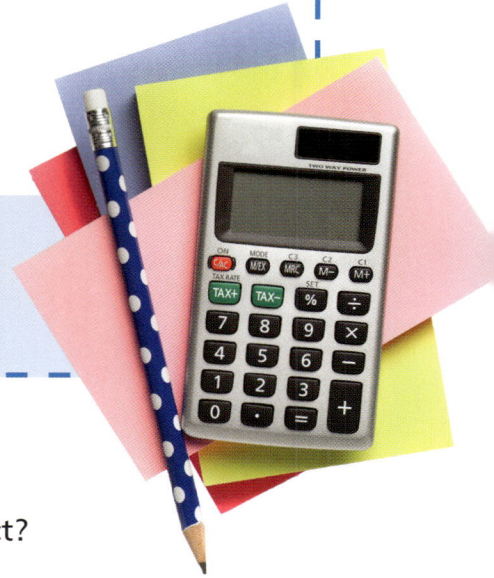

Questions

4   Was your prediction about how the Sofia's graph will look correct?

5   Why are the spikes in Sofia's graph shorter now?

Practical task 1

You will need: a desktop computer, laptop or tablet with spreadsheet software (such as Microsoft Excel) and source file **2.5_Zara_spending**

Zara has made a spreadsheet that tracks her spending. She has made a bar graph to represent the spending so she can easily see how much she is spending on each category. You are going to change the data in Zara's spreadsheet to see what happens to the chart.

1   Open source file **2.5_Zara_spending**.

2   In cell B2 type =22+26 then press Enter.

3   In cell B7 type =4.5+4.85+7.99+6.3 then press Enter.

Write down the changes you see in the bar graph.

Zara buys a T-shirt for $8. Use a formula to add this cost to the correct cell.

You do not need to add up the amounts before changing the data – just use a formula.

Finding specific data in a spreadsheet

We often need to find specific data in a spreadsheet. To do this, we can use search criteria. Search criteria are words or conditions we search for in the spreadsheet to find data that matches.

One well-known example of using search criteria is when you use a search engine to find information on the internet. For example, if you search 'cat in a teacup' on Google Images, one of the results (pieces of data) might be this picture:

Supermarkets use databases to keep track of what each customer buys. They can use this information to send each customer special offers for things they buy often. If a supermarket runs a special offer on pizza, the computer system might search for customers who often buy pizza. Then those customers will get an email about the offer. This way, companies can sell more products, and people who love those products get them cheaper.

If a teacher keeps a spreadsheet with details about all of the children in their class, the teacher could use it to find out which of their learners have birthdays each month and then send those learners a birthday card.

Unplugged activity 2

You will need: a pen and paper

Use the table below to find
learners who meet these criteria.
Write down the learners you find.

1. Learners whose names begin with Z.
2. Learners with birthdays in March.
3. Learners with a nut allergy.
4. Learners with a birthday in July or August
   AND an average test score over 80%.

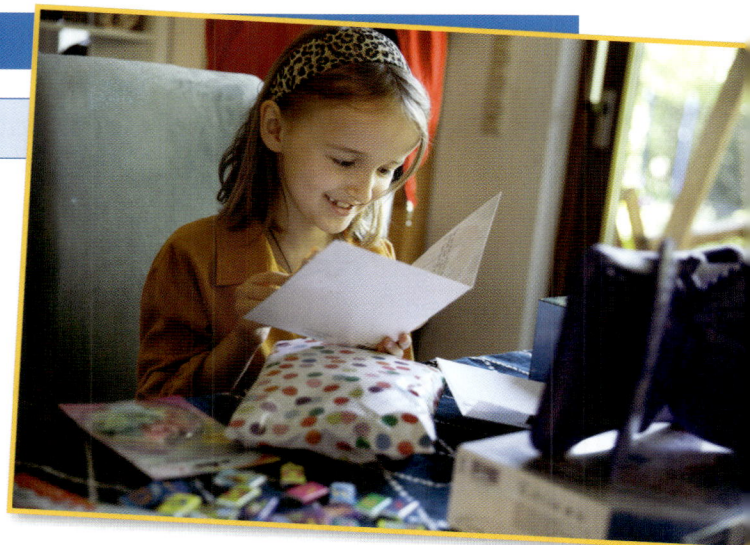

Name	Birth day	Birth month	Class	Allergies	Average test score
Arun	5	June	5A		78%
Chen	6	December	5A		70%
Connor	12	May	5A		86%
Hope	30	April	5A		74%
Jade	14	March	5A		68%
Marcus	3	October	5A		90%
Otis	9	February	5A	nuts	70%
Seb	10	July	5A		76%
Shamim	21	August	5A		86%
Sofia	26	February	5A		86%
Taylor	13	January	5A		74%
Tim	2	January	5A		72%
Wayne	18	March	5A	dairy	90%
Zara	29	September	5A		84%
Zebedee	30	November	5A		86%

Searching using the 'Find' tool

Spreadsheets often contain a lot of data and can be very complex. For example, businesses often use spreadsheets to store a lot of data about the products they make or sell.

Having lots of data in a spreadsheet means it is difficult to find specific data just by looking at the table. If a teacher had 500 learners, they would find it difficult to discover how many learners have a birthday of 14 July by just looking.

In large databases or spreadsheets, it is easier to use the 'Find' tool in the software. This is a bit like a search engine that is built to the software.

Practical task 2

You will need: a desktop computer, laptop or tablet with spreadsheet software (such as Microsoft Excel), source file **2.6_learner_records**, a pen and paper

You are going to look at the records for all the learners in Stage 5 of Marcus's school and search for specific data. Write down your search results on paper.

Name	Birth day	Birth month	Class	Address	Town	Allergies	Test 1 score	Test 2 score	Test 3 score	Test 4 score	Test 5 score	Average score
Arun	5	June	5A	6 Clayfield Avenue	Newtown		8	7	8	9	7	78%
Chen	6	December	5A	72 Richmond Crescent	Fincham		6	8	7	7	7	70%
Connor	12	May	5A	8 Mayfair Close	Totterton		7	9	8	10	9	86%
Hope	30	April	5A	11 Beechcroft Road	Newtown		6	7	6	8	10	74%
Jade	14	March	5A	19 Devon Hill	Sunningdale		6	6	5	9	8	68%
Marcus	3	October	5A	4 Denver Street	Newtown		8	10	7	10	10	90%
Otis	9	February	5A	89 Ashdale Avenue	Newtown	nuts	5	7	6	8	9	70%
Seb	10	July	5A	10 Riverdale	Hillingborough		7	9	7	7	8	76%
Shamim	21	August	5A	256 Banbury Road	Fincham		8	10	9	8	8	86%
Sofia	26	February	5A	45 St Michael's Street	Totterton		9	10	8	9	7	86%
Taylor	13	January	5A	52 West Road	Fincham		6	9	7	7	8	74%
Tim	2	January	5A	12 Finchley Crescent	Dronfield		8	9	7	6	6	72%
Wayne	18	March	5A	92 Hollow Way	Fincham	dairy	9	10	9	10	7	90%
Zara	29	September	5A	26 Morton Street	Blossomdale		8	9	10	7	8	84%
Zebedee	30	November	5A	31 James Street	Sunningdale		10	10	8	9	6	86%
Charlotte	4	August	5A	55 Farmington Drive	Newtown	peanuts	6	7	7	8	9	74%
Rashid	7	September	5A	3 Stow Avenue	Totterton		10	8	9	9	10	92%
Michelle	12	April	5A	8 The Crofts	Dronfield		9	9	9	8	9	88%
Kate	18	June	5A	90 High Street	Fincham		7	5	7	7	6	64%
Faizal	29	May	5A	332 Manor Road	Marcham		10	9	9	10	7	90%

Continued

1   Open source file **2.6_learner_records**.

2   On the Home menu, click 'Find & Select' then 'Find' (or press Ctrl+F at the same time). A pop-up box will appear so that you can input your search criteria.

3   A teacher wants to find information about a learner called Jemima. Type 'Jemima' into the search box and press Enter or click 'Find Next'.

4   Which class is Jemima in?

5   Now the teacher wants to find out how many learners live in Blossomdale and what their names are. In the search box, type 'Blossomdale', then click 'Find All'. At the bottom left of the pop-up box you will see how many results match the criteria. How many learners are there and what are their names?

6   Now use the spreadsheet to find:

   a   the names of the learners who live on Beechcroft Road

   b   the names of the learners with a dairy allergy

   c   how many learners have a birthday in December

   d   learners who have the letters 'son' in their name (select the Name column before doing your search, so that only this column is searched).

How are we doing?

Swap your results for each search with a partner.
Did you get the same answers? If not, why?

Look what I can do!

☐   I understand what happens when I change data in a spreadsheet.

☐   I can use search criteria to find specific data in a spreadsheet.

Project

In this project you will imagine you are setting up a dessert café business. You will collect data using a form, then organise this data in a spreadsheet and use it to help you make decisions.

Step 1: Create a form

- With a partner, decide what kind of imaginary café you will run. Will you serve cupcakes? Or maybe milkshakes? How about ice cream? You could choose pies – or all of these.

- You are going to create a form to find out what customers would want from your café. You will use this data to make decisions about what to serve and what prices to charge. Decide on three pieces of data you will need to collect. For example, you might collect data on:
  - what people's favourite flavours are
  - whether people need non-dairy options
  - how much people are willing to pay per item.
- With your partner, write questions to collect your data.
- Create your form. Think about how easy your form will be to use. What things have you learnt that you could use to help you?
- Get as many learners in your class as possible to fill in your form. You could ask adults too.

Step 2: Create your spreadsheet and make charts

- Put your data into a spreadsheet and organise the data.
- Make bar charts of the data to help you decide what items to offer and what prices you should set.

Continued

Step 3: Make predictions about sales and money

- Now make a spreadsheet to predict how much money you might make. Use the prices you set and make up some sales figures for each item based on your form results.
- Use formulae and functions to calculate how much money your business will make each week.

Step 4: Write a report or presentation to share your business plan with the class

- Use document production tools to create a report or presentation about your investigation.
- Include some of your data tables and charts, and write about the decisions that they helped you make. Make sure you say which data led to which decisions.
- Finish with a sentence about whether you think your business would be a success, and why/why not.

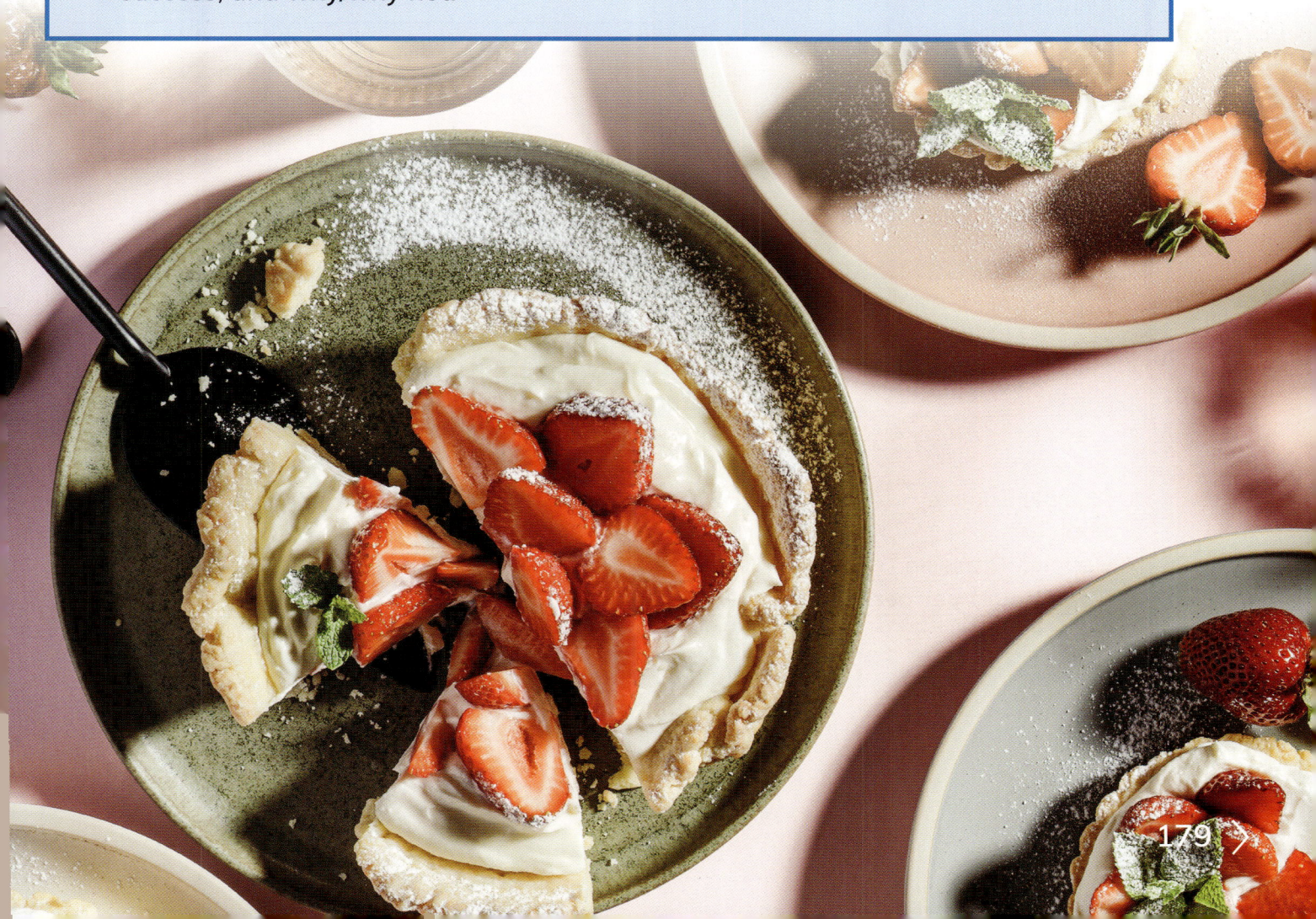

Check your progress

1 What device can be set up to automatically take data readings all day and night at regular times?

2 Give two advantages of using an online form instead of a paper form to collect data.

3 Give two advantages of storing data in a spreadsheet rather than on paper.

4 What is the tool in a spreadsheet called that helps limit the kind of data a cell can have, to avoid errors?

5 Which kind of chart is best for showing categorical and discrete data?

   A Venn diagram   B Line chart   C Bar chart

6 What two changes could you make to this bar chart to make it easier for a room full of people to use?

7 Which cells of this spreadsheet could contain the following?

   a =AVERAGE(B6:E6)?

   b =SUM(C3:C7)?

   c =B3+C3+D3+E3?

Customers

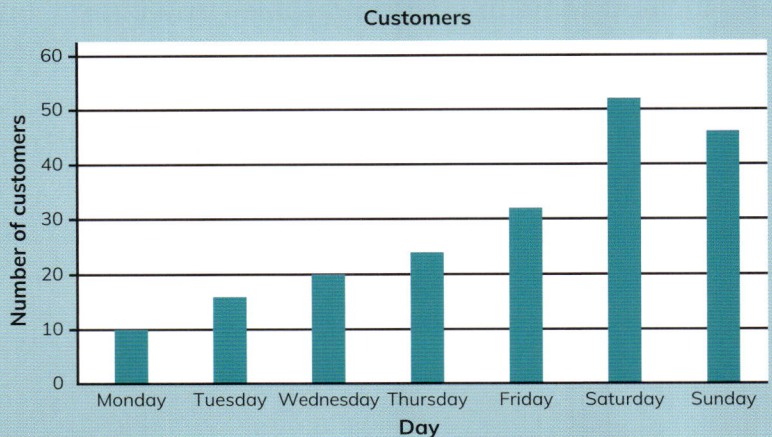

Game name	Hours played				Total hours per game	Average hours per game
	Marcus	Zara	Sofia	Arun		
Gemfinder	0	4	2	3	9	2.25
Buzz Off	1	2	1	3	7	1.75
Rumble Tumble	2	1	2	2	7	1.75
Zoomer	4	1	1	0	6	1.5
Penguin Crossing	3	0	4	1	8	2
Total hours per person	10	8	10	9	37	9.25

3 Networks and digital communication

> 3.1 Network hardware

We are going to:

- **identify hardware devices in a network**
- **understand the role of different hardware devices in a network.**

aerial

internet

router

signal

switch

transmit

wireless access point

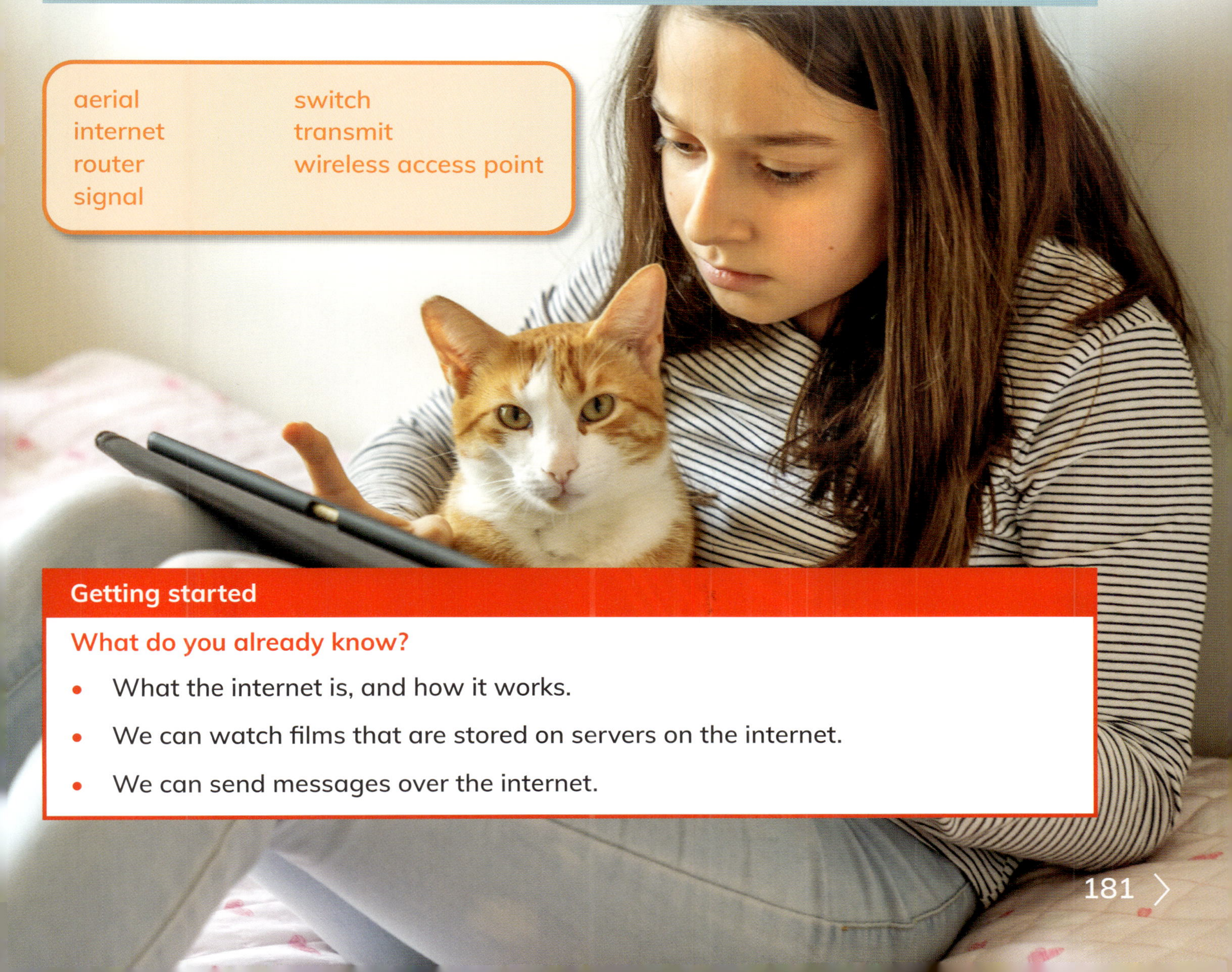

Getting started

What do you already know?

- What the internet is, and how it works.
- We can watch films that are stored on servers on the internet.
- We can send messages over the internet.

Continued

- You have a network of computers at school.

- Devices can connect to networks using wires, or through wireless connections.

- What happens when connections in a network break.

Now try this!

Look around the classroom to identify which wires connect to the computers. Make sure you do not touch any of the wires.

Are there any wireless connections in the classroom? Are there any boxes on the ceiling or on the wall that have flashing lights on them?

Ask your teacher to help you find where these boxes are. Your teacher may take you outside the classroom to find them.

Remember that wired and electric equipment can be dangerous. Do not touch or unplug any wires. If you see something you think is unsafe, tell your teacher.

Network hardware

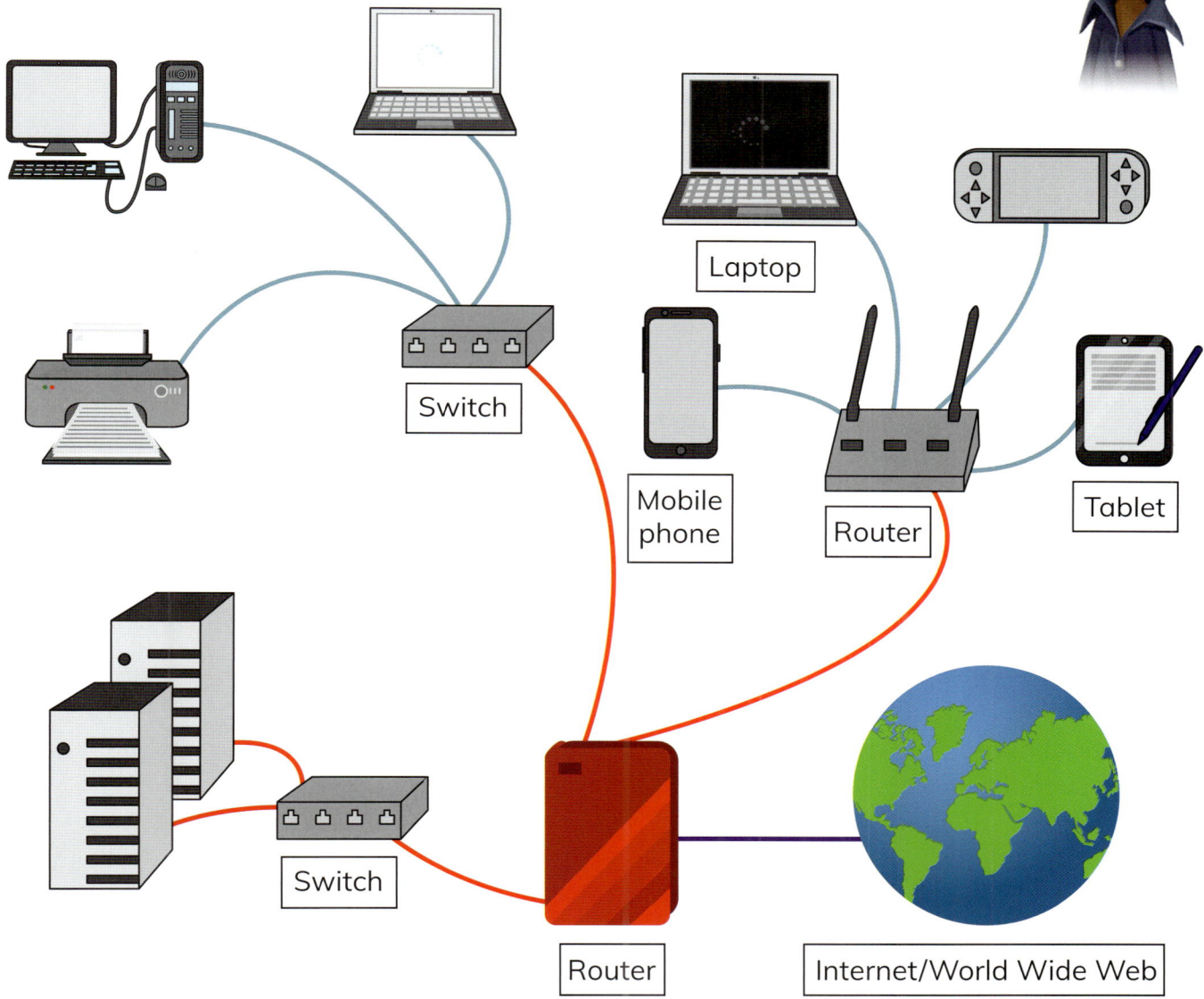

Do you remember the two ways a device can connect to a network?

Laptop

Switch

Mobile phone

Router

Tablet

Switch

Router

Internet/World Wide Web

Computers need to be connected to a network to be able to share files and software. Computers can connect to a network with wires, or without wires.

Connecting with wires

Some digital devices connect to a network using an Ethernet cable.

There are two types of device that often connect to a network with wires: a switch and a router. They each do a slightly different job.

Switches and routers have lots of sockets for cables. This means you can connect lots of different devices to a switch or a router.

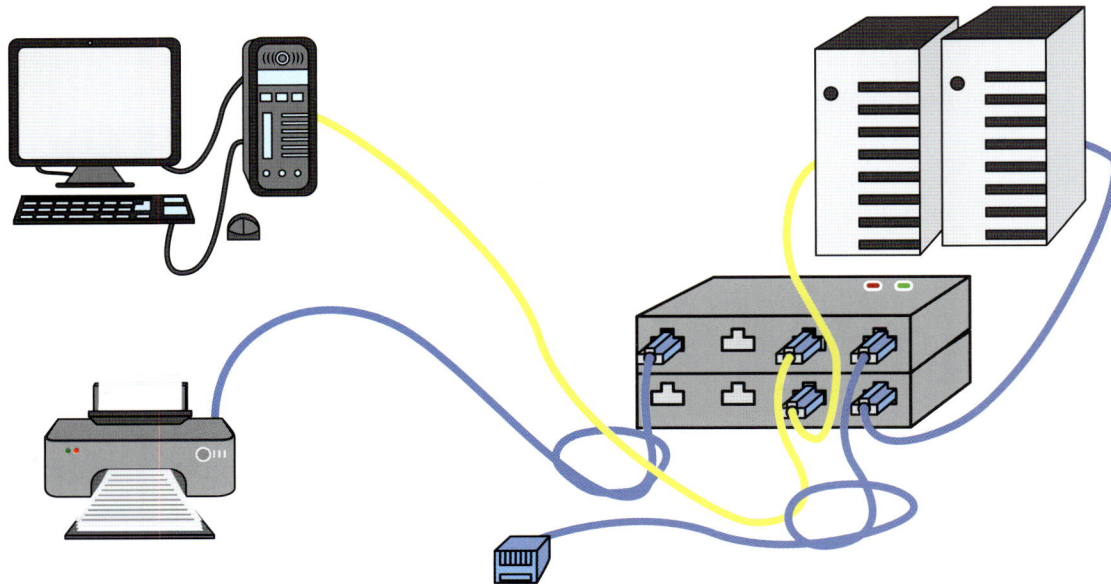

Switches

A switch allows you to connect wired devices to a network, for example your school network or an office network. The switch is used to connect devices such as:

- printers
- servers
- desktop computers and laptops
- televisions.

The switch allows wired devices to communicate with each other by connecting them together. This means they can send and receive data.

Question

1   Look at the picture of a switch. How many devices do you think you can connect to this switch?

> Connecting a device like a printer to a network using a switch allows every computer on the network to access that device.

Routers

A router allows different networks to communicate with each other. The most common use of a router is to connect a smaller network, like your home or school network, to the internet.

For example, a router connects your school network to the internet. This means that any device connected to your school network can access the internet. This allows you to do things like view the World Wide Web on your school computer.

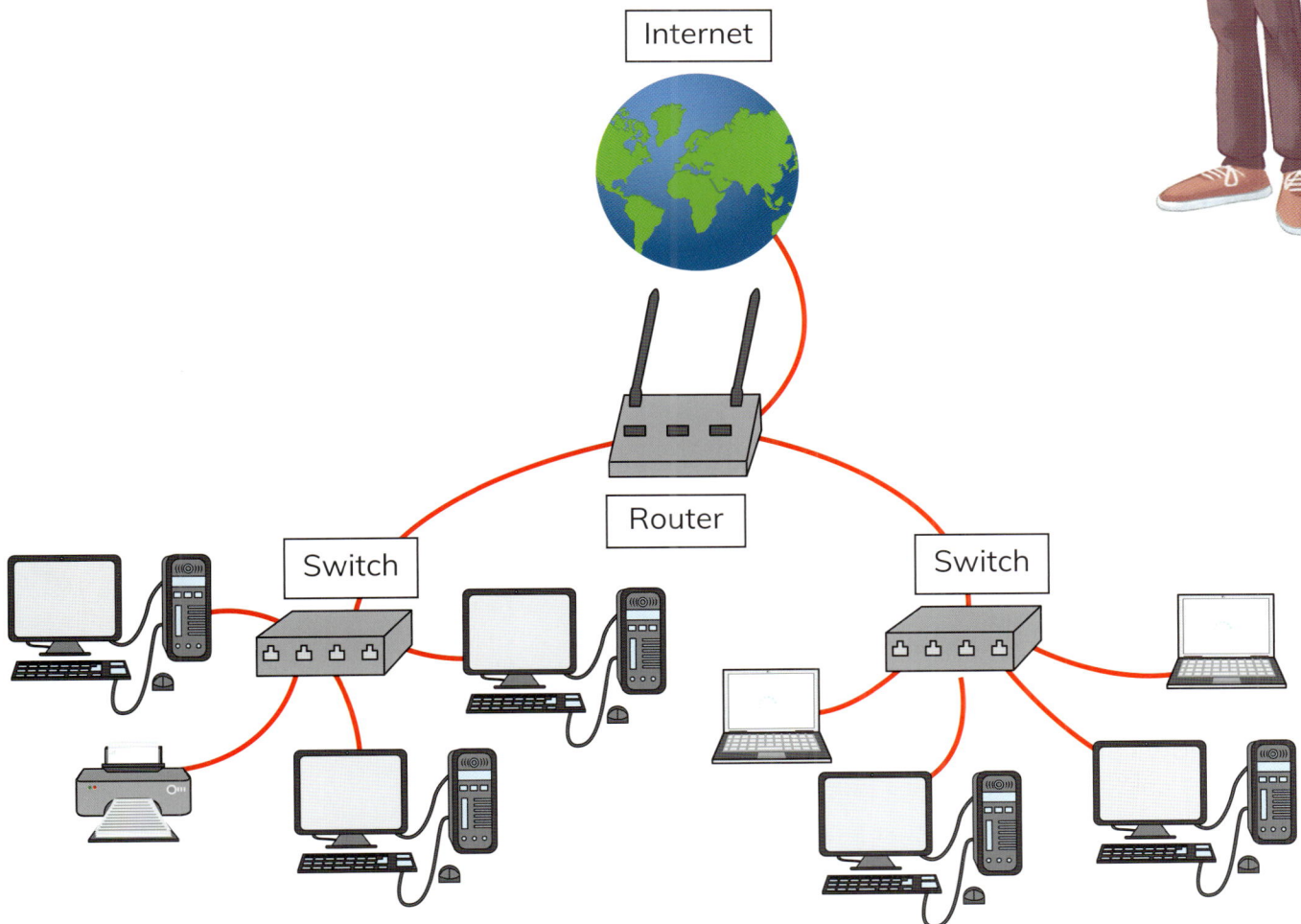

Internet

Router

Switch

Switch

Connecting without wires

A wired switch and a wireless access point do similar things. They both allow computers to connect to a network. However, the wireless access point allows wireless connections.

Some examples of devices that can connect to a network wirelessly include:

- mobile phones
- tablets
- laptops.

An example of a wireless access point is a wi-fi access point. Wi-fi access points allow devices to connect to a network wirelessly. An advantage of wireless access points is that many devices can connect to a single access point without a physical connection, like a wire. A wired switch needs one cable for each device. One wireless access point allows hundreds of devices to connect.

A wi-fi access point is used to transmit (send) data to any device nearby. This means that it sends signals to devices, and it receives signals from devices. Signals are special waves that allow the wi-fi access point to communicate with devices nearby.

Wi-fi sends signals over a short distance. The further away you are from the wi-fi router, the weaker the signal.

Wi-fi access points are often attached to walls and ceilings, and sometimes they have an aerial on them. An aerial is something that allows signals to be sent and received.

> Have a look around your classroom to see if you have a wi-fi access point. Ask your teacher where the nearest wi-fi access point is.

Question

Look at the picture of the wi-fi access point and compare it to the picture of a switch.

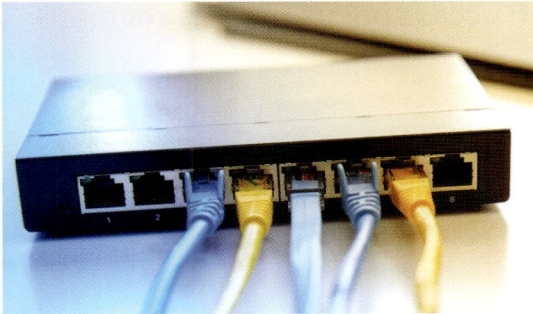

Switch

Wi-fi access point

2   What is the biggest difference between the wi-fi access point and the switch?

Remember, it is only the router that allows devices on a network to communicate with other networks and the internet.

Activity 1

You will need: a desktop computer, laptop or tablet with presentation software or image-drawing software

Use simple drawing or presentation software to draw two networks that are connected together and to the internet. Your drawing should show:

- two separate networks, for example a school network and a home network
- the devices in each network and what they are called. For example:

    - laptop
    - mobile phone
    - television
    - printer
    - wireless speakers
    - servers

Continued

- how the devices are connected to the network
- how the two networks are connected to each other and to the internet.

Think carefully about where you place switches, wi-fi access points and the router.

How am I doing?

Swap your drawing with a partner.

Check:

- they have named all the devices correctly
- the switch, router and wi-fi access points are connected correctly.

If your drawings are different, discuss why that is.

How do you remember the difference between a switch and a router?

Look what I can do!

☐ I can identify hardware devices in a network.

☐ I can explain the role of different hardware devices in a network.

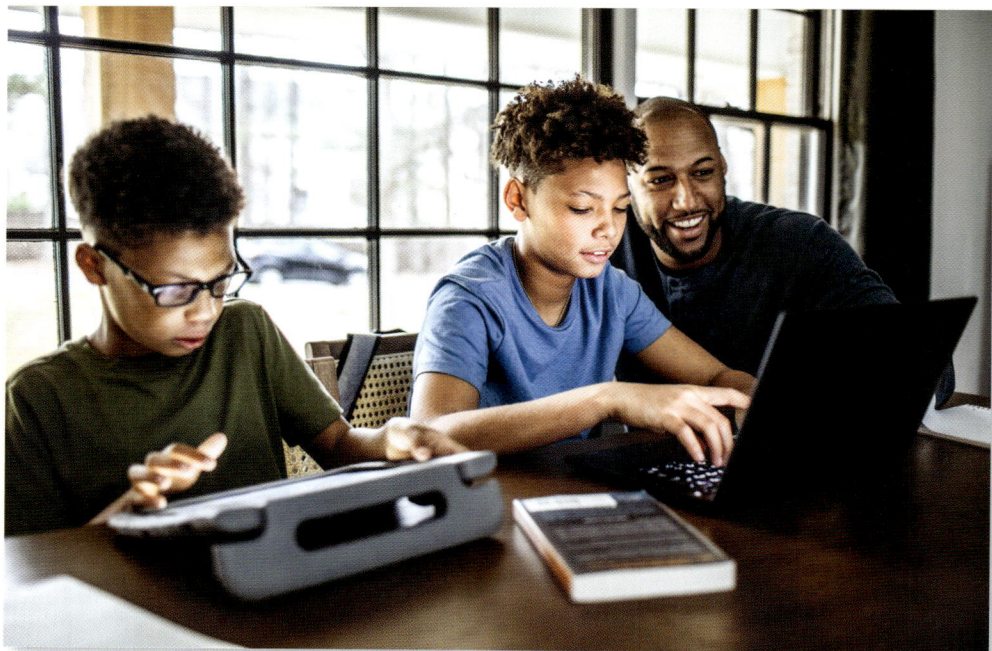

> 3.2 How data travels through networks

We are going to:

- investigate cellular networks

- investigate what an IP address is

- explore how data is split up into smaller chunks called packets

- find out how packets travel through networks

- explain how websites are stored on servers

- explain how websites are accessed.

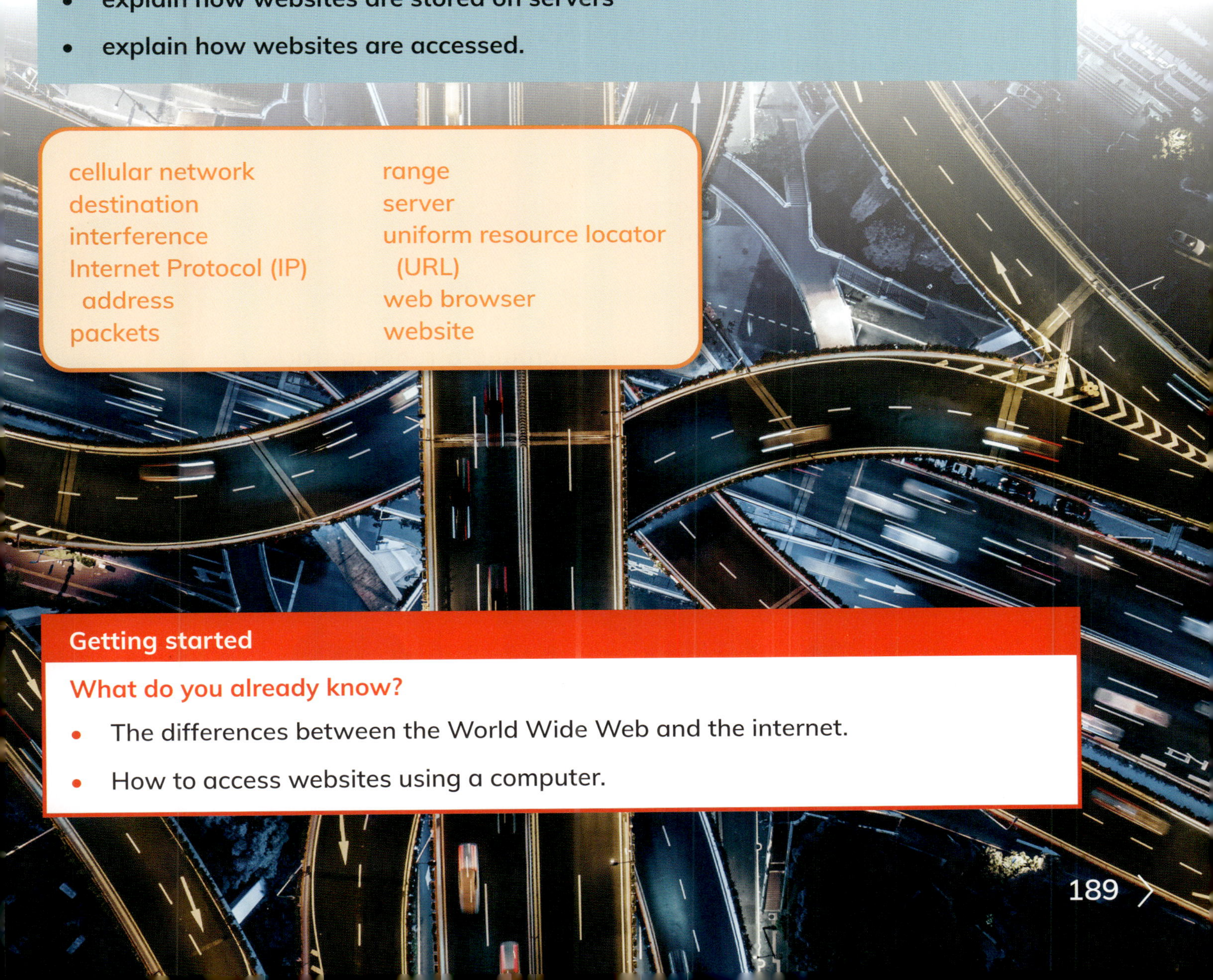

cellular network
destination
interference
Internet Protocol (IP)
 address
packets

range
server
uniform resource locator
 (URL)
web browser
website

Getting started

What do you already know?

- The differences between the World Wide Web and the internet.

- How to access websites using a computer.

Now try this!

Have you ever sent a birthday card to a friend by posting it? What do you put on the envelope so that it arrives at its destination safely? What if you were to send a birthday card to another country?

Write down the things that you think are needed in order for a birthday card to arrive safely at its destination.

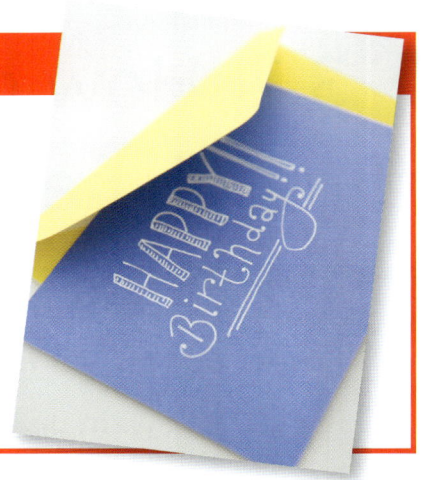

Using cellular networks

A cellular network is a different type of wireless network. Cellular networks cover large areas. They use very strong signals that smartphones can detect over many kilometres.

Cellular networks use tall towers to send signals over large distances. Cell towers can send signals over distances of up to 50 km, but most of the time they tend to reach around 5 km.

Having tall towers means that signals are less likely to be blocked by hills or buildings.

50 kilometres is the same as running around a running track 125 times.

Mobile phones use cellular networks. This allows them to connect almost anywhere, from the top of a mountain to the middle of a city. Other devices use cellular networks as well. For example, some cars use a cellular network. Using a cellular network allows the car to access the internet. The car may use this to download new software to run, or it might allow people to make calls from in-car phones.

The ability to work over large areas is a big advantage of cellular networks. However, they also share the same disadvantages as wi-fi connections. The biggest disadvantage is that they can suffer from interference. This means that the signals may not reach the devices. This can stop a device from connecting to the cellular network or make the connection very slow.

Comparing different connections

Wi-fi, cellular and Ethernet connections are each suited to different uses. For example, you would not want your smartphone to be connected with wires when you were walking around a city!

Each type of connection has a different range.

Let's look at the advantages and disadvantages of each connection.

	Wi-fi connection	Cellular connection	Ethernet connection
Wired	✗	✗	✓
Wireless	✓	✓	✗
Range	Usually around 20 m	Usually around 5 km	100 m
Speed	300–1000 Mbps	100 Mbps	1000 Mbps
Number of devices	30 per access point	Between 60 and 1500	One per wire
Chance of interference	High	Some	Low

> Connection speeds are measured in megabits per second or Mbps. This is the maximum speed that data can be sent at.

Activity 1

You will need: a desktop computer, laptop or tablet with access to the internet and presentation software

Create a digital presentation about the different connections that devices use to connect to a network. Include the following things:

- the three types of connection that you know about
- the advantages and disadvantages of each type of connection
- where you might use each type of connection (for example at home or in school)
- examples of a device (or more than one if you can) that would use each type of connection. Use pictures if possible.

Use the internet to do some research to add more detail to your presentation.

Share your presentation with a partner and get feedback on it.

Use the following questions to provide feedback to your partner.

- Did they correctly identify devices which use wi-fi, cellular or wired connections?
- What were the differences between your presentation and your partner's presentation?

How am I doing?

Think about the feedback you received from your partner about your presentation.

Give yourself a red, orange or green rating based on how well your partner thought that your presentation explained the differences between wi-fi, cellular and wired connections.

- Red means it was unclear and you need to edit the presentation to make it clearer.
- Orange means you have explained it, but there were things you could have done better.
- Green means that you have described the differences well and your partner understood them fully.

Use the feedback from your partner to improve your presentation.

Internet Protocol (IP) addresses

Think about the number of devices around the world that connect to the internet. There are millions and millions. We already know that we can use the internet to send data between these devices. But how do the devices know where to send this data?

The internet uses a system to identify the location of each device connected to the internet. This system is called the Internet Protocol (IP) address system.

An IP address is a set of numbers. The numbers tell the computer the destination to go to and get data from or send data to. These IP addresses are usually automatically created by a program on a computer. You can think of each part of the IP address in the same way as the parts of the address on a letter. The numbers tell you the address of the network and the device to send the data to.

For example, a post code or zip code is usually made up of letters and numbers. Each area has its own unique code. This makes it easier for the people in the post office to quickly see where letters or parcels need to be delivered.

We use a computer program to create IP addresses. This helps to stop an IP address from being used by more than one router.

> Thinking of street addresses may help you to understand IP addresses. However, in real life it is a little more complicated than that.

INTERNET

Data

Data

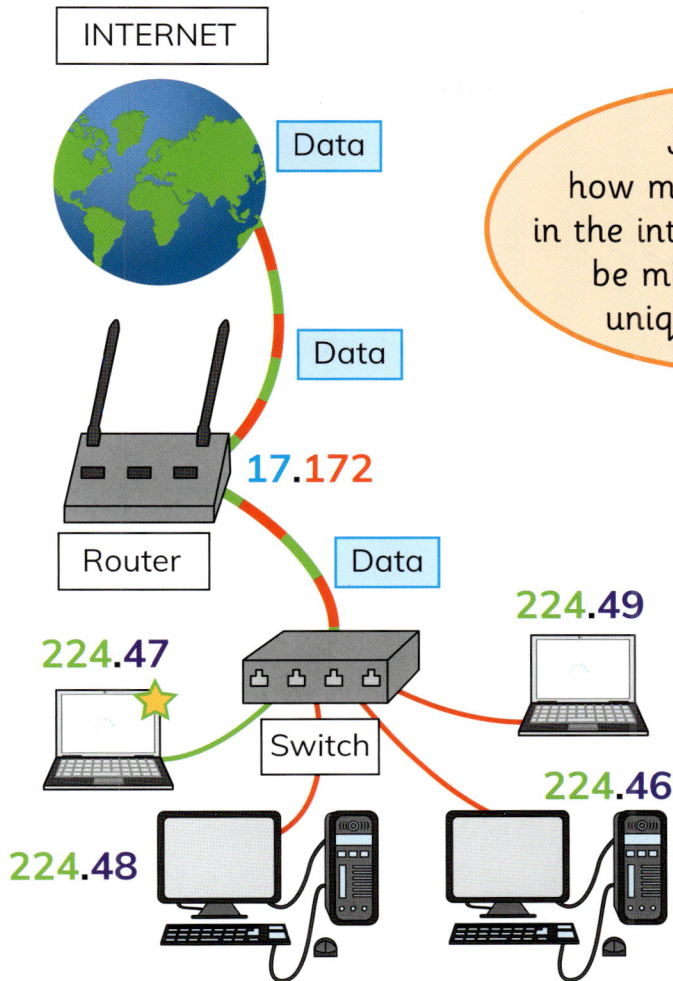

Just think how many devices are in the internet. There must be millions of these unique addresses!

17.172

Router

Data

224.49

224.47

Switch

224.46

224.48

Did you know?

There are two types of IP address. IP4 is an older one – it is starting to run out of addresses! Therefore a new one was created called IP6. This allows for an almost unlimited number of addresses for devices.

Unplugged activity 2

You will need: a pen and paper

43.66.141.66

Work with a partner. Talk about what you know about IP addresses.
Think about the internet and web pages.

Write down one sentence which describes what an IP address does.
Share your sentence with the class.

Transmitting data

When we send data across the internet, it can use different routes to get to the same destination.

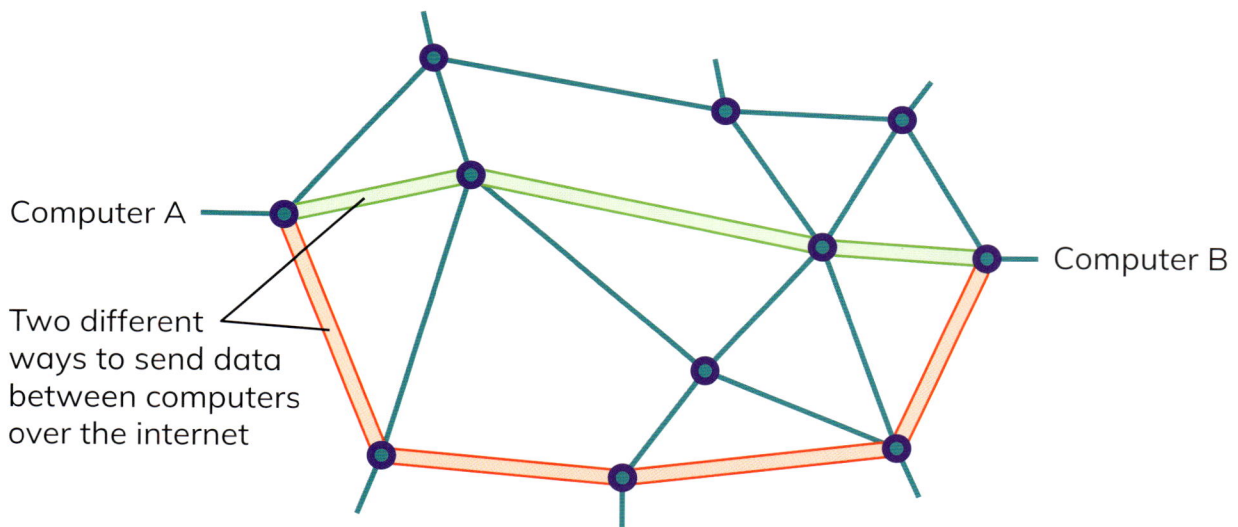

Computer A

Two different ways to send data between computers over the internet

Computer B

But how does this happen?

Before data is sent over the internet, it is split up into packets.
Packets are small chunks of data. They are usually all the same size.

```
10001100           ──────►  10001100
11111110  ──────────────►  11111110
11010010  ──────────────►  11010010
10101000  ──────────────►  10101000
11100111  ──────────────►  11100111
10111110  ──────────────►  10111110
11100001  ──────────────►  11100001
11000111  ──────────────►  11000111
```

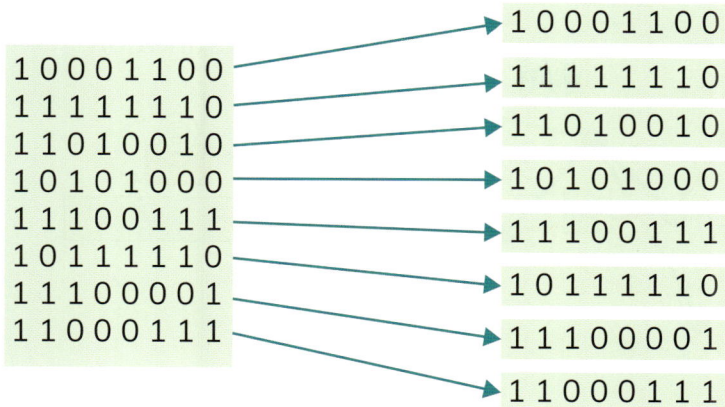

Imagine Arun wants to send a message to Sofia.

When Arun sends the message, it is split into packets.

In this example, the message is split into three packets with nine characters in each one. The number of characters and packets may be different each time.

T H I S   I S   A   M E S S A G E   F O R   S O F I A

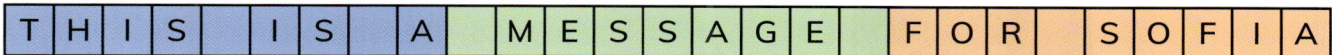

| T | H | I | S | | I | S | | A | | M | E | S | S | A | G | E | | F | O | R | | S | O | F | I | A |

Each packet also includes the IP address that it comes from and the IP address it is going to. This means that if packets are lost along the way, the computer knows which IP address to ask to send those packets again. We can see how the message above is split into three different packets in the image below.

Packet number:	1 of 3
Sent from:	Arun
Sent to:	Sofia
Packet data:	THIS IS A

Packet number:	2 of 3
Sent from:	Arun
Sent to:	Sofia
Packet data:	MESSAGE

Packet number:	3 of 3
Sent from:	Arun
Sent to:	Sofia
Packet data:	FOR SOFIA

When packets arrive at their destination, they may be in the wrong order. This is because each packet may travel to the IP address by a different route. Some routes will be quicker than others and so they will arrive at different times.

The packets of data contain information about the order in which they should be reassembled or put back together again. The computer at the destination uses this information to put the packets into the correct order. When all of the packets have arrived and are assembled in the right order, the computer can use the data.

Sender

Destination

Step 1	Step 2	Step 3	Step 4
Data is split into packets.	Packets are sent to the internet.	Packets travel across the internet. Some may travel more slowly than others.	Packets are put back in order to complete the message.

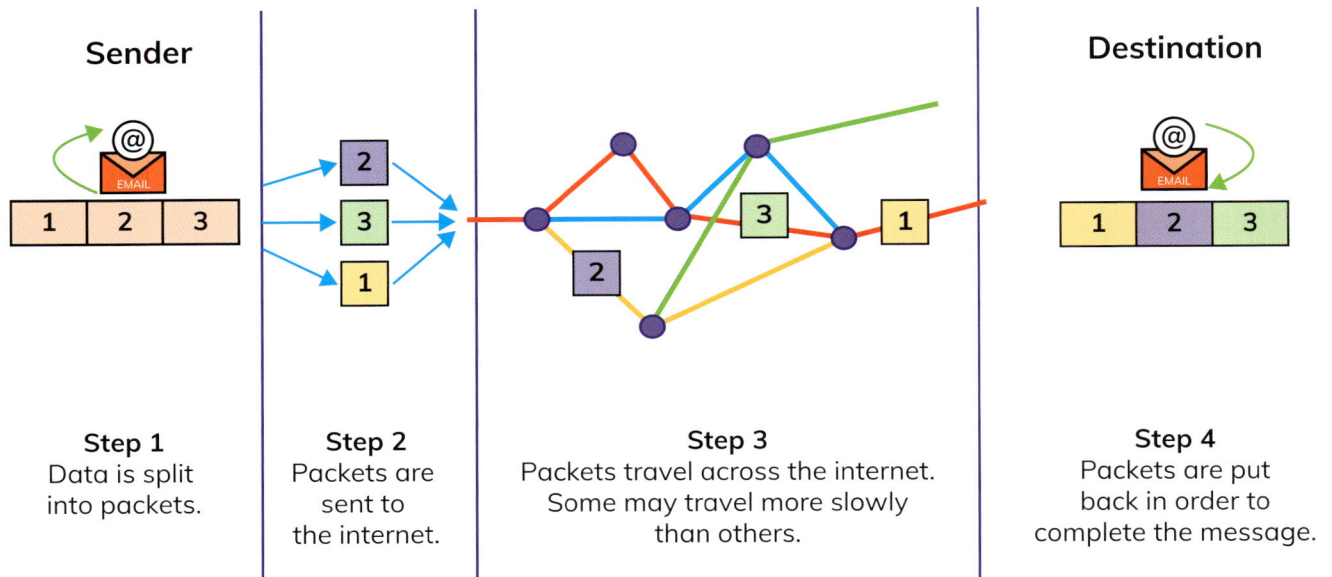

> This diagram shows a snapshot of packets of data travelling across the internet. You can see that some packets arrive sooner than others.

Advantages and disadvantages of packets

Using packets has the following advantages.

- If a packet is lost, a computer only needs to resend a small bit of data again.

- Packets do not take up as much bandwidth, so they can be sent along a greater variety of connections.

- Smaller packets are less likely to get delayed along a network.

As well as the data being sent, each packet contains extra pieces of information. This information is needed by the device which receives the data packets. These extra pieces of information include:

- the IP address that the packet was sent from
- the IP address the packet is being sent to
- the number of the packet that is being sent.

Packet number:	1 of 4
Sent from:	43.64.234.12
Sent to:	34.44.123.321
Packet data:	1101110

Packet number:	2 of 4
Sent from:	43.64.234.12
Sent to:	34.44.123.321
Packet data:	11011001

Packet number:	3 of 4
Sent from:	43.64.234.12
Sent to:	34.44.123.321
Packet data:	11110000

Packet number:	4 of 4
Sent from:	43.64.234.12
Sent to:	34.44.123.321
Packet data:	00110101

There are some disadvantages to using packets.

- The extra information that each packet needs means you use more data in total to send something.
- You need all of the packets to arrive before you can read the data that was sent.

Sometimes packets are lost and do not reach their destination. This means that the data is incomplete and cannot be put back in the right order.

What happens if packets are lost?

If a packet gets lost:

- the receiver computer sends a message to the sender computer asking it to send another copy of the packet
- the sender computer sends another copy of the lost packet
- when the packet arrives at the receiver computer, the data is complete and the receiver computer puts it in order
- the data can then be used.

Destination

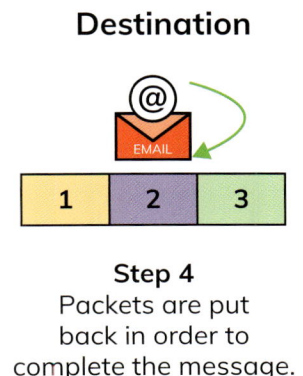

Step 4
Packets are put back in order to complete the message.

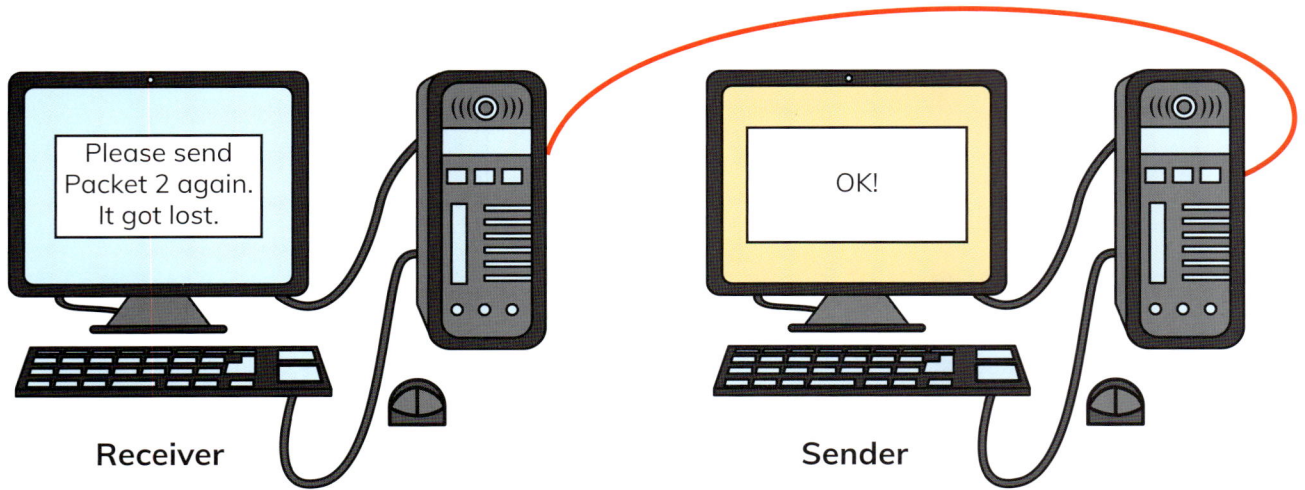

Receiver   Sender

Unplugged activity 3

You will need: a pen and paper, scissors

Work as a class to act out how packets of data travel from a sender computer to a receiver computer.

One of you will be a sender computer (where the packets are sent from). Four of you will be receiver computers (where the packets are sent to). The rest of the class will act as routes for the packets of data.

- As a class, write a short message by copying and completing the message template below.

From:				From:				From:				From:			
To:		Packet:	1	To:		Packet:	2	To:		Packet:	3	To:		Packet:	4

- Write the name of the person that the message is being sent from (pretending to be the sender computer) in the 'From' box.
- Write the name of one of the people it is being sent to (pretending to be the receiver computers) in the 'To' box. This is where your message will arrive.

Continued

- Cut up your message into packets and give them all to the person pretending to be the sender computer.

From: Arun						
To:	Zara		Packet:	1		
T	H	I	S		I	S

From: Arun						
To:		Zara		Packet:	2	
A		M	E	S	S	A	G

From: Arun						
To:	Zara		Packet:	3		
E		F	O	R		Z	A

From: Arun						
To:		Zara		Packet:	4	
R	A					

- The sender computer and receiver computers stand on opposite sides of the classroom.
- The rest of the class spread out between the sender and receiver computers.
- Work together as a class to send the packets from the 'sender' computer to the 'receiver' computers along different 'routes'. Pass the packets to the person who is closest to the destination. If that learner already has a packet in their hand, use a different route.
- The receiver computers put the packets in the correct order and read the message to the class.
- Make sure your message made it to the receiver computer and was put back together in the correct order.

Questions

1 What are the advantages of splitting data into packets?
2 What are the disadvantages of using packets?
3 What happens if some of the packets are lost?

How did you remember the process of sending packets?

What are the difficult parts to remember?

Why did you find these parts harder to remember?

What things did you do to help you remember these parts?

What strategies for remembering how data is sent across a network would you suggest to a partner to help them remember each step?

Accessing websites

A website is stored on a web server. A web server stores all of the pages for a website, and the IP address of the website. Web servers are connected to the internet.

To access a web server using the internet:

- You type a web address into your web browser. Another name for a web address is a uniform resource locator, or URL for short. The URL is written using text. For example: www.cambridge.org.

- Your web browser connects to the web server using the internet.

- Because computers only understand numbers, the URL is converted into an IP address.

- The web browser gives the web server the IP address for the website you want. This address tells the web browser where the website is stored on the web server.

- The web server checks that the web page is there, and then sends the data back to the web browser that asked for it.

Computers use IP addresses for websites because they only understand numbers. Humans use a URL because it is much easier to remember than a lot of numbers!

Stay safe!

Remember to only use websites that you trust and are safe. Always check with a teacher or adult before going on a website you do not know.

How am I doing?

Give yourself a mark from 1 to 5 for the following statements.
1 is 'not confident' and 5 is 'very confident'.

- I am able to say why we use IP addresses and URLs.
- I am able to discuss how devices access cellular networks.
- I am able to describe how data is sent across the internet.
- I am able to give examples of devices that connect to the internet using wires, wi-fi and cellular networks.

Share your marks with a partner. Choose an area where your mark is higher than theirs. Ask what they found difficult about that topic/question. See if you can teach them more about this topic.

Look what I can do!

- [ ] I can describe what a cellular network is.
- [ ] I can state what an IP address is.
- [ ] I can describe how data is split up into packets.
- [ ] I can explain how packets travel through networks.
- [ ] I can explain how websites are stored on servers.
- [ ] I can explain how websites are accessed.

> 3.3 Network failure

We are going to:

- **identify what happens if an internet connection fails.**

cloud storage
corrupted
network

Getting started

What do you already know?

- Network connections can fail.

- How to watch videos or listen to music online.

- How to access websites.

Now try this!

Think about how you use the internet. Discuss the answers to these questions with a partner.

1   What do you use the internet for over the weekend?
2   What do you use the internet for during the week?
3   Have you ever found that the internet stopped working?
    For example, a video may have stopped while you were watching it.

The internet

The internet is made up of all the connections between computers and digital devices. A **network** is a collection of connections between devices. The internet is a massive worldwide network.

People all over the world access the internet every day for work and fun. When you connect to the internet you might be able to access these services on servers:

- websites
- online games
- cloud storage
- banking
- holiday bookings
- online shopping
- messaging services and email.

Cloud storage allows you to save your files and data on someone else's computer. Big companies often have a huge server which has lots of storage space. They allow you to use some of this storage space for your data. Because it is stored on the internet, you can access your data from anywhere in the world – as long as you can connect to the internet.

Internet failures

Sometimes the internet seems to fail. This means that one or more of the internet connections breaks.

Question

1   What would happen if the internet connections failed when you were booking tickets to a concert with your parents?

Minor network failures

When a connection breaks, it stops working and data cannot travel along this route.

Because the internet is made up of many connections and networks all linked together, the data can use a different route to reach its destination.

This means you will not notice when a single connection on the internet fails. For example, if the blue route in the picture breaks, then data can still travel along the red and yellow route to reach its destination.

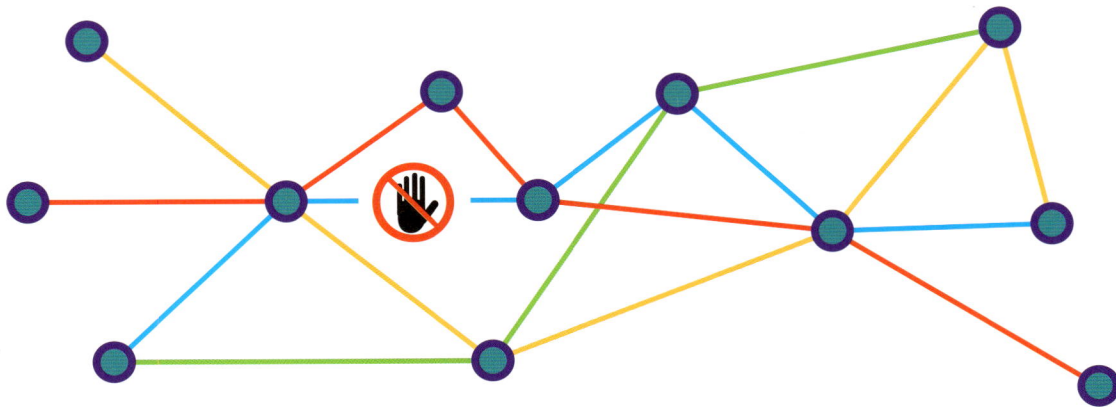

Large internet failures

Sometimes large servers or connections can break. You may notice this when a service you use stops working or becomes very slow. Usually there are other servers which offer the same services, so if one breaks, your computer can simply access another one. This means you may notice that things 'stop working' for a short period of time.

Unfortunately, lots of connections can fail all at the same time. It can take many hours or days to fix internet failures like this.

Sometimes big failures are caused by a single connection failing. This could be the main connection to the server. If there is only one connection, then the data cannot travel along other routes.

Why do connections break?

There are many different ways for connections to break. Breaks are most likely to occur in the connection from your device to the internet.

For example:

- someone accidentally turns off the power

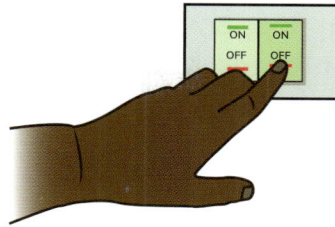

- someone unplugs a cable by mistake

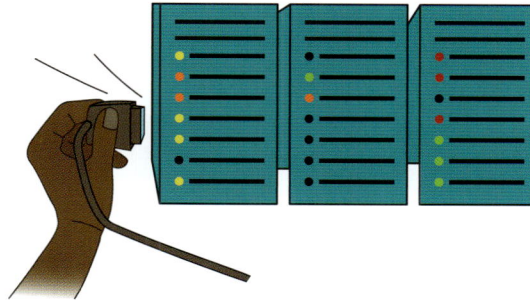

- a fire could cause a server to stop working or damage cables.

The internet is like a set of roads connecting towns and cities. If there are roadworks or an accident on the road, car drivers will choose different roads to use. These roads may be narrower so drivers cannot drive as fast, but they will still allow the drivers to get to where they want to go.

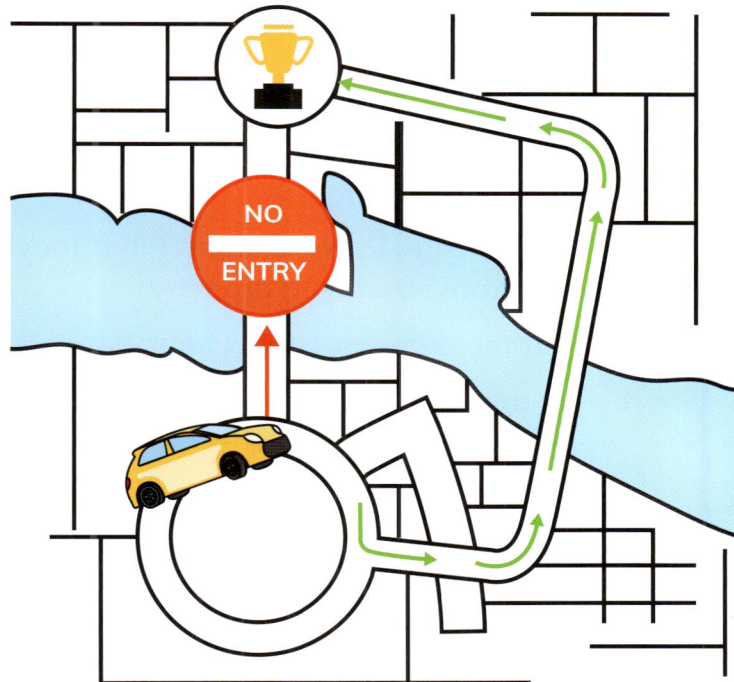

NO
ENTRY

Remember:
if one connection on the internet breaks, there are other connections that can be used to connect to a server.

This is similar to what happens on the internet. Data will travel down different routes, but those routes get busier. Data will still arrive where it needs to go, but it will travel more slowly. You may notice that things take longer to load, or the film you are watching stops and starts again.

> Sometimes when connections fail, people say: 'The internet is broken!' Remember: the internet does not break – it is just the connections between some computers that break.

Unplugged activity 1

You will need: a pen and paper

Read this conversation between Zara and Arun.

> I was streaming a video on my phone. It suddenly stopped working!

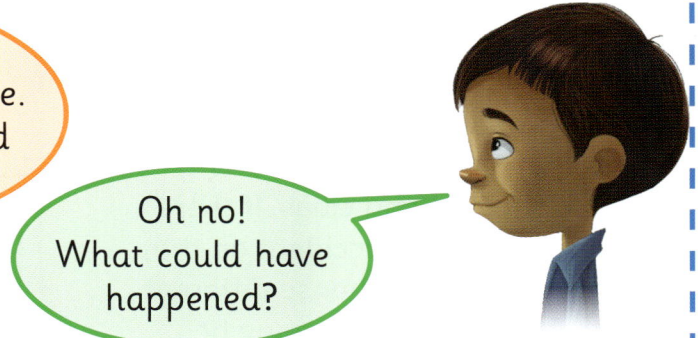

> Oh no! What could have happened?

Use your knowledge to write about what may have happened to stop Zara's video from streaming properly.

Think about the different connections between Zara's phone and the web server.

Share your answers with your classmates.

The effects of network failures

Network failures can have very small effects or very big effects. Network failures that have very small effects happen quite often. For example, if a network fails when you are working online, your work may disappear if you have not saved it recently. Or, if you are playing a game online, the game will stop working.

These network failures are annoying, but they do not usually cause too many problems.

Large network failures that have big effects do not happen as often, for example the failure of a bank network. A large network failure is more likely to happen if there is only one server. To try to stop this, many companies make copies of their servers. So if one server breaks they can use a second server instead.

Effects of larger network failures could include:

- not being able to stream films, radio or TV shows

- not being able to access money in online bank accounts to pay bills or buy goods

- not being able to play online games with other people around the world, or the games may stop working

- not being able to make video calls, or the calls may stop working.

Because large networks like these are very important, companies spend lots of money to try to stop them from failing. They often have backup or 'spare' networks that can be used in case of a failure.

Sometimes data may be corrupted during a network failure. This means that data cannot be used and may be lost forever.

> Large network failures have happened to the PlayStation network and Steam. Millions of gamers could not play the games they wanted to play.

Questions

2   Imagine what would happen if a bank network failure stopped a person from withdrawing their money. How would they feel? What effects would this have on the person?

3   Imagine that you lost all of your homework because there was an internet failure and you could not save your files. How would you feel?

Activity 2

You will need: a desktop computer, laptop or tablet with access to the internet

Use the internet to research a famous internet failure. Make notes about what happened.

Find out about:

- why the network failed
- what happened when the network failed
- how many people it affected
- any other details you think may be interesting. For example, if the company was given a fine or punishment, or maybe it was the largest network failure in the world
- anything that could have been done to stop the network failure.

Use your notes to write a short presentation.
Present your research to your class.

How am I doing?

Ask your classmates for some feedback on your presentation. Ask them for two good points about your presentation. Ask them for one idea to make your presentation better.

List three things you would change in your presentation if you were to do it again.

Think about the differences between small and larger network failures.

Are there parts of network failures that confused you? What things did you think of to help you understand these issues better?

Look what I can do!

☐ I can identify what might happen if an internet connection fails.

Project

Create a quiz game for your classmates about networks and digital communication.

Your quiz game should have three rounds of questions. Each round should have five questions. If the player answers all five questions correctly for each round then they move to the next round.

Each round will have easy, medium or hard questions.

- In round 1, you will ask five easy questions.
- In round 2, you will ask two easy questions and three medium questions.
- In round 3, you will ask three medium questions and two hard questions.

You may ask your teacher for some ideas on easy, medium and hard questions.

Write a set of seven easy questions, six medium questions and two hard questions about networks and digital communication. The questions should be about what you have learnt in this unit. You can add more questions if you want to make your quiz harder.

Play your quiz game with your classmates and see who gets the most correct answers.

Check your progress

1 What device allows a network to access the internet?

2 What allows devices to connect wirelessly to a network?

3 Why do we need IP addresses?

4 Give two advantages of a cellular network.

5 When data is split into smaller pieces, what do we call these pieces?

6 Say two things that a packet should have in it.

7 What is a disadvantage of using packets?

8 What is an advantage of using packets?

9 Give two examples of the effects of internet connection failure.

10 Explain how an email message is sent across the internet.
Use the following key terms:

    IP address   internet connection   routes   packets   destination

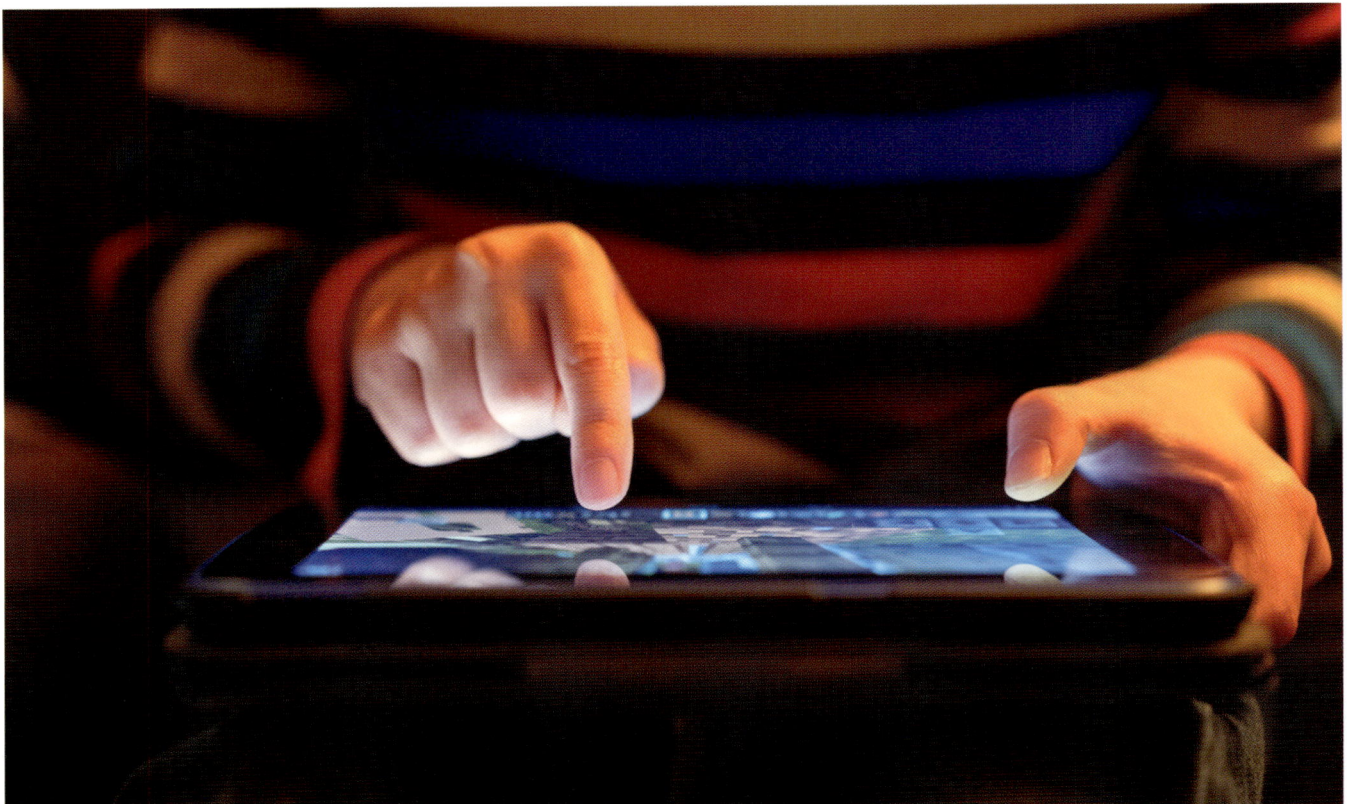

4 Computer systems

> 4.1 Input and output devices

We are going to:

- discuss what input and output devices may be connected to the internet
- discover how input devices control output devices remotely via the internet
- understand that an actuator is a type of output device.

actuator	input	remote
automatically	input device	remotely
cursor	output	sensor

Getting started

What do you already know?

- How to use input devices such as a mouse, keyboard and touch-screen.
- Robots can be used for delivery services and healthcare.
- Where control systems are used.
- Computer systems use inputs to control outputs.

Continued

Now try this!

Look at the picture. It shows a robotic submarine. Scientists are using the submarine to explore a shipwreck deep underwater. The scientists control the submarine from a boat above.

Write your answers to the following questions.

1   What input devices do you think the scientists have to control the submarine?

2   What input devices do you think the submarine has to help it explore the wreck?

3   What output devices do you think the scientists have to help them explore the wreck?

4   What output devices do you think the submarine has to help it to explore the shipwreck?

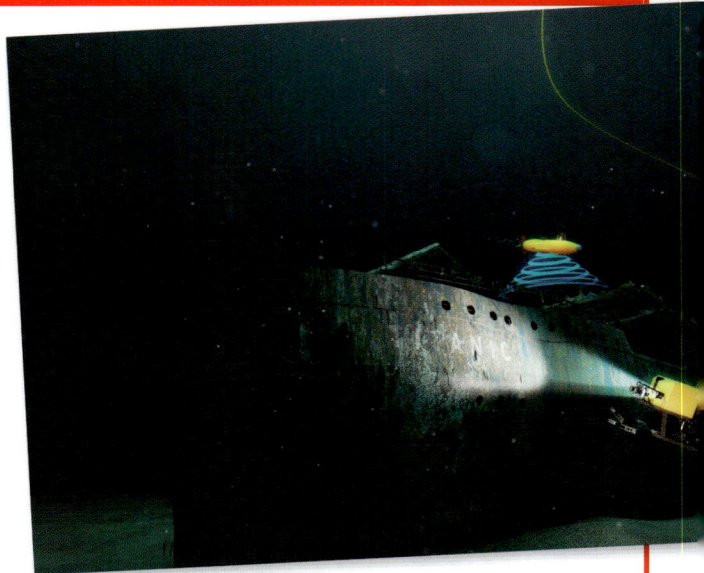

Input devices

Almost all computers need input. Input allows a computer to know what is happening around it. Computers use input to help make choices or carry out actions. This is similar to how we use our eyes and ears to see and hear what happens in the world.

A device that provides input to a computer is called an input device.

A touchscreen is an example of an input device. Touchscreens are found on many portable devices such as smartphones and tablets.

The mouse and keyboard connected to a desktop computer are also input devices. The movement of the mouse causes the cursor to move around on the screen. The keyboard allows us to enter text, numbers and symbols. This input tells the computer what we want it to do.

A sensor is another type of input device. Sensors are used to sense changes in our surroundings. For example, an oven uses a temperature sensor to sense how hot it is inside the oven. When the oven is at the correct temperature, the heater is turned off.

Have you ever been in a car where the headlights come on automatically? The car uses a light sensor to detect when it is getting dark, and it turns the car lights on.

When it is light outside, the car's lights are off.

When it is dark outside, the car's lights are on.

Remote input devices

Input devices can be connected directly to a computer. For example, a mouse, keyboard and touchscreen are all examples of input devices that are directly connected to a computer.

Input devices can also be connected to a computer remotely. This means they don't have to be next to the computer. Remote input devices connect to a computer using the internet. These input devices can be a long way from the computer.

Remote input devices are useful when:

- we want to collect data over a long time (days, months or years)
- we want to collect an input from a location that is a long way from our computer
- it is not safe for humans to use an input device by hand
- we want to collect data to make life easier or more efficient.

Input devices for measuring data over time

A scientist investigating climate change needs to measure the temperature in different places around the world every day and compare them. They need to check the measurements every hour of each day too.

One person cannot do this by themselves. However, if they used lots of temperature sensors, they could put a temperature sensor in each place and connect to them remotely using their computer.

Power stations may use sensors to detect the temperature, how much electricity is being generated and how much fuel is needed. The person in the photo here is checking data from sensors in a power station. Measurements need to be taken in many areas, at the same time, and constantly. It would not be possible for a human to do this on their own.

Input devices far away

We use remote input devices to help us measure data globally. We can use many remote input devices in different countries to measure the temperature of the Earth. For example, scientists working in Malaysia can use remote input devices to measure the weather in Australia and America at the same time. We can also use remote input devices to measure things at the top of mountains or deep in the sea.

To use sensors around the world, we connect them to the internet. The signals from the remote sensors are sent through the internet back to a computer. The signals can reach the computer very quickly.

Space scientists use sensors to collect data in space. These sensors might be on a telescope or a space station, or on a robot like the Mars Rover that explores other planets.

> **Did you know?**
>
> The Hubble space telescope orbits 340 miles above the Earth and travels at 27 000 kilometres per hour.

We can also use sensors to measure the environment on planets that are millions of miles away. The data is then sent back to a computer on Earth using signals. We can use robots, like the Mars Rover, to carry the sensors and move them to new places on the planet surface to take measurements.

> **Did you know?**
>
> It takes up to 22 minutes for an input command to be sent to Mars. If we drove to Mars, it would take over 350 years to get there.

Input devices in dangerous places

Volcanoes are very dangerous places. They produce hot lava and poisonous gas when they erupt. Scientists cannot get close to volcanoes when they erupt. Instead, they use remote input devices, such as sensors, to collect the data they need. This means that they can stay a long way away, where it is safe.

Dangerous locations are not always big and scary. Extreme heights and temperatures can be dangerous to humans, as well as things like engines. Even forests can be dangerous to humans because of the animals that might live there.

Here are some other examples of where sensors can be used in places which can be dangerous for humans:

- A car uses sensors to detect and measure data about the engine to help it run more efficiently.

- An aeroplane uses sensors outside to measure how fast it is going and how high it is flying.

Robots can be used to help rescue people who are trapped in a building. This might be because of a fire, or it could be because of a natural disaster such as an earthquake. Using a robot means that humans do not have to go into a dangerous situation. The sensors in the robot will help it drive around the building safely to find people.

A robot can also fly emergency medical supplies to people who may be trapped after a landslide or a mudslide. It could take several days for humans to get to the people who are hurt or cut off. The robot will have many sensors, such as cameras or temperature sensors. The human pilot can use the information from these sensors to send the robot to the right place.

Input devices at home

Do you have any 'smart' devices at home? For example, a 'smart plug' which is able to turn itself on and off? Or perhaps 'smart lights' which change colour when you tell them to?

Smart devices in the home use sensors so that we can control them.

Many appliances in the home can be controlled remotely with input devices. Heating, lighting, windows and lights can all be controlled with input devices. This helps people by doing things automatically. Something which is automatic operates without input from a human.

It is very useful to be able to control devices in our homes automatically. Imagine you had automatic windows. You could use an input device to check if you had left a window open. You could then close the window remotely if you needed to.

Questions

1. Why are remote input devices useful? Give three reasons.
2. Write down three situations where remote input devices are used.

Sensors and safety

Sometimes, using only one sensor to record input is a risk, for example if the sensor measures data that is important to protect human life.

We need a way to make sure that control systems will keep working if a sensor breaks or sends the wrong data.

To solve this problem, we can use two or more sensors to record the same data and send it to the computer.

Imagine you want to know whether you need to bring your coat to school. You could use a temperature sensor to see what the temperature is. But what if it told you the wrong temperature? You might decide to leave your coat at home, only to find it is actually very cold at school.

If we used three temperature sensors, we could check that they all give the same reading. If one sensor shows that it is hot, and the other two show that it is cold, we know that:

- one of the sensors is likely to be broken

- it is probably cold outside, as two sensors are telling us this.

Many important control systems use multiple sensors to record data. The computer compares them. If one sensor provides different data, the computer will ignore that sensor and use the correct data from all the other sensors.

Activity 1

You will need: a desktop computer, laptop or tablet with access to the internet and word-processing or presentation software

Remote input devices are very useful.

Create a poster showing examples of different input devices. You can use examples from this book or use the internet to search for other remote input devices.

For each example, include:

- the name of the input device
- what data is collected
- where the input device is used
- why the input device is used for this task
- a picture to show the input device being used.

Using input devices to control output

Almost all computer systems need to be given data (input). The computer system processes the input to decide on an appropriate output. Output is any action based on the input.

For example, we know that a mouse connected to a computer is an input device. When you move the mouse around, the movement is the input.

The cursor moving around on the screen is the output. You can see this output on the screen. The input from the mouse is the same as the movement on the screen. If you move the mouse to the right, then the cursor on the screen will move to the right.

When you use a touchscreen device, the screen detects where your finger is. The screen is the input device. The output shows where you have touched, or it moves a cursor on the screen.

Automatic doors use a motion sensor to detect movement. This sends input to a motor, which turns on. The output of this is that the door opens.

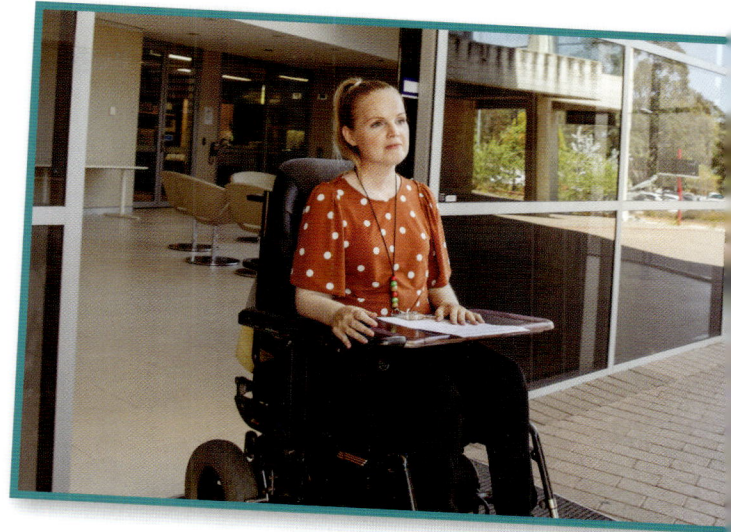

> **Did you know?**
>
> Sensors and output devices can be used to make things happen automatically. Automatic devices make life easier for people. For example, voice controlled devices can help those with mobility problems by opening doors when asked.

There are many examples of outputs in the world around us:

- lights turning on and off
- an alarm sounding
- a robot changing the way it moves
- windows opening and closing.

An actuator is a type of output device. Actuators can be used to open, close or move objects. Actuators are parts of a machine. They perform physical movements. If a device in a machine makes something move, that device is likely to be an actuator.

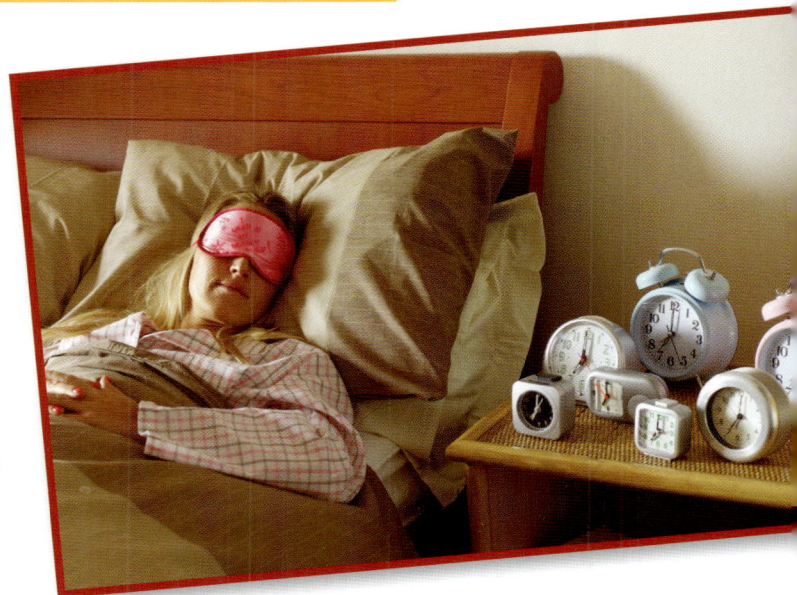

Think about a time when you have been shopping in a supermarket. When you got to the checkout, you probably put your shopping onto a moving belt. The belt moves the items towards the person at the till.

The belt is an actuator. It is a motor and a rubber belt.

Another example of an actuator is one that forms part of the device that moves the flaps on an aeroplane. This actuator uses a motor to pump liquid into a tube. This liquid-filled tube is called a piston. The piston moves the flaps on the plane.

Activity 2

You will need: a desktop computer, laptop or tablet with access to the internet, a microphone and speakers and software to record sound

Work with a partner to plan and record a short discussion about input and output devices used in the real world. Your teacher will show you which software to use.

Think of examples of devices that you find interesting. For example, you could look at input and output devices used in cars, space exploration, boats or farming.

Use the internet to find out about input and output devices in your chosen area.

Your recording should include:

- what input and output devices are

- what an actuator is

- the input and output devices you have researched

- why you think that these input and output devices are used (whether they save time or make a job safer, for example)

- whether any actuators are used.

A hydroelectric dam uses water to create electricity. Input sensors detect how much power is needed. A computer then works out how much water to release through the dam. Then it uses an actuator to open the water gates.

225 >

Continued

How are we doing?

Listen to another pair's recording.

- Have they described input and output devices?

- Have they described what an actuator is?

- Do you think that the examples they give are explained well?

- Have they said why the input and output devices are useful?

- Is their recording clear and easy to understand?

Work with your partner to give the other pair's recording a score out of ten. Write some feedback on how you think they could improve their recording.

Unplugged activity 3

You will need: a pen and paper

Can you think of an example of when you have used a device that has been controlled remotely? Or perhaps you have seen a device being used in this way.

Write a short story to describe when you used a remote device or saw a remote device being used. Make sure you include:

- why the device was used

- how it solved a problem

- what the input(s) and output(s) were.

For example, you may have had a toy remote control car. Think about the input needed and the output of this device. Try to include five new words that you have learnt from this unit.

Swap your story with a partner. Can you identify the input and output on their chosen device? How could they improve their story? Give your partner feedback on their story.

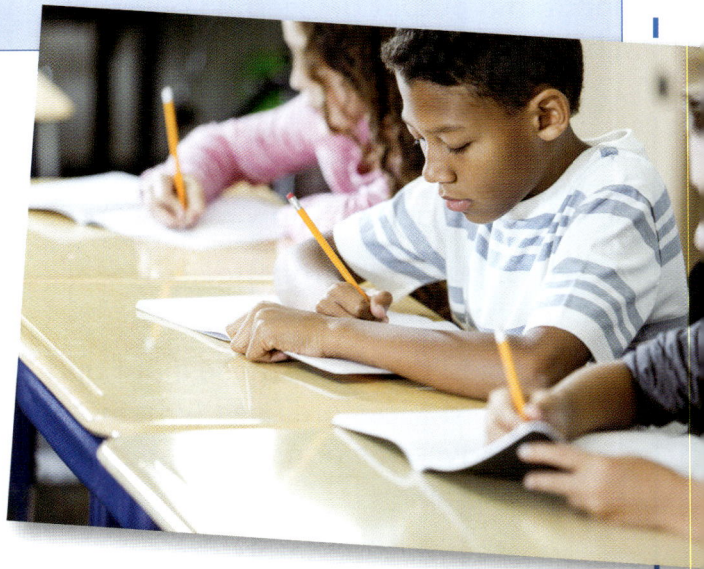

Continued

How am I doing?

How many of the following points did you manage to do?

- I finished writing a story about a remotely controlled device.
- I used five new computing words in my story.
- I included the output and input for the device in my story.
- I identified the output and input devices in my partner's story.
- I gave my partner helpful feedback on their story.

If you did not manage to do all of them, write two sentences on how you could improve in the future.

Look what I can do!

- [ ] I can describe input and output devices that are connected to the internet.
- [ ] I can describe how input is used to make output happen, both at home and remotely, using the internet.
- [ ] I can describe actuators and how they can be used.

> 4.2 How is data stored?

We are going to:

- **identify a range of storage devices**
- **learn how computers store data**
- **discover the units of data storage.**

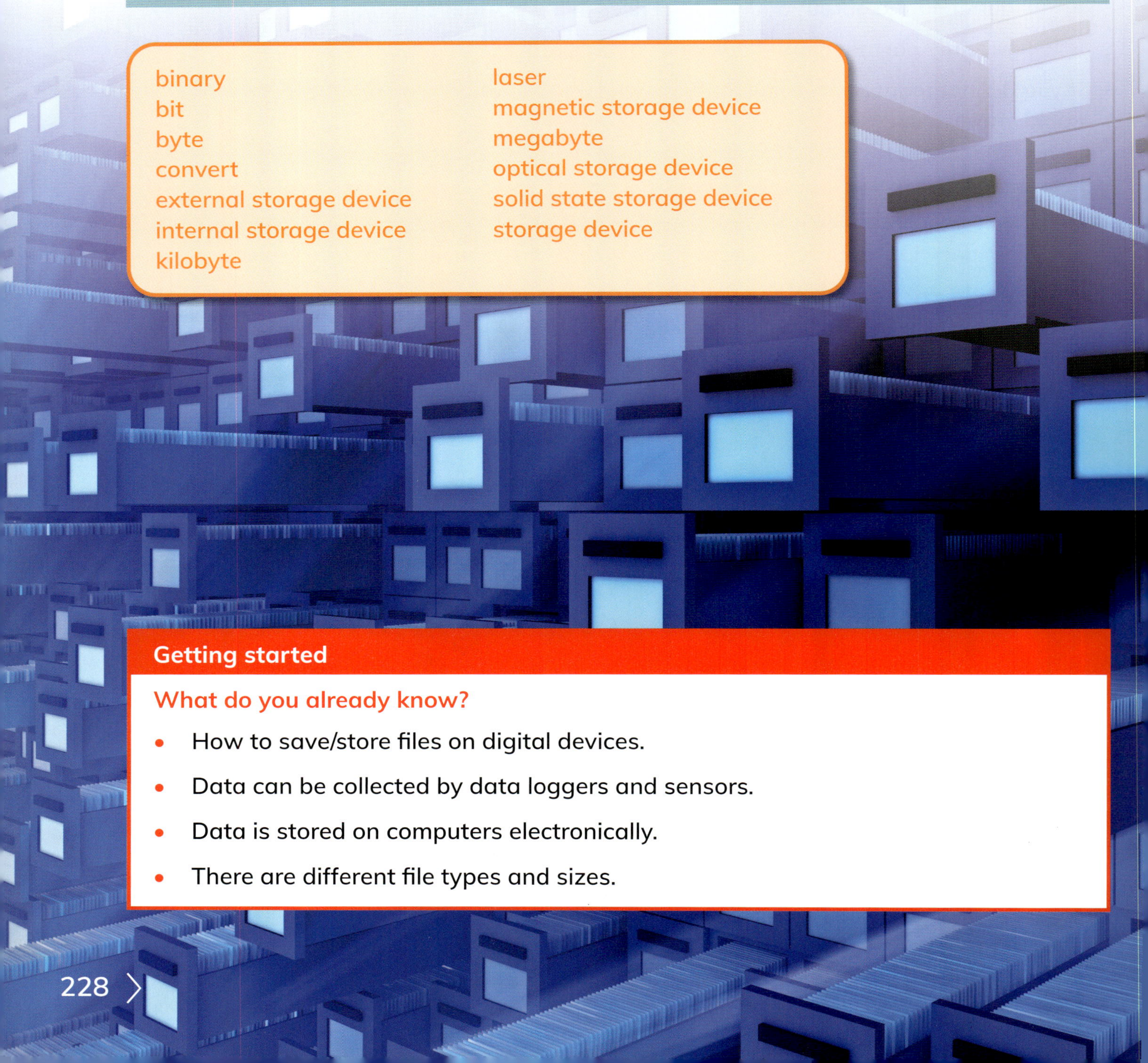

binary
bit
byte
convert
external storage device
internal storage device
kilobyte

laser
magnetic storage device
megabyte
optical storage device
solid state storage device
storage device

Getting started

What do you already know?

- How to save/store files on digital devices.
- Data can be collected by data loggers and sensors.
- Data is stored on computers electronically.
- There are different file types and sizes.

Continued

Now try this!

Look at these different files. Put the files in order, from smallest to largest.

- A three-minute sound file of a pop song.

- A high-resolution photo.

- A movie on a DVD.

- A text document of a 100-word story with no pictures.

Share your order with a partner. Does your partner agree with the order you chose? Why do they agree or disagree?

Storage devices

A storage device allows a computer to save data permanently. There are lots of different types of storage devices.

Internal storage devices

Some storage devices are found inside digital devices. These are called internal storage devices. This means they are found inside devices like tablets, smartphones and desktop computers.

229

External storage devices

Some storage devices are external. External storage devices are found outside of the main computer case or device case. External hard drives and memory sticks are examples of external storage devices. External storage devices have a case to protect the contents. For example, a memory stick has a hard outer case to stop it getting damaged if it is dropped.

Quite often, you will find that portable devices like laptops use external storage devices. This is because laptops are designed to be small and lightweight, so space for extra storage is limited. This means external storage is a better choice. Lots of different external storage devices can be connected to laptops.

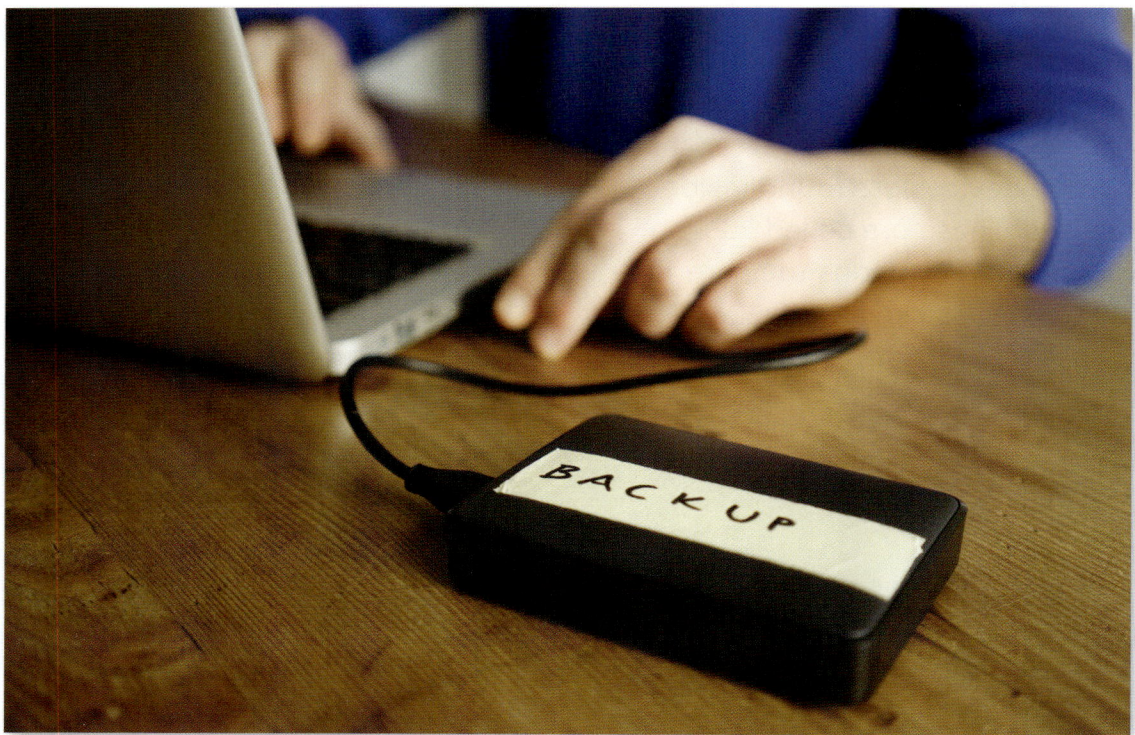

Activity 1

> **You will need:** a desktop computer, laptop or tablet with word processing or presentation software (optional)

Do you recognise any of these devices?

Magnetic hard drive	Solid state drive (SSD)	USB drive
SD card	Tape drive	CD/DVD drive

Research each of the storage devices in the table. See if you can find out the following about them:

- cost
- memory size
- whether it is internal or external (some storage devices can be either external or internal)
- where you might use one.

Share what you find with a partner. Do you have the same answers? If your answers are not the same as your partner's, talk about why they may be different. Make changes to your notes if you need to.

There are three different types of storage device:

- magnetic
- optical
- solid state.

Magnetic storage devices

A magnetic storage device uses magnets and metal discs to store data. The thin metal discs are placed on top of each other, a bit like a stack of pancakes. Between each metal disc is a magnet. The magnet writes the data onto the discs. This data can be removed later if necessary.

Magnetic storage devices are very common and are often used in servers. Magnetic storage is usually inexpensive.

Magnetic devices have moving parts. These parts can be damaged if they are dropped or carried around.

The most common type of magnetic storage is the hard disk drive. This can be internal or external.

Hard disk drives can store hundreds of films and hundreds of thousands of images.

Optical storage devices

An optical storage device uses circular plastic discs to store data. These are called compact discs (CDs) or digital versatile discs (DVDs).

Optical storage drives use a laser to make small marks on the plastic disc (the optical storage device). A laser is a thin beam of very powerful light. The beam of light is able to burn marks onto the plastic discs. These marks can also be read by the laser and turned into numbers that a computer can understand.

Optical storage devices, such as CDs and DVDs, are not used very often now. They were used mostly to store music and films. A DVD usually stores a single film or a few thousand images. Now, most people download or stream music and films straight to their tablets or smartphones from servers. You might not have any DVDs at home.

Some older laptops still have DVD drives and some older cars have CD drives to allow people to listen to music. Some very old desktop computers may still use external CD and DVD drives.

Optical storage can be damaged easily. It is easy to scratch or damage the plastic discs used to store the data. The plastic discs can be removed from the storage devices and carried around. This is good if you want to move your data to another computer or give it to a friend. But if the plastic discs get scratched or damaged the data can be lost.

CD and DVD drives can be internal or external.

Solid state storage devices

A solid state storage device uses circuits to store data. Solid state storage was invented more recently than optical and magnetic storage. It is the most expensive type of storage.

This type of device has no moving parts, which means that solid state storage is less likely to be damaged if it is dropped. Solid state storage devices are commonly used in desktop computers, laptops and tablets.

Solid state storage devices work much faster than optical and magnetic storage devices.

Solid state devices can be internal or external. Many people own portable external solid state storage devices. These are called memory sticks. They are small 'sticks' of solid state storage which connect to devices such as desktop computers and laptops. They also allow users to move files between devices.

Memory sticks can store a lot of data on them. Some of the most expensive memory sticks can store around 250 films or over 200 000 photos.

One disadvantage of memory sticks is that they are easy to lose because they are so small.

Did you know?

Some of the largest storage devices can store an average of 300 million images. This is the same amount of storage that you would get on around 85 000 mobile phones.

Unplugged activity 2

Work individually to think about each of the following devices:

- a laptop
- a mobile device (like a mobile phone, tablet or games console)
- a desktop computer.

Try to answer these questions:

1 What storage devices would you expect to find on each one?
2 What would each storage device be used for?

Discuss your answers with a classmate and see if you have different ideas.

How is data stored?

We now know that storage devices allow computers to store data.
But how is the actual data stored?

What does this mean?

I don't know!

Computers store data using binary. Binary is a number system.
It uses two numbers: 1 and 0.

A computer stores data in its memory. Computer memory is
made up of lots of switches. Each switch can either be on or off:

- If a switch is on, the binary value is 1.

- If a switch is off, the binary value is 0.

The binary value stored in one switch is called a bit. A bit is the
smallest unit of data storage.

Storage devices each use a slightly different way to tell a
computer whether each bit is 1 or 0.

Did you know?

When you store files on a computer, the files are converted to binary. All files (including text files, image files and spreadsheets) are stored as lots of 1s and 0s.

For example, in optical storage, data is stored by the marks made on the plastic disc. A mark represents a 1 and no mark means 0.

Here is an example of eight bits of storage for an optical storage device.

0	0	0	0	0	0	1	1

In this example, we have six data bits with no mark. This would be six 0s. Then we have two marks, which would be two 1s. This gives us 0 0 0 0 0 0 1 1. The computer can read this data and then process it.

Storage devices can store data for a long time. Data remains on the device unless we delete it. This means that if you throw a memory stick away, someone could still read the data stored on it.

Units of measurement

We know that the smallest piece of data is a bit. Each bit is either a single 1 or a single 0. Computers store lots of bits together to make larger units of storage.

Data is nearly always stored in units larger than a single bit.

A byte is a collection of eight bits together.

A kilobyte is 1000 bytes.

A megabyte is 1000 kilobytes, or 1 million bytes.

Stay safe!

Data stays on storage devices unless we delete it. Make sure you delete files and personal data from old storage devices.

megabyte = 1,000 kilobytes   largest

kilobyte = 1,000 bytes

byte = 8 bits

bit   smallest

Most units of measurement are based on the byte. You will see the word 'byte' at the end of each unit of measurement.

Activity 3

> **You will need:** a desktop computer, laptop or tablet and access to a computer folder that your teacher will give you

Have a look at the computer folder that your teacher will show you. See if you can answer these questions.

1 What types of files are stored in this folder?

   A pictures

   B text documents

   C presentations

   D sound files

2 Which files are largest?

3 Which files are smallest?

4 How many megabytes of storage do all of the files take?

Imagine you have run out of storage space.

5 What files would you delete to make more space?

6 Why have you chosen those files? What things did you consider when you made these choices?

Converting units of storage

We can use information about different units of storage to convert one unit of storage into another unit of storage. When we convert something, we change it from one thing to another.

For example, we can work out how many kilobytes there are in 10 megabytes like this:

- We know that 1 megabyte is 1000 kilobytes.
- Therefore 10 megabytes is 10 × 1000 kilobytes (or 10 000 kilobytes).

Questions

1   How many bits are in one byte?
2   How many kilobytes make a megabyte?
3   How many bits are in 4 bytes?
4   How many kilobytes make 3 megabytes?
5   How many bits are in 1 kilobyte?

> 1 kilobyte = 1000 bytes and so 5 kilobytes is 5,000 bytes.

What is the most difficult piece of information to remember about units of storage?

Can you think of a clever way to remember this?

Look what I can do!

☐   I can identify a range of storage devices.

☐   I can describe how computers store data in binary.

☐   I can identify the units of data storage.

› 4.3 Processing data

We are going to:

- **discover how computers use the input-process-output model**
- **look at different examples of the input-process-output model.**

> input
> output
> process

Getting started

What do you already know?

- Some examples of control systems and where they are used.
- That output devices provide information.

Now try this!

With a partner, consider the following:

- traffic lights
- automatic doors in shops or on trains.

Describe the inputs and outputs for each of these examples.

Input-process-output

All computer systems have an input, process and output.
This is known as the input-process-output model:

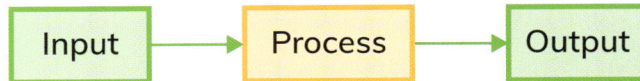

```
Input  →  Process  →  Output
```

The computer receives input (data) from an input device. Input devices can be things like buttons or sensors. The input tells the computer system what is happening.

Some sensors only send data when they are pressed – like a button. Some sensors may send data to the computer all of the time.

When a computer receives an input, it will process it. This means that computer programs make decisions about how to respond to the data provided. The way the computer responds depends on how it has been programmed.

Finally, the computer will give an output. The output could be to flash a light, or turn an actuator on or off. Remember, an actuator opens, closes or moves objects.

In the image here, the computer received input from a temperature sensor. The sensor sent data to the computer about the temperature.

Did you know?

Data travelling through the internet can travel at speeds of 200 000 km per second. That is fast enough to travel around the Earth five times in just one second.

The computer program then processes the input and calculates what action the computer system should take. In the picture, the computer calculated that the temperature in the office was too hot.

Finally, the computer system provides output. In this example, the computer gave instructions to switch the fan on.

> **Did you know?**
>
> Computers can detect temperature through sensors called thermistors. They affect the flow of electricity depending on how hot it is.

Input-process-output in humans

We use the input-process-output model all the time as humans. We have five senses to collect input:

- touch
- sight
- smell
- hearing
- taste.

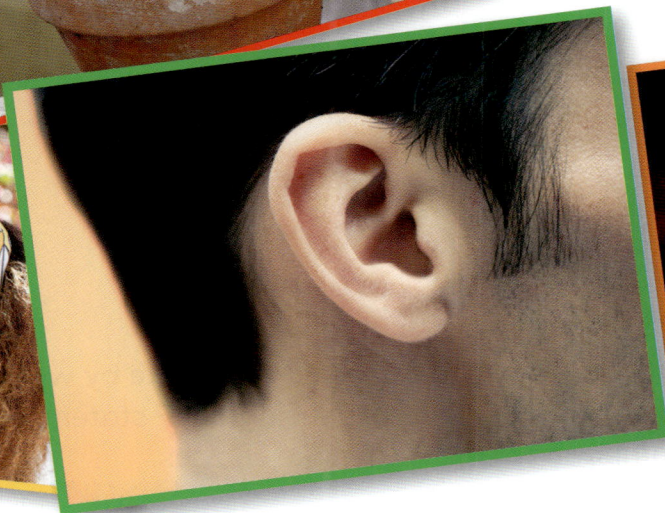

For example, for hearing:

- Input – you hear a fire alarm.

- Process – your brain understands there may be a fire in the building. It sends signals to your body to move.

- Output – you move to the fire exit.

Unplugged activity 1

Think about your journey to school.

Work with a partner to identify one input-process-output that you do for each of the five senses during your journey to school.

Processing data

When computers process data, they make choices.

We can program the choices that the computer can make by writing programs. In Topic 1.3, you made a program using an IF statement. IF statements allow computing devices to make choices.

Look at the following algorithm. What do you think the input, process and output are here?

1	IF the temperature is WARM
2	THEN open the window
3	ELSE close the window

This program has a very simple choice. Computer programs are usually more complicated than this, and allow a computer to make many difference choices.

Examples of the input-process-output model

The input-process-output model is something we see all around us. Here are some examples of where you may see the input-process-output model in real life.

Area	Input	Process	Output	Example
Printing	Clicking the print button in word-processing software	Documents are converted into binary and sent to the printer	The printer uses the binary data to print text and images on paper	Printing photos from your smartphone Printing schoolwork
Recording sounds	Microphone detects sound near the computer	Sounds are converted into digital forms Different effects could be used on the recording	A digital audio track	Recording a voice message for your friend on a smartphone Recording a pop song

Area	Input	Process	Output	Example
Farming (control system)	A sensor checks the water content of the soil	Computer works out if the soil is wet enough	An actuator controlling a water spray is turned on or off	Automatic watering systems in fields Indoor plant growing
Traffic lights (control system)	Motion sensor detects when cars are waiting at traffic lights	Computer works out where cars are and how long they have been waiting	Traffic lights change	City centre roads Train tracks
Swimming pool (control system)	Sensors detect if a person is sliding down a water slide	Computer works out if anyone is sliding down the slide	If there is no one on the slide, it shows a green light. Otherwise it shows a red light	Swimming pools
3D printing	A file which has a 3D model drawn in it	The file is converted into data for the printer to understand	Actuators feed plastic, metal or concrete into special printing nozzles	Parts for cars Shoes Houses

Questions

1 What happens if an input device gives the computer the wrong reading, or it breaks?

2 What steps can we take to stop the wrong inputs being given to a computer?

Activity 2

You will need: a desktop computer, laptop or tablet with word-processing or presentation software

Work with a partner to make a poster.

Your poster will show the input-process-output for a computer system that looks after a pet automatically.

Your poster should include the following.

- What the pet needs to be happy and healthy.
- What input devices you need to collect data on your pet's needs, for example a weighing scale to see if the food bowl is empty.
- What processing takes place, for example if there is enough food left for breakfast.
- What outputs the system provides, for example an actuator opens the food hatch to allow more food to enter the bowl.

To create your poster:

- firstly, think about what pet you want to pick
- then make notes on the ideas above, including what the pet needs, input devices, processing and outputs
- collect or draw some images to use in the poster
- finally, create your poster.

Continued

How am I doing?

Share your poster with a partner. Look at the input-process-output that they have thought of.

- Can you think of one more input-process-output for the pet they have chosen?
- What improvement can you suggest to make their poster better?
- Why have you picked this improvement?

Take the feedback you get from your partner and make an improvement to your poster.

Look what I can do!

☐ I can discuss how computers use the input-process-output model.

☐ I can give a range of examples of the input-process-output model in real life.

> 4.4 Artificial intelligence (AI)

We are going to:

- investigate what artificial intelligence (AI) is
- discover how AI allows computers to copy human intelligence
- explore the use of AI in predictive text or speech to text.

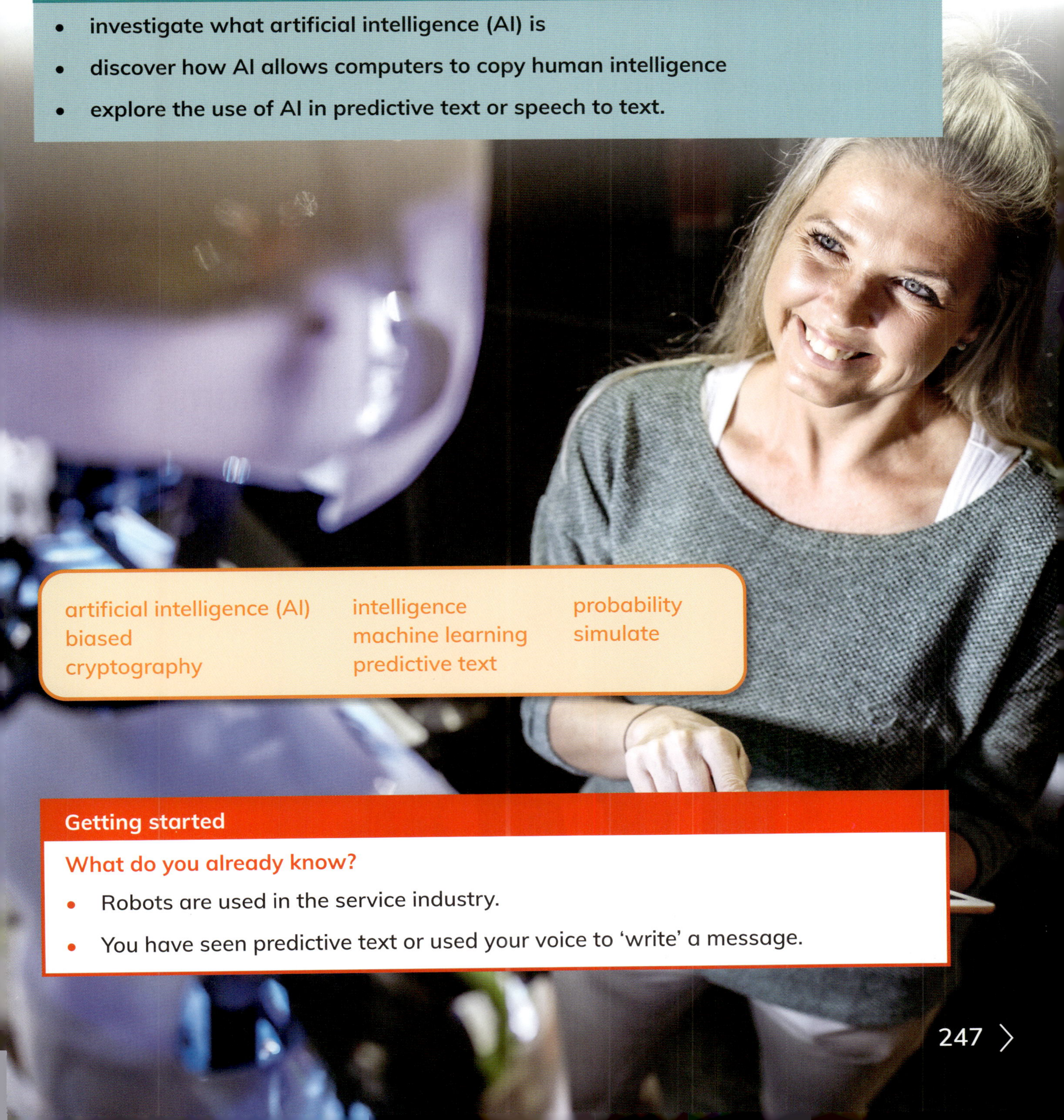

artificial intelligence (AI)   intelligence   probability
biased   machine learning   simulate
cryptography   predictive text

Getting started

What do you already know?

- Robots are used in the service industry.
- You have seen predictive text or used your voice to 'write' a message.

Continued

- How the input-process-output model works.

- You have explored automatic systems in vehicles such as trains or cars.

Now try this!

We have to make choices in our lives. Sometimes it is difficult to know the correct choice to make. Sometimes there is not a correct choice.

Imagine you are waiting at the bus stop with your friend, ready to go to school. The bus arrives and there is only one seat left.

Do you get on the bus, or do you let your friend get on the bus?

Can computers be as clever as humans?

As humans, we do lot of things automatically, without thinking. For example, if we see someone in trouble, we often automatically try to help them. Imagine a classmate has hurt their leg – you would want to help them walk to a bench to sit down.

Humans are also very good at learning. We learn what did not go well and often change our actions the next time. For example, you might eat an ice cream too quickly. This gives you a headache because it is so cold. Next time, you know to eat the ice cream more slowly.

Humans have intelligence. Intelligence is when we use skills or knowledge in a sensible way. Computers run on programs written by humans. Often these programs do not change, and the computer can only carry out the commands in the program. This means that computers are not intelligent.

Computer scientists have now developed programs that allow computers to think and act like humans. This is called artificial intelligence (AI).

Artificial intelligence is a way to simulate (copy or recreate) human intelligence. When a computer acts like a human, it behaves in the same way or 'pretends' to be like a human. Computers with AI can perform tasks automatically on their own, just like humans. They can also learn. This means they can change how they respond to certain inputs. This learning allows them to become more intelligent. This is known as machine learning.

Unplugged activity 1

Work with a partner. Discuss the following questions.

1   What are the advantages of computers learning how to think more like humans?

2   Where do you think using AI would be most useful in life?

3   What disadvantages might there be to computers learning how to act more like humans?

Programming AI

Learning to trust a computer to do the correct thing is difficult. Humans program computers to think and learn. This means that the programs may have mistakes in them. Sometimes these mistakes can be small and will not result in anything serious happening. However, sometimes the mistakes may be big, and this can cause accidents.

This means you need to trust a human to write a computer program that provides the correct instructions.

In Topic 1.3, you made programs that had choices using IF THEN ELSE. This coding is a simple way to make a program more intelligent. It is a very simple form of AI. For example, you can use IF THEN ELSE to program a small automatic vacuum cleaner.

> IF there is a wall
>
>   THEN Turn left
>
>   ELSE Keep going forwards

However, this does not make a very intelligent vacuum cleaner. We would need to add many more lines of code to simulate human intelligence.

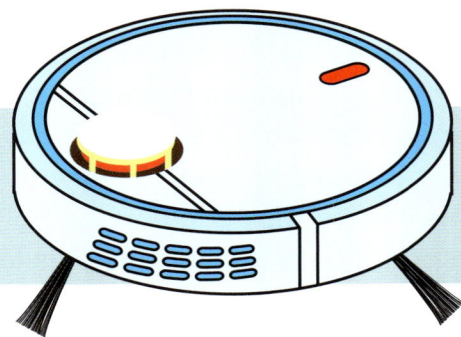

You didn't tell me what 'Left' is!

Questions

1 Who would you trust to do the following things? Choose between a human being and a computer that uses AI.

   a Make breakfast.

   b Drive you to school.

   c Select songs that you might like to listen to.

   d Operate on a person in a hospital.

2   For each example, say why you decided on a human or a computer with artificial intelligence.

3   Discuss your answers with a partner. Which tasks did you both agree to let a computer do for you? Which tasks did you not trust a computer to do? Why was this?

> You have already learnt about robots. Robotics and AI are different areas of computing. Most robots use algorithms that do not change. Computers often use AI to change how they respond to inputs. Sometimes, AI is given to robots to help them adapt to their surroundings.

Making the correct choices

There are two things that every programmer must try to think about when programming computers with AI:

- allowing the program to learn, predict and make better choices in the future

- making sure the decisions that the program makes are fair and suitable.

Making predictions

A big challenge with AI is to create programs that allow computers to predict what will happen next. They must also make the best choices depending on what inputs they receive. The computer can learn and change what it does if necessary.

251

What thought process did you go through to make 'the right choice' about getting on the school bus?

Is it always possible to make the right decisions? How did you reach the decision you made? Were you happy with the strategies you used? Did you find it hard to make a choice? What might affect your strategy for making choices if you did this exercise again?

Unplugged activity 2

You will need: a pen and paper

Think about the decision you made at the start of this topic, about whether you got on the school bus or whether you let your friend get on the bus. What did you choose to do?

Now think about the following statements:

- You have an important piece of homework to hand in.

- Your friend has an important test in the morning.

- You have already been late for school once this week.

Work with a partner. You will pretend to be the two people waiting for the school bus.

Discuss which person should be allowed to get on the school bus. Think about the statements above.

Write down your thoughts and how you decided who should get on the bus. You must both agree on the final choice.

Discuss your decisions with the other people in your class.

Making fair choices

Sometimes programmers working on AI can accidentally make programs that are biased. This means that they treat some people or actions differently – for example, one outcome of a program might be more likely than the others.

Imagine you wanted to join a local basketball club and had to fill in a form. The form is processed by a program with AI. Unfortunately, the AI in the program is biased.

The AI learnt that people who are very tall are usually better at playing basketball. It says you cannot join the basketball club because you are not tall enough. This system is biased because it mostly selects people based on height, and not how good they are at basketball.

Artificial intelligence in the real world

Artificial intelligence is being used a lot in the world we live in. When we search the internet for music to listen to, AI can learn about what songs we tend to like, and then suggest more songs for us.

Artificial intelligence can also be used to help us carry out tasks and help those with disabilities.

For example, AI can respond to your voice control devices in your house according to instructions. It may learn when you wake up and make sure that the lights are already turned on. It may learn what temperature you like in your home, and turn the heating on and off automatically for you.

Artificial intelligence can help those who have difficulties with vision. They can use AI to talk to their phones to get directions. The AI will understand what they say, open navigation software and locate the correct address. It can then use speech to direct them to the correct location.

Predictive text

We use simple forms of AI in our lives every day. Quite often, we may not even know we are using AI. Your mobile device probably has AI programs on it.

Predictive text is an example of AI. Predictive text programs read what you have written and then suggest what you may want to say next.

These programs learn what we say most often. They use probability to predict what we will write next. Probability is how likely something is to happen.

For example, when writing a message to a friend you might often start the message: 'Hello! How are you?' But sometimes you might write: 'Hello! Is it raining?'

Because you write 'Hello! How are you?' more often, the computer predicts this is what you will write, and it gives you options to choose from to complete the sentence. The options you use more often will usually be first to appear.

Arun

Hi Marcus!

Hi Arun, How are

you | things | your

Speech to text

Artificial intelligence can also be used to convert our speech to text. In speech to text, the computer learns how we speak. For example, it learns how our voice sounds and what words we often use in a sentence.

The computer converts what we say into text in a document, text message or email.

Sometimes the computer gets this wrong. It suggests the wrong words as text. It might also put punctuation in the wrong place.

We can tell the computer about these mistakes to help it learn what was wrong. This means it is less likely to make the same mistakes next time. In this way, the AI gets better the more it is used.

Speech to text can help people who find it difficult to use a keyboard. For example, they may have limited movement in their hands.

By using a headphone and a microphone, they can use voice commands to control their device, and use speech to text to write long documents.

Talking like humans

Another big challenge of AI is to get computers to talk like humans.

In 1952, a scientist called Alan Turing created a test to see whether a computer could think like a human. The test was called the Turing test. The test checked if it was possible to tell whether you were talking to a human or a robot.

> **Did you know?**
>
> Alan Turing was an English mathematician and computer scientist. He was an expert in cryptography and artificial intelligence. Cryptography involves disguising text by converting it into special code.

Many websites now allow you to talk to a computer in order to help you. They call these 'virtual assistants'. You can type questions in a box and the computer gives you the reply.

255 >

Activity 3

> **You will need:** a desktop computer, laptop or tablet with word-processing software or presentation software

Think about tasks that you do in day-to-day life. For example, jobs that you do to help around the house.

How could AI help you to complete these tasks?

Pick one task that you think would be easier with AI.
Use a computer to type a report about how the AI helps.
The report should include:

- the task you have chosen

- how AI will help

- the disadvantages if the artificial intelligence does not make the correct decisions.

Read your report to the class.

How am I doing?

Look at the report you wrote. Think about what you heard in other reports by your classmates.

Do you think you covered all of the disadvantages of using AI in your report?

Having heard the reports of other learners, is there anything you would add to your report?

Look what I can do!

- [ ] I can say what AI is.
- [ ] I can describe how AI allows computers to simulate human intelligence.
- [ ] I can explain how AI works in predictive text or speech to text.

Project

A local shop wants to use drones to send parcels to its customers.

A customer will be able to order items from the shop online. The shop will then pack the items into a parcel. The drone will fly the parcel to the customer.

The drones will be controlled by AI. The AI will:

- work out which parcel to take
- fly the parcel to the correct house
- drop the parcel off in the customer's garden
- fly back to the shop
- work out when to recharge its batteries.

Work with a partner. Plan and create a digital presentation to argue whether AI should or should not be used to control the drones.

Share your presentation with the class.

At the end of the presentations, vote on whether AI should or should not be used for the drones.

Check your progress

1 Why do computers need input devices?

2 Give one advantage of a remote input device.

3 Give two places where we may use input devices to help us.

4 What does an actuator do?

5 Give two different groups/types of storage devices.

6 Which type of storage device uses a laser?

7 How is data recorded on a storage device?

8 What is the correct size order of data storage units?

   A   byte, bit, kilobyte, megabyte   C   bit, byte, kilobyte, megabyte

   B   bit, kilobyte, byte, megabyte   D   megabyte, kilobyte, bit, byte

9 Why is data stored in binary?

10 What happens at the process stage in the input-process-output model?

11 Say one way we can stop a computer using incorrect input from an input device.

12 What does AI allow a computer to do?

13 Give two reasons why people may not trust AI.

14 Explain one way that AI could help someone who has a disability.

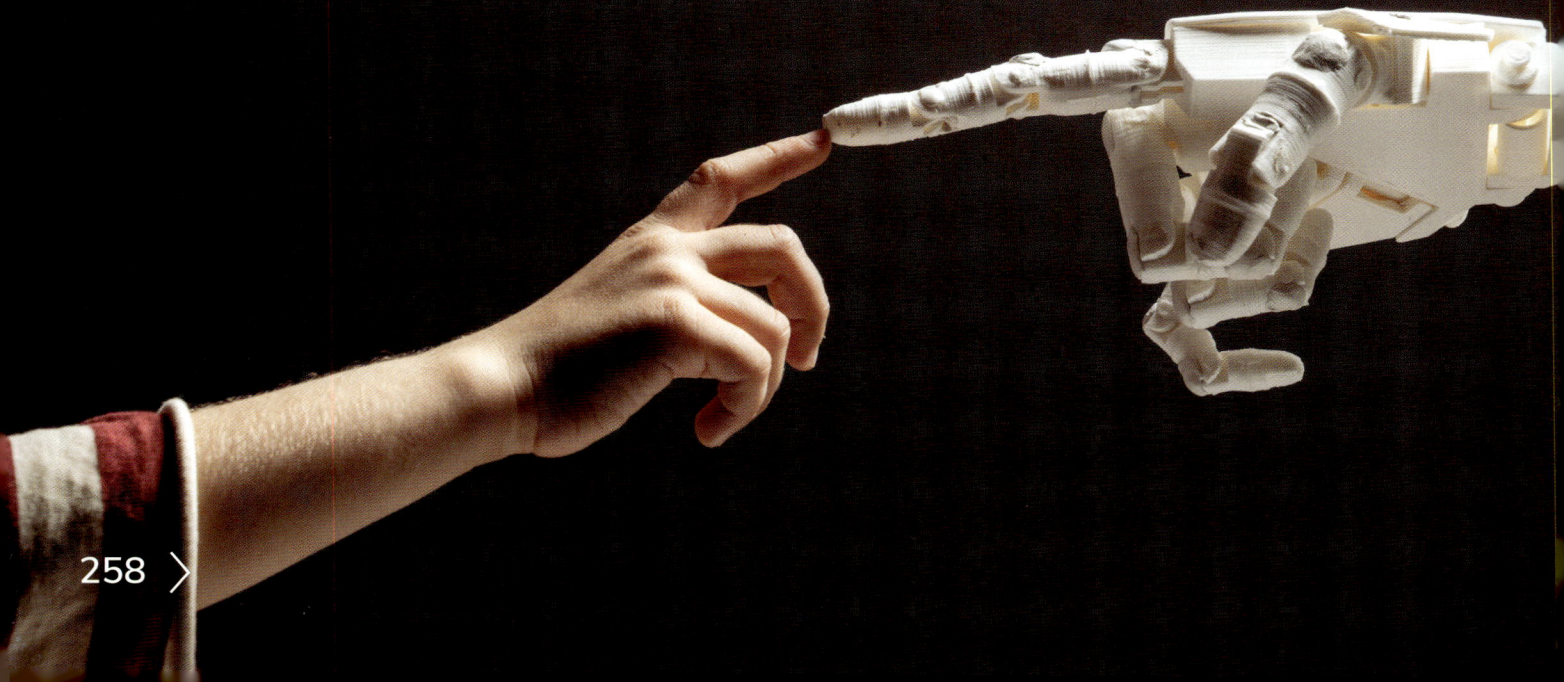

Glossary

actuator an output device that moves or controls something 223
The door was opened with an actuator.

aerial a rod that allows signals to be sent and received 186
My wi-fi router has three aerials on it.

analyse to look closely at data, find patterns in it and think carefully about what it means 123
We analysed the data we had collected and found that puzzle games were the most popular.

analysis the act of studying something in detail to understand more about it. 97
We performed an analysis of the game to understand how we could have played better.

arithmetic the use of numbers in calculations and counting 28
I have worked out the price, but I need to check the arithmetic.

arithmetic operator a symbol that instructs a computer about what type of calculation to perform on values 28
The + symbol is an arithmetic operator for addition, and the − symbol is an arithmetic operator for subtraction.

artificial intelligence (AI) a way of simulating human intelligence in a computer 249
Artificial intelligence allowed the computer to decide what to do when the cat ran in front of the driverless car.

assign when we give a value to a variable. 15
We assign the value 'Mike' to the variable Name.

automatically done without human input 125
The train doors open automatically.

average a value in the middle of a set of values; a way of representing the pattern of the whole set in one value 134
The average journey time was 12 minutes.

megabyte	a unit of digital storage which is the same as 1000 kilobytes or 1 million bytes *My sound file was one megabyte in size.*	236
network	two or more devices connected together that share resources and communicate *I connect my laptop to the network to save my work.*	205
numerical data	facts and information expressed as numbers, for example 2, 14, 3.6 or −60.87 *It can be useful to store numerical data in a spreadsheet.*	123
object	something that has its own shape and form and has different behaviours *A table is an object that has four legs and a level top.*	78
operator	a mathematical symbol used in calculations to do a particular action, like adding or dividing *The multiplication operator we use with computers is *.*	161
optical storage device	uses a laser to read and store data on a plastic disc *A DVD drive is an optical storage device.*	232
output	information that you get out of a computer system after data has been processed *A printer is a common output device that lets you print information onto paper.*	70
packets	small pieces of data that travel through a network *Sofia's email was split into many hundreds of packets when she sent it.*	196
predictive text	the ability of a program to suggest words that you may want to use when writing a sentence *I use predictive text when I write text messages.*	254
probability	the chance that an event will happen or will not happen *There is a small probability it will rain today.*	254
process	calculations or instructions that a computer carries out *A computer will use the input data and carry out a process to produce an output.*	70
project life cycle	the different stages of a project starting from analysis and followed by design, development, testing and evaluation *Each stage of the project life cycle for creating the video game involved different people.*	97

Acknowledgements

The authors and publishers acknowledge the following sources of copyright material and are grateful for the permissions granted. While every effort has been made, it has not always been possible to identify the sources of all the material used, or to trace all copyright holders. If any omissions are brought to our notice, we will be happy to include the appropriate acknowledgements on reprinting.

Thanks to the following for permission to reproduce images:

Unit 1 Peter Dazeley/GI; H&C Studio/GI; Kali9/GI; Prostock-Studio/GI; Andresr/GI; Nick David/GI; Edwin Tan/GI; Jordi Salas/GI; Peter Dazeley/GI; Westend61/GI; RichVintage/GI; Ana Maria Serrano/GI; Richard Sharrocks/GI; Artpartner-Images/GI; Zero Creatives/GI; Kukkaibkk/GI; Willowpix/GI; Jordan Lye/GI; Destillat/GI; Wikimedia; Mint Images/GI; Andy Ryan/GI; JuSun/GI; Peter Cade/GI; OsakaWayne Studios/GI; Ojo Images/GI; Laura Olivas/GI; MoMo Productions/GI; Jackyenjoyphotography/GI; IndiaPicture/GI; Tahreer Photography/GI; David Clapp/GI; Dowell/GI; Germán Vogel/GI; D3sign/GI; Monkeybusinessimages/GI; Mayur Kakade/GI; Andresr/GI; ER Productions Limited/GI; SOPA Images/GI; Donald Iain Smith/GI; China News Service/GI; John M Lund Photography Inc/GI; Skynesher/GI; Maskot/GI; Hill Street Studios/GI; Cavan Images/GI (x2); Juanma Hache/GI; Morsa Images/GI; Alvarez/GI; Izusek/GI; RichVintage/GI; Jose Luis Pelaez Inc/GI; We Are/GI; BongkarnThanyakij/GI; Ariel Skelley/GI; Phynart Studio/GI; Sakchai Vongsasiripat/GI; Maskot/GI; Bill Hinton/GI; Rafael Mayrink Goes/GI; Aang Permana/GI; Winhorse/GI; MikeSleigh/GI; South_Agency/GI; Baona/GI; Andriy Onufriyenko/GI; **Unit 2** KTSdesign/GI; Robert Kneschke/GI; JGI/Jamie Grill/GI; PM Images/GI; Arterra/GI; Maska82/GI; Alex Tihonov/GI; Mike Kemp/GI; Nora Carol Photography/GI; Waldo Swiegers/Bloomberg via GI; John Keeble/GI; Nikada/GI; Anchiy/GI; SDI Productions/Gi; FG Trade/GI; moodboard-Mike Watson/GI; Zak Kendal/GI; GK Hart/Vikki Hart/GI; Dave Queva/GI; Paul Starosta/GI; Tirc83/GI; Arterra/GI; Urbancow/GI; Image Source/GI; Fly View Productions/GI; Roberto Westbrook/GI; Eclipse_Images/GI; Bob Thomas/GI; Kajakiki/GI; Imagenavi/GI; Mike Watson Images/GI; Elva Etienne/GI; Peter Finch/GI; MirageC/GI; Andriy Onufriyenko/GI; Artur Debat/GI; Gam1983/GI; RLT_Images/GI (x3); Blend Images – Todd Wright/GI; Andriy Onufriyenko/GI; MirageC/GI; Tetra Images – Mike Kemp/GI; Jasmin Merdan/GI; Erik Isakson/GI; TommL/GI; Andresr/GI; Peter Dazeley/GI; Martin Poole/GI; Jacobs Stock Photography Ltd/GI; Elva Etienne/GI; Ron Levine/GI; Samere Fahim Photography/GI; Matthias Kulka/GI; Rivers Dale/GI; Jena Ardell/GI; Istetiana/GI; **Unit 3** Uchar/GI; Piranka/GI; Vnosokin/GI; Casezy/GI; Thanasis/GI; Mario Marco/GI; Momo Productions/GI; AerialPerspective Images/GI; Jamie Grill/GI; Anilyanik/GI; Oscar Wong/GI; Peter Dazeley/GI; Javier Zayas Photography/GI; DBenitostock/GI; Jayk7/GI; John Lamb/GI; Riska/GI; Bgwalker/GI; SOPA Images/GI; Wongmbatuloyo/Gi; Christopher Hopefitch/GI; **Unit 4** Neustockimages/GI; Mmdi/GI; Maskot/GI; Westend61/GI; Sinology/GI; Monty Rakusen/GI; LHJB Photography/GI; Dima_zel/Gi; Mark Garlick/Science Photo Library/GI; Salvatore Allegra Photography/GI; Magnilion/GI; Juanma hache/GI; Mikroman6/GI; Stefan Cristian Cioata/GI; Thomas Barwick/GI; SolStockGI; Peter Dazeley/GI; Tom Werner/GI; Santiago Urquijo/GI; Franckreporter/GI; Kali9/GI; Wang Leng/GI; 3alexd/GI; Muriel de Seze/GI; Jeffrey Hamilton/GI; Halfdar/GI; MihailDechev/GI; Yevgen Romanenko/GI (x2); MarkSwallow/GI; Aolr/GI; Blackred/GI; Narumon Bowonkitwanchai/GI; Michaela Begsteiger/GI; Sakchai Vongsasiripat/GI; Don Farrall/GI; Yevgen Romanenko/GI; Jim Craigmyle/GI; JakeOlimb/GI; Lazyleric/GI; Witthaya Prasongsin/GI; Tara Moore/GI; Sergio Mendoza Hochmann/GI; Tara Moore/GI (x2); Rebecca Nelson/GI; Wakila/GI; Smile/GI; Pete Starman/GI; Ray Wise/GI; Ratnakorn Piyasirisorost/GI; Devrimb/GI; Catherine Delahaye/GI; Karina Mansfield/GI; Westend61/GI; Floresco Productions/GI; Sue Barr/Gi; Maskot/Gi; Tom Odulate/GI; Westend61/GI; Reggie Casagrande/GI; Maskot/GI; Pictures from History/GI; Selimaksan/GI

Key GI = Getty Images

Cover image by Pablo Gallego (Beehive Illustration)

Scratch is a project of the Scratch Foundation, in collaboration with the Lifelong Kindergarten Group at the MIT Media Lab. It is available for free at https://scratch.mit.edu

Illustrations and photos showing the BBC Micro:bit are created and used with permission from the Micro:bit Educational Foundation

Screenshots from Microsoft Excel are used with permission from Microsoft

Printed in Great Britain
by Amazon